봉준호

BONG JOON HO

Dissident Cinema

봉
준
호

Karen Han

Foreword by David Lowery

Little White Lies   Abrams, New York

CONTENTS

FOREWORD BY DAVID LOWERY

When I reflect on Bong Joon Ho's work, I think of memories that appear like unexpected wraiths: a little boy, looking up at his mother, wanting to trust her, or two wild eyes, peering from a secret door. I think of a sad-happy family meal, plucked out of time. I think of tall grass blowing in the wind, cold and desolate in one instance, a golden reprieve in another, along with broad smiles and eyes welling up with righteous fury. Sighs of sad acceptance, too; those are always there. I think of bodies in childlike repose and noodles stirred violently in a bowl. I think of a mother pig nudging her baby toward freedom.

And I think of the funeral scene because it was the funeral scene that got me.

The Host was my introduction to Director Bong and, when I saw it, the image of that central family unit descending into blubbering sobs as they eulogize Song Kang-ho's not-actually-dead daughter knocked me out of my already slightly wobbly center of gravity. What movie was I watching? How could this mostly sober monster movie veer into absurdity with such guileless abandon? Which lane was the filmmaker in? I'd already reckoned with an opening scene plucked from a 1950s creature feature, followed by a title sequence wrought with the moribund severity of an urban melodrama. Now, as if taking a cue from Song's bleached hair, Director Bong was pushing his cast into cartoonish levels of grief, taking a moment of great sensitivity, and almost daring us not to laugh at it. I didn't know how to handle it.

But I also couldn't forget it. It was still on my mind when I saw *Mother*. This film, too, features a funeral scene, which likewise devolves into chaos. The dissolution is far more aggressive this time, moving from tears to an outright brawl, but it made sense to me. Why? Perhaps the indignity of grief is less unsettling when its pathos remains severe; perhaps it was this very severity, and the strange, surprising grace that ebbs up around it, that made it easier for me to embrace the film as a whole, just as the science-fiction context of *Snowpiercer* somehow made perfect bedfellows out of grungy class warfare and Tilda Swinton's incredible dentures. I watched these films and understood what Director Bong was doing. I knew what lane he was in, even when, as in *Okja*, he is figuratively and literally veering around within it.

(*Okja*, for the record, reduced *me* to blubbering sobs. Perhaps I should have taken note.)

In any case, by the time I backtracked to *Memories of Murder* and *Barking Dogs Never Bite*, and, like the rest of the world, was repeatedly exhilarated by *Parasite*, I knew Director Bong to be one of those filmmakers whose formal and thematic concerns form the backbone of an oeuvre that is not nearly as disparate as it might seem from the outset—a predilection I found personally inspiring! *Of course* a police procedural would lead to a horror film! *Why wouldn't* a child's fairy tale about factory farming set the ideal stage for a Hitchcockian castigation of caste? I'd come to recognize the sense of humor that infuses his most bitter representations of our social constructs, and to take comfort in the compassion that somehow swaddles his razor-sharp articulations of moral injustice. Through his work, I came to better understand that a perfect calibration of tone can nonetheless encompass wild vacillations, that a great movie might exist in multiple genres at once, and that when an equally great filmmaker guides their cast towards the furthest extremities of human behavior, there is surely, undeniably a reason for it. I knew all of this, and yet . . .

The Host and its funeral scene were still stuck lopsided in my memory. An outlier in my appreciation of his work. I'd been a burgeoning cinephile when I first saw that film; my skills of cinematic comprehension had been narrower than I would have liked to admit. In the wake of *Parasite*, I figured it was high time to return to it and see if I'd missed something.

Of course, I had.

I'd missed that the film was not merely a monster movie, but as incisive a social critique as *Parasite*. I'd missed that the creature was not just a fearsome beast, but an animal as worthy of empathy as the titular pig would later be in *Okja*. I'd missed that this funeral I can't stop talking about was a signifier, not only of Bong's intent with this particular film, but of his designs as a filmmaker, for never in his worldview is any sentiment consigned to a singular interpretation, just as bathos is never any more or less valid than pathos, just as his heroes are never so righteous that they can't be capable of terrors, just as he doesn't let us turn our back on those characters when we realize what they've done.

I'd missed all of that and, most of all, I'd missed that he was teaching me how to watch the rest of his movies.

Thank goodness the lesson sunk in regardless!

INTRODUCTION

In the days leading up to *Parasite*'s history-making Academy Award wins in 2019, Bong Joon Ho, its director, had this to say about the class thriller:

> *The true horror and fear of* Parasite *isn't just about how the present-day situation is bad but that it will only continue to get worse. [. . .] After I die, will it get better? I don't know. I'm not so hopeful.*

As reflections of the world that we live in, Bong's works often circle around that sense of impending doom, sometimes venturing into bleak, even cruel territory. The loglines of his movies speak for themselves: A father whose daughter is kidnapped by a grotesque monster fails to save her; a supposed hero admits that he's eaten children; two detectives cause an innocent man's death—and nearly kill another—while trying to catch a serial murderer. What's remarkable is that, despite what these surface descriptions might suggest, it is impossible to categorize Bong as a cynic, or see his films purely as tragedies. In fact, it is arguably impossible to categorize him at all—he walks between the raindrops of conventional genre and style with enviable ease, defying any labels, rebuking attempts at moralizing, and building stories that function both as political allegories and cultural histories.

What makes his status as something of a dissident truly exceptional, however, is that his clear-eyed view of the world never succumbs to nihilism. The final part of the above quote, given in a Vulture profile, makes that abundantly clear, as well as serving as a sort of guiding light:

> *Still, we have to try to live happily. We can't cry every day.*

OPENING THE YELLOW DOOR

Born on September 14, 1969, in Daegu, South Korea, Bong Joon Ho discovered a passion for cinema early on, watching movies on TV.

"My mother was a little bit of a compulsive germophobe," he recalls, as to why television was his primary conduit into film, "and because, in the movie theater, you don't have a lot of sunlight, she insisted that it was filled with a lot of germs." His channel of choice was the American Armed Forces Network, which would broadcast Western films, including works by Sidney Lumet, Brian De Palma, and Sam Peckinpah, albeit in censored form, leaving the young Bong to imagine what had been edited out. This early exposure to the world of cinema would blossom into obsession—after enrolling at Yonsei University in 1988, he sold donuts at the school cafeteria for six months in order to save up enough money to buy a Hitachi camera, and would fall asleep holding it.

At Yonsei (incidentally the same school one of the characters in *Parasite* pretends to have attended), he would study sociology, though film remained his true love. Along with a handful of other students from neighboring universities, he cofounded a film club, Yellow Door (so named because the club room door was painted yellow), and was in charge of managing the club's video collection and bootlegging films. He would also shoot his first short films while at Yonsei, a stop-motion film called *Looking for Paradise* (which unfortunately seems impossible to track down) as well as a live-action film titled *White Man* (1994)—the latter short would serve as a launching pad for Bong to attend the Korean Academy of Film Arts.

To date, Bong has made seven feature works: *Barking Dogs Never Bite* (2000); *Memories of Murder* (2003); *The Host* (2006); *Mother* (2009); *Snowpiercer* (2013); *Okja* (2017); and *Parasite* (2019). In speaking to the press, he hasn't been shy about revealing the real-life experiences that have influenced his films. *Parasite*, for instance, was born out of his (brief) time as a math tutor for the son of a wealthy family. *Barking Dogs Never Bite*, filmed in the very same apartment complex that Bong lived in after getting married, was inspired by his childhood memory of finding a dead dog on a building roof, as well as his brother's travails in the world of academia. I mention this to give context to context—Bong was born into a Korea that was still under the rule of a military dictatorship, and entered college the year after the June Democratic Struggle (a period of mass protests—held in response to the then-president's military regime and the torture and death of student activists—that led to the establishment of the current government of South Korea). "Every day was the same," he has said of his time as a student. "Protest during the day, drink at night. Except for a few people, we didn't have much faith in the professors at the time." His experience was such that he has said he sometimes smells tear gas in his dreams, as it had been deployed so frequently against student protestors. (It feels like no coincidence, as such, that the image of noxious gas seeping into the frame recurs throughout

his oeuvre.) An incident for which he was arrested—joining a union demonstration—was behind his decision to take two years of mandatory military service in the middle of his enrollment at Yonsei, as that was the condition for a suspended sentence. That is to say, as much as filmmaking seems to be in his blood, so is an awareness of social structure and a puckish, anti-authoritarian streak. Even his sociology degree—which he admits to being not entirely passionate about—plays a part in his personal evolution: "Although I wasn't really interested in sociology, I was always interested in society, particularly because, at the time, Korea was going through a very dynamic period. When I was in college, in the late '80s and early '90s, Korea saw the end of the military dictatorship. We had our first democratic administration come in, and that's when pop culture, cinema, and pop music really exploded into the mainstream consciousness." *Memories of Murder*, which takes place in a similar time period, provides some cultural background for those less well-versed in contemporary Korean history, as the protests that occur as a team of detectives attempt to solve a serial murder case serve to address government corruption on multiple levels.

White Man—and the short film *Incoherence* (1994), which Bong produced while attending the Korean Academy of Film Arts—would place Bong squarely in the Korean New Wave. As the South Korean government pulled back on censorship and control over the country's film industry, artists who had come of age with the push for democracy began rising to prominence, eschewing restrictions on subject matter and tackling subjects that had previously been considered risky or otherwise off-limits. Among their number was Director Park Chan-wook (*Oldboy, The Handmaiden*), who was so impressed by Bong's first two short films that he reached out (though the two filmmakers wouldn't manage to actually work together until *Snowpiercer*, on which Park served as a producer). The relative success of the shorts also helped Bong land a job as an assistant director (and cowriter) on Park Ki-yong's 1997 debut feature *Motel Cactus*. And yet, Bong's transition into the Korean film industry wasn't entirely smooth—for some time, he eked out a living as a wedding videographer. ("I filmed really well. If the parents cried, I did a closeup, and if there was someone who looked like the groom's ex-girlfriend, I did a closeup on them, too.") Even after directing his first feature, 2000's *Barking Dogs Never Bite*, his financial straits were such that one of his former college classmates would buy him rice.

Memories of Murder, released in 2003, would mark a turning point, as the film was both critically acclaimed and successful at the box office. It cemented Bong's place as a filmmaker to watch, and has even been credited with saving one of the companies that produced it, Sidus Pictures, from going bankrupt. *The Host*, which followed in 2006, was also a hit—in fact, it became the highest-

2017

grossing South Korean film at the time—and served as Bong's international breakthrough. As his stock as a filmmaker increased, the subsequent limelight would also make his professional life more difficult. The themes present in *Memories of Murder* and *The Host*—namely, government incompetence and corruption, as well as an unflattering portrait of the American political class, all common throughout Bong's work—landed him on a secret government blacklist. Created under the conservative president Lee Myung-bak, whose term lasted from 2008 to 2013, and expanded under President Park Geun-hye (in whose 2017 impeachment this would play a small role), this blacklist was meant to deprive the artists on it from receiving government funding. Fortunately, Bong had gained enough of a reputation as a director that he was able to secure private backing—though his situation was an exception rather than the rule.

That said, finding a true foothold abroad was something of a protracted process for Bong. His fans may recall this choice quote from his Best Foreign Language Film acceptance speech at the 2020 Golden Globes: "Once you overcome the one-inch-tall barrier of subtitles, you will be introduced to so many more amazing films." Though it's a broadly applicable sentiment, it also feels particularly apt considering Bong's journey as far as Western media is concerned. Despite how his films are now lauded for their "universal" themes, a glance at contemporaneous reviews and appreciation of his films up until *Parasite*'s historic Oscar wins (the film would become the first non-English language film to take home Best Picture, as well as winning Best International Feature Film, Best Original Screenplay, and Best Director) reveals relatively scant interest and, more dispiritingly, the sense that their status as "foreign films" equated to a certain level of inaccessibility or inherent disadvantage. For example, the *New York Times* review of *Memories of Murder* opens with: "[The film] is such a taut, effective thriller it's a shame you have to read subtitles to gauge just how good a movie it is." Great praise—until you reach the sentence's baffling end. Though filmmakers such as Quentin Tarantino have championed Bong's work, and Bong's oeuvre has grown to include two international coproductions (*Snowpiercer* and *Okja*, the latter of which was released on Netflix), for a long time, that one-inch-tall barrier was enough to keep Bong from achieving wider recognition and appreciation. Granted, he has been fairly nonchalant about his international success, notably referring to the Oscars as a "local" ceremony.

To that end, writing about Bong for *Time*'s feature on the hundred most influential people of 2020, Tilda Swinton, who has appeared in two of Bong's works to date, had this to say:

> *This is the filmmaker who, this year, has risen into the 2020 vision of the entire cinepassionate planet like a new sun. Whip-smart, highly skilled, supremely cineliterate, exuberant, irreverent, self-*

determining, deeply romantic, with a voracious delight in the absurd, highly principled, precision-tuned, compassionate to the last: his films have always been all this. It just seems to be time for the world to catch up.

She is, of course, right on the money, and almost amusingly so. In the wake of *Parasite*'s Oscar win, Bong fever has reached new heights—the rise of the "Bong Hive" (of which I humbly profess to be the founder), a blanket term for the director's fans, is just the tip of the iceberg. Three of his films are now a part of the prestigious Criterion Collection (*Parasite*, *Memories of Murder*, and *Okja*), and conservative politicians in Daegu (which he has, since moving away, referred to as "Korea's most conservative city") have proposed everything from building a museum to renaming streets in his honor—a far cry from the contempt and condemnation that similarly-minded officials demonstrated toward him before.

BONGTAIL

Bong has long had a telling nickname in the Korean film industry: "Bongtail." A portmanteau of his family name and the word "detail," the title refers to his extreme attention to detail, which extends to practically every aspect of production. He storyboards his films personally—a few have been published, and a quick look through the pages, which read like a comic, makes it abundantly obvious just how clearly Bong can see his films in his head before there's even a camera present. As with the Coen brothers, he doesn't shoot any coverage, i.e., there's no "extra" footage. Editor Yang Jinmo, who worked with Bong on *Snowpiercer*, *Okja*, and *Parasite*, has said that, as a result, he sometimes uses somewhat unconventional methods: "Because Director Bong uses only the essential, bare necessities—this is something I've never shared before—sometimes when a certain shot is at the latter end of the emotion, I would use to the very end after Director Bong calls cut."

Then, of course, there's just how carefully constructed his screenplays are. Nothing is ever without purpose, and even the most banal details often return later on, to tremendous effect. Take, for instance, the role that Hite beer cans play in *The Host*. Initially, they're a way of demonstrating the protagonist's happy-go-lucky style of parenting, as he offers beer to his underage daughter without a second thought. But the next time we see a can of beer, it has taken on a new significance as a heartbreaking reminder of familial love and safety. And even on a broader scale, such as the puzzle-box construction of *Parasite*, Bong's films are so meticulously made that it's easy to imagine a single missing element causing the whole thing to tumble down—and further evince just how singular a talent he is.

In these respects, "Bongtail" feels apt, but the kind of image that the name conjures (Bong, who has professed disliking the name, has explained that he thinks it sounds "petty") lies diametrically opposed to the kind of person that Bong seems to be. In researching and speaking to his collaborators for this book, the portrait that emerges is of an unfailingly patient and thoughtful artist—in other words, the opposite of the kind of interiority and arrogance that "Bongtail" may suggest. And if anything, his public appearances—his red carpet interviews and acceptance speeches during *Parasite*'s awards campaign, in particular—make him out to be a bit of a joker. Asked, at the Oscars, how he came up with the story for *Parasite*, his answer was, "I'm a fucking weirdo," followed by a mischievous giggle. Later that same night, he would end his Best Director acceptance speech—throughout which he seemed to be in a state of shock—with the immortal line, "I will drink until next morning."

That all those traits seem contradictory to one another, or at least not easily contained within a single person, is perhaps as Bong-ian as can be. With seven features under his belt, his distinguishing traits as a director can arguably be defined as such: a superhuman facility for moving between tones and genres; an unflinching examination of the world we live in; and a refusal to oversimplify the stories he tells. His heroes are rarely, if ever, uncomplicatedly good, and his villains are almost never evil simply for the sake of being evil. As far-fetched as some of the stories he's told have been, all of the characters he's brought to life have been recognizably human in some way—and so are the themes he winds into his work. This is a not inconsiderable feat given that his films have retained—for lack of a better descriptor—an unapologetic Korean-ness. *Memories of Murder* addresses specific events in Korean history; *The Host* is partially built on the uneasy relationship between Korea and America; *Parasite* is chock-full of details that non-Korean viewers are likely to miss, such as a nod to the castella cake bubble that burst in Korea in the mid-2010s, as well as the specificity of noodle dish "jjapaguri," which is translated as "ram-don" in English for the sake of ease of understanding.

The point here is that Bong has never compromised as an artist for the sake of a more "universal" appeal (an idea which, in itself, is something of a fallacy), even when forced into a corner. The release of *Snowpiercer* was infamously fraught—boiled down to its essence, producer Harvey Weinstein wanted more Chris Evans, more narrative hand-holding, and less runtime, and Bong refused. And the fact that *Okja* was picked up by Netflix (then still a relatively nascent player in terms of original content) had at least a little to do with the assurance of directorial control. Even at the beginning of his career, he was something of a contrarian: He was urged by producers to change the ending of *Memories of Murder*

(he didn't); and even his first feature was a source of bafflement for producers (he recalls his wife asking, "Did they really agree to make this?" after reading the script). The result is an impressive, inimitable body of work—one that, most excitingly, is still growing.

CRYING EVERY DAY

Even though Bong's films uniformly avoid uncomplicated happy endings, and sometimes do end in despair, they evoke a vast wellspring of feeling rather than a descent into cynicism. Not only is Bong a master at prompting unexpected emotional responses (laughter in moments of horror, in particular), but of the specific kind of adrenaline rush that comes from seeing a sequence so perfectly executed that it acts as a reminder of just why cinema remains such an enduring and beloved art form. I think, especially, of seeing *Parasite* for the first time when it screened for critics at the 2019 Cannes Film Festival. As the Kim family carried out their plan to get rid of the Parks' housekeeper by capitalizing on her peach allergy, the atmosphere in the Debussy theater began to buzz. As the sequence reached its finale, the gathered audience burst into ecstatic applause. The characters were clearly behaving reprehensibly, but the climax to the astonishing "Belt of Faith" sequence is carried out so deftly and built up so beautifully that experiencing it for the first time was a total revelation. (Applause would break out one more time during the film's runtime, following the "ram-don" sequence, for similar reasons.)

This kind of alchemy isn't, broadly speaking, exclusive to Bong's films, but is specific to him when it comes to drawing emotion out of his audience not in moments of triumph but in some of the most painful experiences he puts his characters through. Of all of the scenes in Bong Joon Ho's films, there is one I often find myself coming back to. In *The Host*, a family of oddballs find themselves up against both an uncaring government and a hungry, mutated monster. Midway through the film, Gang-du (Song Kang-ho) hands his father Hee-bong (Byun Hee-bong) a shotgun with which to dispatch the creature. As the beast barrels down the sidewalk, Hee-bong raises the gun and shoots—to no effect. The gun doesn't have any cartridges left in it. As he realizes this—and his adult children come to the same grim conclusion—he turns to face his kids, waving his hand both in farewell and as a missive for them to keep running. In the next instant, the monster is upon him. That single shot—of Hee-bong facing the camera, the monster rapidly approaching behind him—has stuck with me ever since I first saw *The Host* in the mid-2000s. It's hard to explain just why—it must partially, I'm sure, have to do with first seeing the movie at a fairly impressionable age, but it's also a scene that, to me, perfectly encapsulates Bong's specialty as a filmmaker. The split second in which we see Hee-bong resigning himself to his fate, Gang-du's horror as he counts the cartridges against his head and realizes what he's done, Hee-bong's shooing gesture—every little moment and cut adds to the bittersweetness of the scene. Even though something awful is unfolding, there's a note of tenderness that's ever-present through it: Hee-bong doesn't react with anger to his son's mistake—his actions are informed by love for his family right up until the end. The paradox present in the scene—the tragedy of what's occurring versus selfless love and sacrifice for one's family—is exactly what makes it so affecting.

Despite the darkness he confronts us with, Bong's films all retain that sense of humanity and empathy. That is, even when it seems as though things are hopeless, even at rock bottom, we have to hang onto some sense of hope and love for each other. We can't cry every day.

72e FES
NTERNA

플란다스의 개
BARKING DOGS NEVER BITE

1.

→ Opposite
Character introduction 101: In the outrageous opening sequence of his directorial debut, Bong Joon Ho delivers a masterclass in objective empathy, as embittered, depressed, and morally out-to-sea Yun-ju (Lee Sung-jae) resolves to take out all his worldly frustrations on the cutest little Shih Tzu imaginable, then struggles to actually go through with anything.

In screenwriting parlance, "saving the cat" refers to the practice of having the protagonist do something heroic—e.g., saving a cat—so as to instantly garner sympathy.

In the opening scene of Bong Joon Ho's debut feature, *Barking Dogs Never Bite*, we are introduced to our hero as he attempts to kill a dog.

Released in 2000, *Barking Dogs Never Bite* is the most neglected entry in Bong's oeuvre despite its status as his first cinematic missive to the world. Even Bong himself has gone out of his way to dissuade audiences from seeking the film out. "This is a very stupid black comedy movie," he told the crowd just before screening a clip for the 2020 BAFTA Screenwriters' Lecture Series. "Please don't see the whole movie."

"Stupid" is a harsh, if characteristically self-deprecating, description. Though *Barking Dogs Never Bite* is perhaps a little more blunt in its construction than Bong's later works, it's no less interested in matters of class, and the desperate measures that are born out of desperate times. Granted, the desperation that Yun-ju (Lee Sung-jae) is feeling is relatively quotidian. He wants to become a professor and, from one of his colleagues, discovers that the price of professorship is not hard work but a bribe of $10,000. On a more immediate level, he also wants to be free from the irritating yapping of the dog that lives somewhere in his apartment complex, an issue he decides to resolve by doing away with the dog in question.

Bong, who cowrote the script with Song Ji-ho and Derek Son Tae-woong, establishes these motivations immediately, as the very first scene features Yun-ju on the phone, his voice floating over a shot of verdant trees as he tells a friend that he might just not be cut out for life as an academic. "I'd like to go hiking and take a nap on the mountain," he says wistfully. As his imaginary idyll fades into his friend's admonishments that he isn't thinking about professorship in the right way, so too does it become clear that Yun-ju is not actually in the forest, now, but surveying it from his apartment. His breath creates a fog on the glass between him and the outside world while the incessant barking of a dog breaks any remaining sense of serenity. In the next sequence, while taking out the recycling, he comes across a Shih Tzu whose owner is nowhere in sight, and he grabs it with the intention of ending its life—or, rather, improving his own by removing the sound of barking from it.

Watching a character kill (or at least try to kill) a dog sets a high bar when it comes to making them sympathetic or tolerable enough to spend a whole movie with, yet Bong somehow defies the odds by ramping up the pitch-black humor that is now a trademark in his work. Yun-ju doesn't hesitate to snatch the dog, but when it comes to actually killing it, he falters. His morals just about remain intact. After chickening out of dropping the dog from the roof of his building (not least because an old woman almost catches him in the act while she goes about drying some radishes), he then dashes down to the basement and tries to hang it. When that also turns out to be too brutal a method of execution, he locks it in a cabinet and leaves it there to starve. It's difficult to argue that he's not heartless, given that he does leave the pooch to die, but his bumbling, uncertain attempts at getting the job done point to a torn conscience, complicating the cruel and, ultimately, selfish act of killing another person's pet.

The tightrope act of keeping Yun-ju even remotely sympathetic becomes more difficult when it's revealed that it's a different dog that has been getting on his nerves—the Shih Tzu, in a terrible stroke of irony, is incapable of barking thanks to a throat operation. He feels guilty when he finds out, but not guilty enough not to enact a plan to abduct yet another dog, this time the actual culprit, and throw it to its death. But Yun-ju isn't a totally lost cause—almost none of Bong's characters are. Cut-and-dried notions of good and bad rarely exist in Bong's cinematic world, and none of the characters in *Barking Dogs Never Bite* are truly villains (except from an ardent dog lover's perspective). As Yun-ju's journey progresses, he comes into contact with characters who seem a little eerie or menacing, but that perception has everything to do with misunderstanding their circumstances rather than their actual natures. Everyone is doing what they believe they must in order to survive.

2.

→ **Right**
The punchline of *Barking Dogs Never Bite* is that, despite all the mayhem, upset, and personal degradation he has caused, Yun-ju is emotionally back to square one, even after having achieved his single life goal: to secure tenure as a professor.

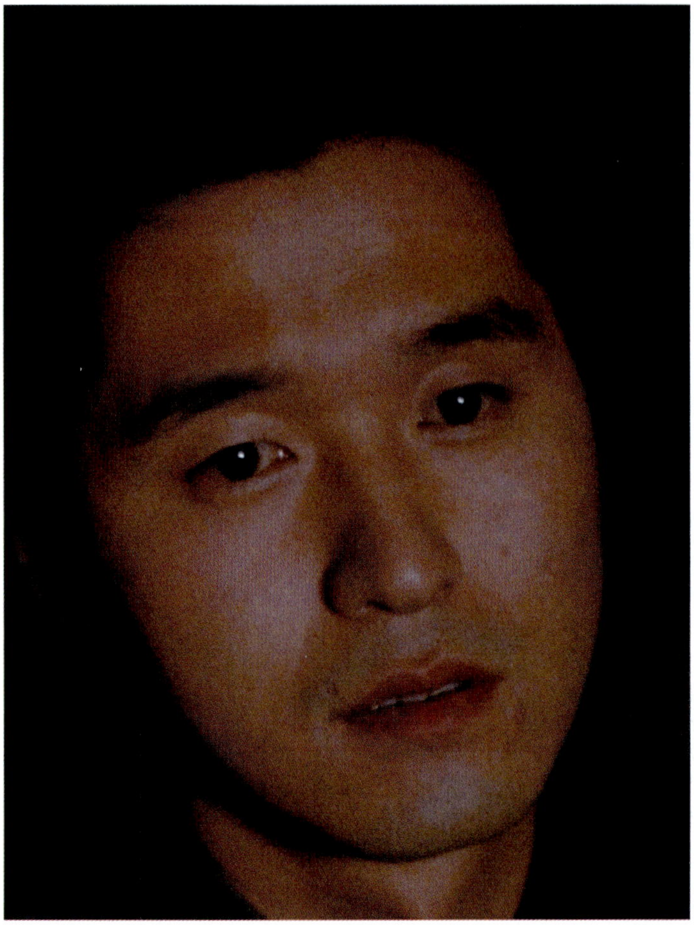

The film's Korean title, *Dog of Flanders*, is a reference to Marie Louise de la Ramée's 1872 novel, and for those familiar with the story, it offers a less-than-subtle hint as to the movie's circuitous progression of events as well as its bittersweet ending. The book focuses on a boy and his dog, but rather than culminating in triumph, or an otherwise heartwarming finale, it ends with the pair, without a penny to their name, freezing to death on Christmas Eve. The events of *Barking Dogs Never Bite* never rise to such dire levels, but Bong too avoids a happy ending. Yun-ju gets his professorship, but still seems unfulfilled. In his final appearance, he stares out the window as his students, preparing for a lecture, close the curtains. The shadows they cast creep across his face until he's left in darkness, that sense of gloomy separation mirroring the film's first scene. His dream of going hiking still seems far off, and is instead fulfilled by Hyun-nam (Bae Doona), a young woman working in the apartment's maintenance office.

Having witnessed Yun-ju's second canine murder (though she only gets a clear look at the back of his head), Hyun-nam becomes obsessed with the idea of apprehending the mysterious dognapper. Her dreams are a little bigger than Yun-ju's—she wants to be famous, or more specifically, be on TV—but she lacks any truly practical plans to achieve them. (Yun-ju, meanwhile, has a concrete, if morally questionable, plan of action to pursue.) After seeing a news report about a bank teller foiling a would-be robber, she becomes convinced that catching the canine killer would serve as her ticket

3.

← **Left**
British author Marie Louise de la Ramée's 1872 novel *A Dog of Flanders* is extremely popular in Korea, and *Barking Dogs Never Bite* is Bong's own satirical, contemporary homage to this classic tale of a boy and his dog.

4.

↓ **Below**
Bae Doona's wide-eyed waif Hyun-nam aspires to be famous but refuses to do any of the necessary groundwork. Her presence in the film is almost as a voyeur; she Is the one person who sees the bigger picture of a recent spate of dognappings.

to fame. (In one of the film's funniest touches, her imagined heroism plays out with virtually the same fight choreography as the CCTV footage from the news report.)

Though she's not the sharpest tool in the box—she can't figure out which end of a pair of binoculars to look through, and consistently falls for prank calls—Hyun-nam at least means well. Just as Yun-ju's character is established in the span of roughly five minutes, so is Hyun-nam's: While on the train, she offers her seat to a woman carrying a baby, only to have the woman resist and shrug her off. What she doesn't realize—and what the audience has seen—is that in the moments before, as Hyun-nam was dozing, the woman was begging for change. She has to keep moving in order to make any money. Under other circumstances, Hyun-nam's gesture might be viewed as considerate and cordial, but in that moment she's an obstruction. Lacking context for the woman's refusal, Hyun-nam is a little shocked. She's trying to do a good thing, and can't understand why she's been rebuffed.

In the end, Hyun-nam doesn't really get what she wants, either—she's cut out of the news broadcast she'd expected to be in—but the shot of her walking through the woods with her friend Jang-mi (Go Soo-hee), which plays under the credits, isn't as melancholic as Yun-ju's final scene, as if to suggest that the things we believe we want aren't as important as how we treat each other while in pursuit of them. To wit, in the film's final shot, Yun-ju, standing on a forest path, uses a mirror to reflect light back at the camera. Perhaps it's a bit on the nose as an entreaty for the audience to take a look at themselves, but it's earned after the film's less-than-happy ending.

For Bong, the line between haves and have-nots is at its blurriest in *Barking Dogs Never Bite*, as the most well-off of the characters are middle class, rather than extravagantly rich in the vein of the Park family in 2019's *Parasite*, or the first-class train passengers in 2013's *Snowpiercer*. There's never any question that $10,000 is a lot of money for Yun-ju to be forking over

5.

← **Opposite**
Yun-ju finally does dispatch a dog mid-film—in a scene that perhaps prompted Bong to include an assurance of animal welfare as an opening intertitle—but is promptly brought back down to earth as his wife brings home a dog for the couple as a surprise.

6.

↓ **Below**
Though Yun-ju's wife Eun-sil (Kim Ho-jung) is initially portrayed as something of a nag, the source of her frustration—her husband's unwillingness to rise beyond what he perceives to be the unfairness of everything in the world—is fair game.

for the sake of career advancement, and he and the apartment's janitor (Byun Hee-bong) commiserate over their shared annoyance about the dogs living in the complex. (Pets technically aren't allowed, but people ignore the rules to suit their whims.) Both imagine that the dog owners must be rich to have the money to raise such expensive toy dogs and, as the janitor notes, "The dogs eat better than I do." As it transpires, however, the first of Yun-ju's victims belongs to a child who skips school out of desperation to find her missing pet, and the second belongs to an old woman with no other family, who passes away from the shock of discovering her dog's demise, leaving behind only her dried radishes. She's not so affluent that she won't chase a couple of grapefruit when she sees them rolling down the street, practically throwing herself onto her knees to catch one. Yun-ju's victims are no richer than Yun-ju himself, who, in a twist of fate, becomes the owner of the film's third missing dog after his pregnant wife, Eun-sil (Kim Ho-jung), unaware of her husband's activities, brings home a toy poodle. As he walks it in the apartment courtyard, he locks eyes with the janitor, then turns to walk in another direction, aware of his perceived hypocrisy and the class division that has now risen between them.

If anything, Yun-ju is the most well-off character in the film. Initially, he's not making any money but gets by thanks to Eun-sil's pay from her office job. By contrast, Hyun-nam lives with her family and whiles away most of her days hanging out with Jang-mi, who runs a small convenience shop. The janitor, meanwhile, takes his breaks in the gloomy basement of the building and, in one of the film's grimmer reveals, makes stew out of both of the dogs that Yun-ju has dispatched. And that stew, while unattended, also feeds a homeless man (Kim Roi-ha) who is squatting in the basement. He's at the very bottom of the apartment complex's social ladder, virtually invisible to its residents, except for the children who follow and throw things at him whenever he emerges out in daylight. Yun-ju witnesses this harassment firsthand, but does nothing about it and, fittingly, at the end of the movie, lets the other

man take the fall for the dog murders rather than fessing up to what he's done.

When Eun-sil's dog inevitably goes missing, it's by accident rather than the product of malice, as Yun-ju is too busy scratching off a lottery ticket—that could win him the $10,000 he needs—to notice that the toy poodle has wandered off. The disappearance heralds a major shift in how the audience is encouraged to see Yun-ju. His actions, as mentioned, are always couched in some understanding of why he's going through with them. On top of it all, he has to deal with the nagging of his wife, who is written as a relatively two-dimensional harridan until this specific moment. She's demanding something in every scene, whether it's that he shell walnuts for her before going out to drink with his friends, or that he not come home too late, or that he return to the grocery store to pick up something they've forgotten.

In reality, however, nothing that she asks of him is too taxing or unreasonable, and it isn't as if he's an exemplary and generous husband otherwise. A moment of sincere kindness occurs when he's drunk, as he kisses her round belly when she's asleep, but even then, the moment is more about him, as he tells the baby bump that he's going to be a professor. Aside from that scene, he doesn't acquit himself well; he fails to notice that something is weighing on his wife, and fails to account for the consequences of killing the dogs, who have done nothing but do what dogs normally do. Eventually, when he is finally forced to face his mistakes, the confrontation speaks to the degree of tunnel vision from which he suffers. Yun-ju snaps when Eun-sil accuses him of losing the dog on purpose, throwing a hammer in her direction (a gesture that's no less shocking for the fact that she throws a plate of walnuts at him first) and berating her for spending money when he's desperately scraping together the cost of a professorship. In tears, Eun-sil explains that she was laid off for being pregnant, and that the dog was the one thing she bought for herself with just $300 out of the $13,000 she was given as severance pay. The rest, she tells him, she intended to use to pay for his bribe.

What makes this particularly painful—or at least frustrating—is that Yun-ju believes himself to be a good person. In the movie's final act, on the way to deliver $10,000 to the university, he slips one bill out of the cake box he's using to transport the money and gives it to the same beggar that Hyun-nam tried to help at the beginning of the film. It's an act of kindness, but one that could be interpreted as being born out of guilt, too. Though he tells himself that he'll never become the kind of person who'd take a bribe as he suffers the indignity of offering one, the promise means less and less given everything he's done. Nobody in the film, particularly those less fortunate, is as selfish. When Hyun-nam discovers Yun-ju's dog in the homeless man's possession—he plans to eat it—she takes the dog and flees in terror. When he catches up with her, it's not to attack her or steal the dog back. He simply asks if the dog is hers, and when she answers that it isn't, he tells her that they can eat it together.

His apprehending soon thereafter feels all the more tragic as a result—he's not responsible for a single one of the canine murders he's being arrested for, and doesn't attempt to defend himself. When interviewed about his motives, he simply says that, in prison, he'll be able to have pork for lunch and fish for dinner: He'll be well fed in a way that he isn't as a free man. The news report also mentions that he's being investigated for other crimes, and will be undergoing psychiatric evaluation because he can't keep his story straight. The idea that his recollections might not be consistent because he's innocent never crosses anyone's mind purely because of his social status. Even the janitor, who is interviewed for the segment, is happy to pile on, though just before his clip ends, he expresses concern about the interview being broadcast for fear of appearing bad at his job for failing to notice a squatter on the premises. Everyone—except Hyun-nam and the homeless man—is happy to step on the shoulders of the person on the ladder rung below them in order to stay afloat.

In speaking about his inspiration for the film at the same BAFTA lecture where he called the film

7.

↖ **Top left**
Radishes are dried on the roof and dog meat is stewed in the basement. Even through food, Bong finds a way to emphasize the hardscrabble lives of various characters, adding a subtle class critique to the themes of entitlement and high-rise living.

8.

↓ Below
Hyun-nam puts her own life in danger to foil the plans of a hungry dognapper (Kim Roi-ha), but is perhaps fixated more on the fame she hopes this will bring her than she is in the satisfaction of civic duty.

9.

↖ **Opposite and above** Bong is known for his keen sense of spatial awareness, as well as an ability to synchronize the placing of the camera with the choreography of the actions he is capturing. This sequence, in which Yun-ju distracts a pensioner (Kim Jin-goo) so he can steal her dog, is executed with the director's soon-to-be-customary balletic precision.

"stupid," Bong recalled that, while in elementary school, he went onto the roof of a "luxurious" apartment complex only to discover the slightly burnt corpse of a dog. "To see that was so shocking, and it was quite a traumatic memory," he said. "I remember at the time I thought, *Who would do such a thing?*" For most, the answer would likely be some kind of monster, so it's indicative of Bong's storytelling interests that he created a film not about an unredeemable killer but about a group of people all struggling to get by. Of course, there are also less traumatic inspirations: Bong mentioned that around the time he was writing the film, his brother had just finished his PhD and was struggling to become a professor, à la Yun-ju, and that the apartment complex in which the movie was filmed was actually the one he lived in as a newlywed in the mid-'90s. ("It shares a lot of details with my own everyday life, particularly with the recycling scenes.")

That all of its themes are pulled from close to home makes it all the easier to identify swaths of *Barking Dogs Never Bite* as a blueprint for Bong's ensuing films. Certain images return in his later work, too, such as the cloud of pesticide that floats across the courtyard as Yun-ju walks the toy poodle. Early on in *Parasite*, the Kim family leaves the windows of their sub-basement apartment open as a man sprays pesticide outside, reasoning that they're getting a free extermination. Still, they break into coughs as soon as the fog of chemicals fills their home, making it obvious that the pesticide is not meant for human consumption. And though the clouds of chemicals in *The Host* (2006) aren't pesticide—rather, a biological weapon called Agent Yellow, in reference to Agent Orange, the chemical used by the US military during the Vietnam War—the visual is deployed for a similar effect. The people being gassed are insignificant. Because they're not wealthy, the fact that they might die, or otherwise suffer negative effects, isn't of any concern to the people doing the spraying.

The scene provides some of the most striking visuals in the film, as Yun-ju and the dog disappear into a white froth. The clouds consume him in a medium shot, then float away from him in a wide shot.

10.

← Left
The geometrically precise exterior shots of the apartment complex highlight the compartmentalized nature of high-rise life and, in their symmetry, recall the work of American filmmaker Wes Anderson.

11.

← Opposite
A recurring motif in Bong's films—that of people being immersed in noxious gas—is introduced at the mid-point of *Barking Dogs Never Bite*, signaling Yun-ju's dangerously numbed state of mind as he walks (and subsequently loses) his wife's new toy poodle.

12.

↓ Next Page
Oblivious to the fact that Yun-ju is the dognapper she's been hunting for, Hyun-nam helps him put up posters after his dog goes missing—and is ultimately fired from her job for spending so much time worrying about the lost pooches, whereas Yun-ju faces no real consequences.

위험

It leaves him in the center of a circle of clear space as the chemical fog recedes like concentric ripples in water. There aren't as many stylistic flourishes in *Barking Dogs Never Bite* as in Bong's later films, but the few moments that do break free from more straightforward filmmaking help distinguish it. There are the Wes Anderson-esque shots of the apartment building, for instance, which treat the floors like rows on a spreadsheet as a way to keep track of the people moving around them like numbers moving from cell to cell. Then there's the film's sole flashback, which occurs when Yun-ju is told of the mishap that befell one of his colleagues on a drunken night. Having delivered his bribe and become a professor, this friend drank so much during his meeting with the dean that, while vomiting onto the subway tracks, he was struck by a train. The events play out in uncharacteristically dramatic fashion, filmed in extreme, saturated colors and using low angles to set the flashback apart from the rest of the movie. Similarly, the scene in the basement in which the janitor tells the story of "Boiler Kim," a repairman who was supposedly murdered and then sealed into the building's concrete after pointing out that the developers had used cheap materials to cut corners, is shot with lighting that gives it an almost noirish feel. Byun's face is lit from below as darkness surrounds him in classic "scary story around a campfire" fashion, the camera tracking his every moment so as to emphasize this one-man show, and it becomes more and more apparent as the story unfolds that this isn't a tale about a murder, per se, but, fittingly, about greed.

The events of *Barking Dogs Never Bite*, though certainly not common occurrences, aren't as obviously outlandish as *Okja*'s (2017) super pig project or *The Host*'s river monster, and for most of its runtime, the camerawork is relatively sedate in reflection of the everyday subject matter. As such, the sense of speed and motion present in the film's two chase sequences feels that much more visceral. The first occurs when Hyun-nam sees Yun-ju throw the old woman's dog from the roof. She rushes to apprehend him, her urgency—and Yun-ju's panic—communicated by a shift into shaky,

13.

↑ Above
Lively, cacophonic jazz plays over the film's two slapstick chase sequences. In both cases Hyun-nam attempts to catch a suspected dog-killer as they dash through the cramped corridors and byways of the apartment block. In the first instance, Yun-ju escapes. In the second, it's Hyun-nam's friend Jang-mi (Go Soo-hee) who actually takes the perceived criminal down.

14.

← Opposite
The gory anecdote of a PhD candidate who had too much to drink before riding the subway is cheekily used to foreshadow Yun-ju's own tawdry fate, and also suggests that his definition of "success" is some way off the mark.

handheld camerawork. The film's jazzy score (composed by Jo Seong-woo, and unlike any music Bong has used since) becomes frantic, with discordant trumpets and cymbal crashes growing louder and louder. As Hyun-nam gets closer to catching her prey, slow motion kicks in, as if building up to a heroic moment. But it's not to be. A door that Yun-ju has just passed opens, and Hyun-nam, who dashes straight into it, is knocked flat on her back. The second chase unfolds as Hyun-nam, having found Yun-ju's dog, flees from the homeless man, with Jang-mi stepping in to take him down. (Go, who is likely best known to Western audiences as the prison bully in Park Chan-wook's *Sympathy for Lady Vengeance*, brings the opposite energy to bear here; she's the warm-but-tough best friend, and though she's tackling and putting the wrong man into a headlock, she becomes the closest thing the movie has to an action hero.) Slow motion kicks in, again, when Hyun-nam returns the toy poodle to Yun-ju. It's the film's cartooniest moment, as, in slo-mo, a deliriously relieved Yun-ju turns around to tell his wife the good news, music swelling as the reunion plays out. Everything is resolved—but just for a moment. Jang-mi, standing behind the grinning Hyun-nam, turns to look into the apartment courtyard, where the homeless man is being led away by the police. The audience knows that the wrong man has been apprehended, and the music comes to a stop as he loses one of his shoes and entreats the police to let him retrieve it.

The slow-motion scene that follows is much less triumphant. Drunk on his way back from meeting with the dean, Yun-ju is helped home by Hyun-nam, who has since lost her job at the apartment office for spending too much time looking for the missing dogs. Stricken with guilt upon finding out that Hyun-nam has been fired for a wild goose (dog) chase that he was responsible for (and perhaps by the parallelism in Hyun-nam's declaration that she'd like to go hiking in the mountains), Yun-ju confesses his sins in the most roundabout way possible. He encourages her to look at his silhouette from behind and begins to run, asking her if he doesn't look familiar. "We ran together

15.

↑ Above
As the missing toy poodle is returned to Yun-ju before being eaten by a man who has been living in the apartment basement, the film's tragicomic register reaches new heights: Their reunion plays out in slow-motion as a beaming Hyun-nam looks on. Only Jang-mi seems to have mixed feelings about the affair, as she notices the unhoused man (who, all things considered, is innocent) being carted off by the police.

16.

→ Opposite
Yun-ju, overwhelmed by guilt, attempts to confess to Hyun-nam by demonstrating how he runs, hoping to jog her memory—a great example of the way Bong constantly returns to and develops seemingly innocuous plot threads and images.

like this before," he tells her. As they pass a group of joggers all dressed in white, the sequence shifts over to slow motion, with Yun-ju's arms resuming their stiff-handed swings, mirroring the shot of his running during the first chase. Hyun-nam comes to a stop, her jaw dropping. It looks like realization is dawning upon her, but even when Yun-ju comes to a stop, saying, "Yes, it was me," Hyun-nam only points to the ground. "One of your shoes is missing," she says, before going to find it for him. Does she not understand what he's trying to tell her? Does she forgive him for what he's done? To say that Hyun-nam understands would be the easy route, but from the very start of the film, it's been established that, though she means well, she'll miss any clues that aren't handed directly to her. Without Yun-ju explicitly stating that he's responsible for killing two dogs—and without Hyun-nam speaking her realization (or lack thereof) aloud—whether or not Hyun-nam has put the pieces together is left up to interpretation. As is his wont, Bong avoids a tidy, uncomplicated ending.

At the time of its release, the film was such a disaster at the box office that Bong recalls fearing being chased out of the industry. Though he describes the film as "stupid" now, he gave a less dismissive response as to why *Barking Dogs Never Bite* bombed in a 2007 interview with *Cineaste*. "Audiences then didn't appreciate black humor," he said. "Recently the producer of that film [Cha Seung-jae] has speculated that if *Barking Dogs Never Bite* had been released two or three years later, it would have been more successful. There has been a shift in sensibility among Korean audiences." Given that *Barking Dogs Never Bite*, upon inspection, reveals itself as the urtext to Bong's later, more lauded work, Cha seems to have been right.

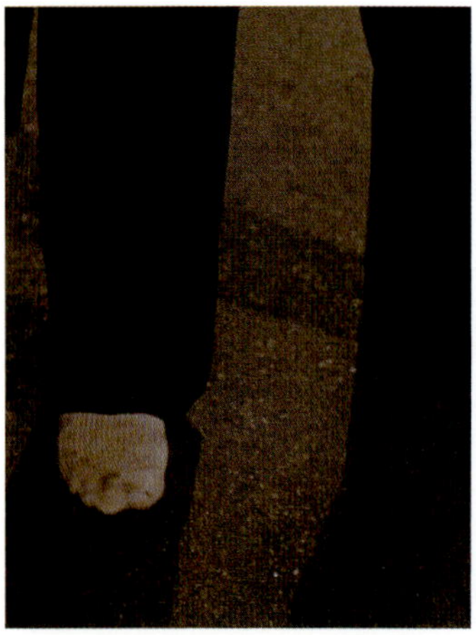

17.

↖ **Above and left**
As the film draws to a close, the two protagonists have, in some sense, achieved their dreams, yet are in a worse place than when they started. Still, both find a scintilla of respite in their grudging acceptance of life's natural chaos.

2000
Barking Dogs Never Bite
1h 50m

Director	Bong Joon Ho
Writers	Bong Joon Ho Song Ji-ho Derek Son Tae woong
Key Cast	Bae Doona Lee Sung-jae Kim Ho-jung
Budget	$10 million *Estimated*
Producer	Cha Seung-jae
Music	Jo Seong-woo
Cinematography	Jo Yong-gyu
Film Editing	Lee Eun-soo
Production Design	Hang Lee

FRIENDS NOT FOOD

PANAVISION

INFLUENCES
PULP FICTION (1994)

Upon its release in 1994, Quentin Tarantino's *Pulp Fiction* was a sensation, not least because of the film's unusual structure: The events of the story are told out of order, and further fractured by the fact that we follow three separate (though interrelated) plot strands. The main protagonists are hitman Vincent Vega (John Travolta), his business partner Jules Winnfield (Samuel L. Jackson), and prizefighter Butch Coolidge (Bruce Willis). The movie, split into seven parts, begins and ends on the same diner hold-up, as the five chapters in between jump around in time and in character focus.

Among those influenced by the film was a twentysomething Bong Joon Ho, then still a student, who was so smitten that he would attempt to emulate it in his 1994 short film *Incoherence*, which follows three different men in different circumstances before bringing them all together in a final segment. "The film school that I went to—in the same building as my classroom, there was a screening room," Bong recalled. "I would open the door for my lecture hall, and go straight to the screening room and watch films. *Pulp Fiction* was playing there, and I remember being so shocked at just the incredible screenplay of that film."

Though Bong's feature works aren't so blatantly partitioned or experimental in scope (relatively speaking), that early love for *Pulp Fiction* is revealed in his skill at building intricate ensemble pictures. Even in his early works—take *The Host* (2006), for instance—the secondary and even tertiary cast members are still well fleshed out and have their turn in the spotlight. And even though, again, there aren't any chapter breaks present, the multiplicity of themes at play in his work creates layers that only become more rewarding with each rewatch. Tarantino would further serve as inspiration for Bong in terms of casting. In a talk between the two directors at the 2013 Busan International Film Festival, Bong said that his equivalent to Tarantino revitalizing Travolta's career with *Pulp Fiction* was casting Byun Hee-bong, who has, at time of writing, starred in four of Bong's films: *Barking Dogs Never Bite* (2000); *Memories of Murder* (2003); *The Host*; and *Okja* (2017). Byun's last film credit prior to *Barking Dogs Never Bite* was 1993's *A Surrogate Father* and, before that, a few films in 1988. "He was out of film work for ten years and acting in TV," Bong said, of his choice to seek Byun out, "but I knew he still had this power and presence that should be seen on the big screen."

The admiration between the two filmmakers is mutual, as Tarantino (who attended the Busan festival on a whim specifically to meet Bong) had this to say about Bong's work, echoing a sentiment that has been fairly common in Western assessments of Bong's films: "Of all the filmmakers out there in the last twenty years, he has something that [1970s] Spielberg had, where he can do many different types of stories. But no matter the type of story, there's always this level of comedy and entertainment that is there."

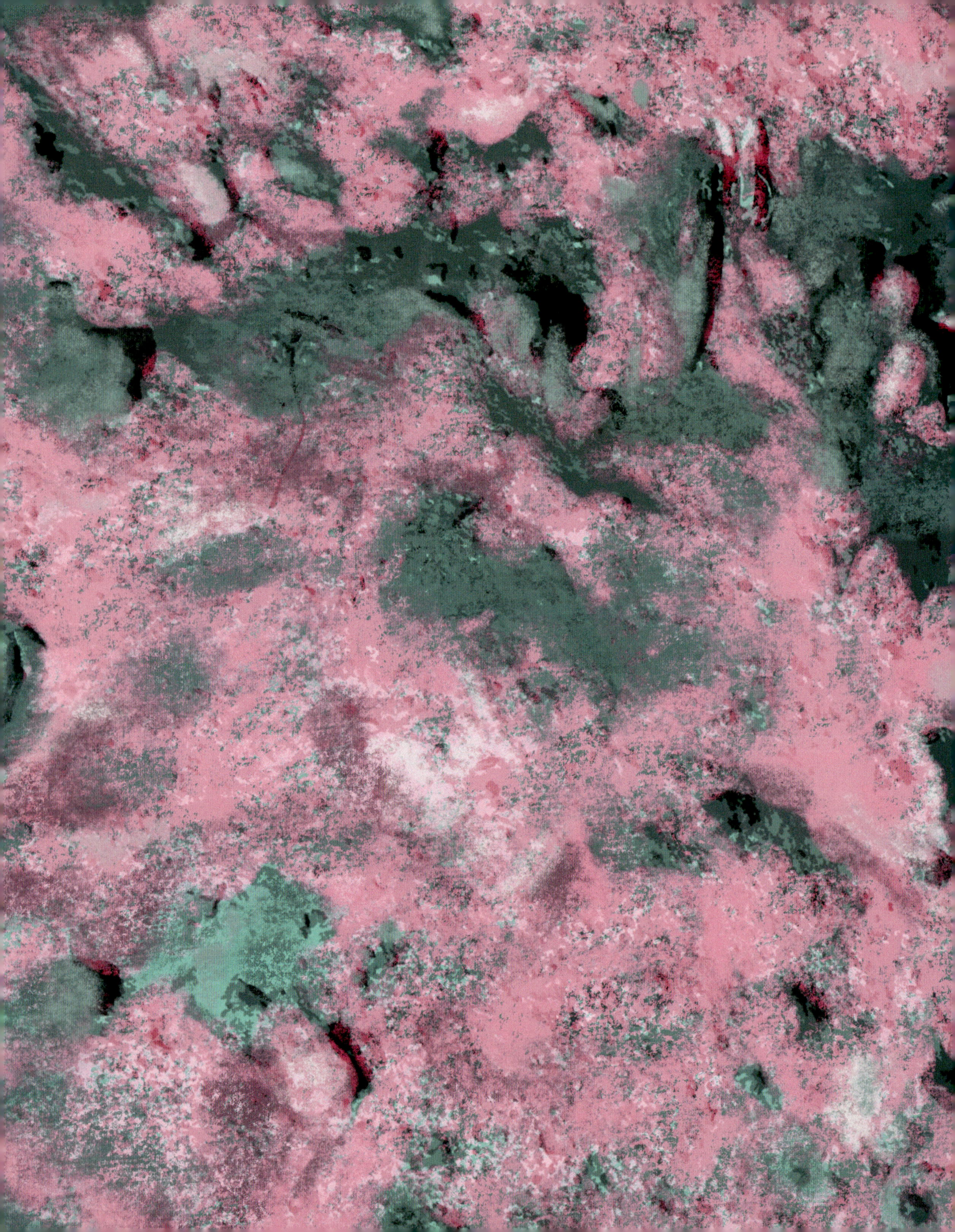

살인의 추억
MEMORIES OF MURDER

18.

→ Opposite
A horribly tense sequence in which a woman is being stalked at night showcases Bong's ability to co-opt fragments of genre convention (in this case, the classic slasher movie), but to orchestrate them with a unique sense of dynamism and formal brio. The killer is revealed, but only for a fraction of a second, creating a visceral sense of tension and fear.

On a dark, rainy night, a woman walks alone through the countryside. As she grows paranoid that she's being followed, she comes to a stop, casting the beam of her flashlight around her. Her figure takes up the right side of the screen, her silhouette framed against a seemingly endless field.

In the empty space to her left, a figure slowly rises from the grass. The black shape—just a head and shoulders, tiny in the frame—barely lingers, pausing only for a moment before sinking back into obscurity. The woman doesn't notice, but the reveal changes everything for the viewer. Suddenly, every inch of grass has become a potential hiding spot.

The eerie hush is now more frightening than any rustling or screaming, in the same way that the monsters of our imagination are inevitably more gruesome and terrifying than anything ever committed to the screen. In the shots that follow, which vary from close-ups on the woman (the sense of claustrophobia increased by the way the umbrella she's holding limits the depth of field) to wide-frame compositions that paint her as a speck against the vast field, it's impossible to find any hint of safety. The killer could be anywhere.

The scene is heart-stopping without ever resorting to jump scares, and the level of craft on display places the film leagues beyond most contemporary horror movies. But Bong Joon Ho's 2003 film *Memories of Murder* doesn't quite fall into the horror or thriller genre. Though it's most easily described as a crime drama, as it tackles South Korea's first (and certainly most infamous) serial murder case, it is, in Bong's own words, a portrait of Korea in the 1980s, and a story about failure.

Bong Joon Ho is one of a rare handful of auteurs whose filmography is nearly impossible to rank. ("Nearly," because 2000's *Barking Dogs Never Bite* generally takes the bottom slot—less because of any glaring artistic failings but more simply because fewer people have seen it.) But of his oeuvre, his second film, *Memories of Murder,* is one of the most talked about. Quentin Tarantino, for instance, has named it (along with 2013's *The Host*) as one of his top twenty favorite movies made between 1992 and 2009, and it is consistently on lists of the best films of the 2000s, including those of *Sight & Sound* and *Film Comment.*

The film is loosely based on the Hwaseong serial murders that occurred between 1986 and 1991, which have been compared to the Zodiac Killer case in the United States because the identity of the killer remained a mystery for so long (until 2019). Bong's version of the story follows a pair of fictional detectives who struggle to solve the case, and whose initial bristliness toward each other turns into shared desperation as the body count rises.

Given its subject matter, *Memories of Murder* is an inherently grim and somber work, but its broader scope opens the door for Bong's tendency to weave seemingly disparate tones together; parts of the film are, somehow, laugh-out-loud funny, not for the sake of lightening the mood or turning the movie into more of a comedy, but because such contradictions are a natural part of life. The layers present in the film also underline Bong's description of the film as a reflection of Korea in the 1980s. At the time, the movement for democracy was reaching its peak after decades of authoritarian rule, martial law, and coup d'états, and the turbulence of the era can be sensed in the civil defense drills and protests that unfold in the background of the movie. Both that historical context and willingness to play with tone are inextricable from the character studies that ultimately give the film so much of its bite, even if, as a fictionalization of real events, it's not clearly anchored to an exact year or location. "I wanted to emphasize time more than place," Bong has said, "but I didn't want to be too specific about it—so I ruled out the idea of showing President Chun Doo-hwan on television, for instance."

In his director's statement for the film's 2020 rerelease, Bong wrote, "The victims and their families, innocent suspects who were hauled and tormented, failed detectives who found themselves in despair, people of those times who trembled with fear. . . . This case

19.

← **Opposite**
The long, bumbling, and largely circuitous road ahead is foreshadowed in an early comic set-piece in which rural detective Park Doo-man (Song Kang-ho) performs a flying kick on a man attempting to ask a woman for directions, only to discover that the man is, in fact, a detective sent from Seoul to assist the investigation.

occurred in the dark era of military dictatorship in the '80s, and truly created a further and darker abyss. But what is surprising is that if you take a step back, this case is an intertwined web of tragedy and black comedy—the eerie comedy that blooms within the air during the most absurd of times. The film is an uncanny, yet natural, mixture of horror and comedy because we were truly living in such times."

Though it may be true that the events the film depicts evoke such mixed emotions in the people who lived through them, Bong deserves equal credit for marshaling the material in a way that doesn't feel exploitative of a major tragedy, and with such skill that the movie was still a hit with Western audiences, who aren't as familiar, if at all, with the history that the film is addressing. That is to say, *Memories of Murder* is an incredibly layered work, a major accomplishment not only as a sophomore outing but also as a truly great film, and the striking images that Bong creates—the alchemy that goes into bringing the script to life—can't be attributed solely to the act of re-creating history.

Park Doo-man (Song Kang-ho) and Seo Tae-yoon (Kim Sang-kyung) are opposites in almost every way. Doo-man, a countryside detective used to life in a small town, has never handled a case of this magnitude before (at the start of the film, the killer has already claimed two victims), and the ace up his sleeve is simply his claim that he can "read people" just by looking into their eyes. By contrast, Tae-yoon, a city boy from Seoul who comes to help with the investigation, relies on facts and science above anything else; his mantra is "Documents never lie."

The representative traits of each character come across as simple on paper. Even a secondary detective, Cho Yong-koo (Kim Roi-ha, who also starred in *Come to See Me*, the play upon which the film is loosely based) is fairly easily defined, as his rough interrogation methods involve a lot of kicking, and he prizes his steel-toed boots. But these seemingly blunt characteristics are never cartoonish in the context of the film, thanks in equal parts to the actors, who commit to their roles wholeheartedly, and to the script, cowritten by Shim Sung-bo and Director Bong, which immediately sets about turning those expectations upside down.

At a key moment, Doo-man and Tae-yoon pursue their second suspect (Ryo Tae-ho), whom they find masturbating at the scene of one of the murders. When the man disappears into a crowd at a nearby worksite, Doo-man finds him, but it has nothing to do with supernatural intuition. That he puts a group of workers in a lineup and picks out the right man is just for show, an attempt to prove to Tae-yoon, who looks down upon the local cops, that he's worth his salt as a detective. In reality, before gathering the men together, Doo-man has already picked the man out, having spotted his red underwear peeking out from his pants. The key to the scene is that the audience is fully in on the deception. Even from the beginning of the movie, it's dubious just how sharp Doo-man's "shaman's eyes" are—he completely misreads Tae-yoon upon their first meeting, putting him on the receiving end of a flying kick and attempting to arrest him. As the cool and collected outsider, Tae-yoon seems a little less incompetent, but when it comes to finding documents that actually lead them closer to the truth, it's the station's single female police officer, Kwon Ki-ok (Go Seo-hee), who manages to find something resembling a paper trail. As in most of Bong's films, it's a woman who has her wits about her while the men flounder. And, perhaps unsurprisingly, given the movie's theme of how the Korean people—specifically, these small-town women—were failed by their government at the time, it takes a while for the male detectives to bother listening to Ki-ok at all.

In a talk given during a 2015 residence at the Jacob Burns Film Center in New York, Bong described the Hwaseong serial murders as the source of a "bone-deep" hurt and mass national trauma. *Memories of Murder* reflects that sense painfully clearly; the film ends without a clear resolution, while the arc of the film involves the destruction of something that each character holds dear. At the movie's climax, Doo-man and Tae-yoon confront Park Hyeon-gyu (Park Hae-il), whom, after their protracted and constantly stalled investigation, they believe to be the killer. Presented with lab results that say the killer's DNA does not correspond exactly with Hyeon-gyu's and therefore can't be called a conclusive match, Tae-yoon, in despair, proclaims, "The document is a lie. I don't need it." Though he's spent the movie up to this point tut-tutting the habits of the small-town detectives as they coerce suspects into confessions through violence, he turns his gun on Hyeon-gyu, only for Doo-man, who has been complicit in brutalizing suspects, to stop him from shooting. Equally stunned by the verdict, Doo-man tells Hyeon-gyu to look into his eyes. The music drops away, leaving just the sound of the rain as the camera holds on Hyeon-gyu's face, then on Doo-man's.

"Fuck, I don't know." Doo-man's intuition fails. He can't tell if he's looking at a killer or an innocent man.

As the detectives let Hyeon-gyu go, the lab papers are torn apart by the wheels of a passing train, as if underlining just how futile the investigation has been. The murderer is still at large, and the things that the detectives once so fervently believed in—whether ideals, superstitions, or objects—have failed them. Whatever romance or sense of heroism there is in the fact that the detectives each have a sort of calling card is erased by their very human limitations. It isn't just that Doo-man is a fool—we've known that from the beginning—it's that even Tae-yoon, the man of science to Doo-man's man of faith, reaches his limit with nothing to show for it. They don't have enough resources to be able to effectively pursue the case, and lose what little they do have in their hunt for answers. Even Yong-koo (given the moniker "Detective Combat Boots" in the film's press materials) loses his leg.

Bong has said that as he began storyboarding *Memories of Murder*, it became clear that the film was a "road movie for faces," beginning with Doo-man's claims about being able to read a suspect by face alone. "The

20.

← **Left**
Memories of Murder marks the first of many collaborations between Bong and Song. By this time, Song's popularity had skyrocketed following turns in *No. 3*, *The Foul King*, and Park Chan-wook's *Joint Security Area* (Song pictured here on the right), whereas Bong had just experienced the flop of his debut feature. However, Song fondly remembered their first meeting—in 1997, while Bong had still been an assistant director—and agreed to take part in the film.

actors' faces and how we shot them inevitably became a very important aspect of the film." Park Hae-il, for instance, was cast for his "innocent face with his doe eyes," which Bong believed would only make the idea that he might be a killer even scarier.

The face upon which the camera focuses the most frequently is that of Song Kang-ho. *Memories of Murder*, which was released in 2003, marks the first collaboration between Song and Bong (who have since been fondly dubbed the "Ho-Ho brothers" by the Korean press for the shared syllable in their given names), but their first meeting dates back to 1997. At the time, Song, who got his start in theater, had only just begun acting in movies, and one of the few film roles he had under his belt was a supporting role as a gangster in Lee Chang-dong's *Green Fish* (1997). As Bong describes it, Song was so good—and still such an unknown quantity—that audiences assumed that Lee had cast a real gangster. Bong, who was then working as an assistant director on Park Ki-yong's *Motel Cactus* (1997), was so struck that he reached out to arrange a meeting despite the fact that Park "didn't really know who Song Kang-ho was and didn't care."

The meeting left a strong impression on both men. "We didn't audition him or ask him to read dialogue or anything, he just came by and I made him coffee," Bong has said, noting that, almost immediately after that fateful meeting, Song rocketed to fame with *No. 3* (1997), *The Foul King* (2000), and *Joint Security Area* (2000). "For my second movie, *Memories of Murder*, I

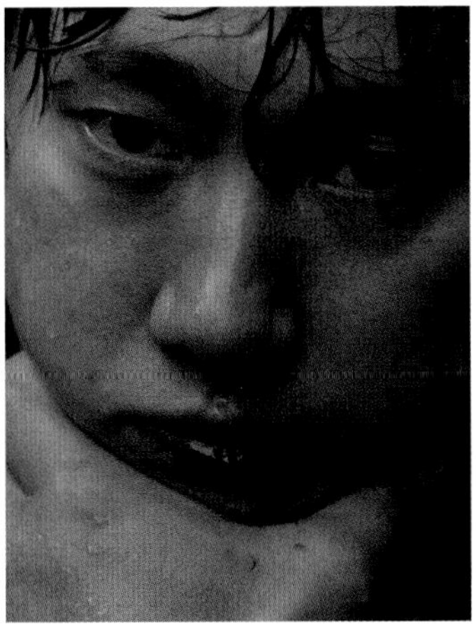

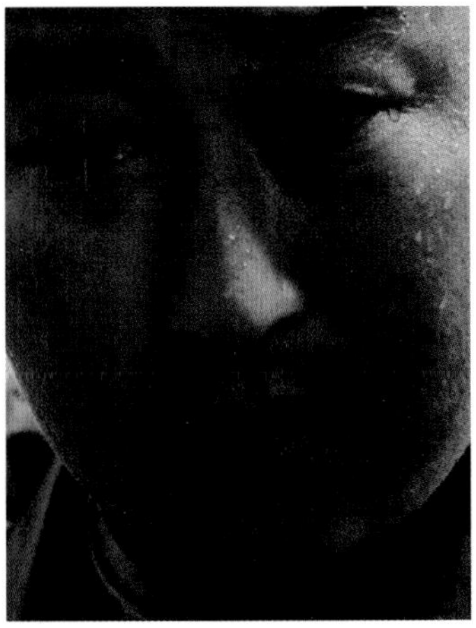

21.

✓ **Left and below**
A key motif throughout the film is the belief of detective Doo-man in his ability to "read people" and intuit the truth—a signifier of the dramatic disconnect from his more scientifically-minded partner, Tae-yoon (Kim Sang-kyung).

thought, *I'd really love to work with Song Kang-ho*, but my debut had been a disaster. I thought I was about to get chased out of the industry, and he was a star. But he remembered that meeting fondly." For his part, Song describes Bong as having been "exceedingly polite and courteous when we spoke." In an interview with Vulture, he continued, "It completely upended my notions of how an AD [associate director] acts. Usually ADs have a bit of a rough edge to them, and they tend to condescend to supporting actors or bit-part actors. When we first discussed working together for *Memories of Murder*, this was a huge factor for me." Speaking with the newspaper *Kyunghan Shinmun*, Song also recalled that their first meeting passed without discussing movies at all, and that afterward, Bong left a long voice message in which he apologized for the fact that they weren't going to cast Song in *Motel Cactus*, but expressed a wish to work together in the future.

Watching *Memories of Murder*, it's impossible to imagine anyone else in Song's shoes. (In fact, Bong wrote the part of Doo-man with Song in mind: "He has a face like people from that era.") As with all of Doo-man's eye-to-eye soul searches, the moment in which he tries to divine Hyeon-gyu's innocence is captured in straight-on shots of Song's and Park's faces. These sorts of close-ups dominate the film, and comprise its final scene, too. In an epilogue set in 2003, Doo-man, now a salesman, finds himself back at the first crime scene. As he looks into the ditch where the first body was found, a young girl asks him what he's doing, saying that another man had done the same thing not long ago, and had told her that he'd done something there in the past. As we've seen just minutes previously, Doo-man leads a completely different life now, living in an apartment with his wife, son, and daughter, and his "shaman's eyes" are now only used to tell whether or not his son is lying when he says he hasn't been playing computer games all night. But as soon as he realizes that the little girl is talking about the killer, a whirlwind of memories and emotions seems to come flooding back, and a long beat passes, as though he were contemplating whether or not it's worth re-excavating all of that pain

and sorrow. He has a new career, new children, a new existence—but the damage caused by the murders, the regret of having never caught the killer, is a wound that will never completely heal.

"Did you see his face?"

The girl nods.

"What did he look like?"

"Well . . . kind of plain."

"In what way?"

"Just . . . ordinary."

For a moment, Doo-man looks out onto the fields, his features trembling. When he turns to stare into the camera, the look lands like a sucker punch. Unlike the previous close-ups, which always had a subject on the other side of the lens, this gaze is focused directly on the viewer. A roil of emotions is visible on Doo-man's face—years of grief in a single expression. "When we were shooting the movie, we talked about how, when the movie comes out, the criminal will watch the movie in theaters," Bong has said, of that final image. "That's why we shot that last shot where the failed detective looks into the camera, so that he's looking out at the audience and at the killer in the theater, and the killer is looking back at him."

The Hwaseong serial murder case is so infamous that there have been several movies and TV shows made about it (*Gap-dong*, *Signal*, and *Confession of Murder*, to name a few), and most have fudged the ending, making up a killer so that the story delivers a contrived sense of closure. *Memories of Murder* may not offer that kind of conclusion, but the final shot of Doo-man's face lands so effectively precisely because of that lingering uncertainty. In his Jacob Burns Film Center talk, Bong told the audience that producers discouraged him from making the film, saying that making a movie where the killer isn't caught was impossible, or that he ought to make up a murderer and then have the detectives apprehend him. "Many innocent people were tortured and accused of being the criminal. . . . It was a

22.

← **Opposite**
In conjunction with its central mystery, *Memories of Murder* deals with masculinity at its most toxic. For instance, the one female officer at the police station, Ki-ok (Go Seo-hee) is often relegated to serving coffee and must endure the sexist comments of her coworkers. Despite their dismissal of her, she offers some of the best leads in the investigation.

mass trauma for all Koreans," Bong explained. "I didn't think I could take that producer's advice and go with a fake ending."

That's not to say that taking such a route was easy—telling a story that ended without answering the big question at its center was a challenge, and one that Bong ultimately cracked with the help of a gift given to him by writer Tony Rayns while showing *Barking Dogs Never Bite* at the London Film Festival: a copy of Alan Moore and Eddie Campbell's 1999 graphic novel *From Hell*. The work paid as much attention to the historical context and social conditions as to the gruesome crimes committed by its subject (Jack the Ripper, another infamous unidentified serial killer). It's that wider perspective that makes *Memories of Murder* so affecting, and keeps it from feeling like an unresolved story despite the detectives' failure—and, in fact, Bong said that while researching the Hwaseong case, "I came to feel that the general social–political situation of that time was as much to blame as any individual."

Speaking about the film for its Criterion Collection release, Bong recalled that actor Park Hae-il wanted to play Hyeon-gyu as if he were innocent and asked Bong for permission to do so. Bong agreed, noting that the movie couldn't end with any definitive answer as to whether or not Hyeon-gyu truly was the killer, but that "99 percent will want to believe, or must believe, that it's [Hyeon-gyu]." To further keep the murderer's identity as ambiguous as possible, multiple actors (including Park) portrayed him throughout the film, making it difficult for even the audience to pinpoint anything about the nature of the killer.

Bong has estimated that the movie, to which he dedicated six months of research, is about half–and–half when it comes to the balance between fictional details and historical accuracy. ("The reality was funnier and more bizarre than anything in the film," Bong has said. "A shaman advised the cops to strip naked at the seashore and bow to a bowl of sacred water. The chief of police actually did that. And while doing it they were mistaken for North Korean spies and had to run.") He reduced the time span in which the murders took place, for instance, to just one or two years, as well as reducing the number of victims. But many of the fictional details have real–life inspirations that shed some light on just how devastating the case was. Describing the interviews he did with the real–life detectives on the case in preparation for the movie, Bong called them "badass" figures who nonetheless were reduced to crying like children when expressing their shame and regret over their failure. Even Bong became obsessed with the killer while researching the case, coming up with a list of questions he'd ask if they ever came face–to–face, carefully planning out an order in which to ask them, and carrying that list around with him.

The shocking thing is that unlike the Zodiac Killer, the perpetrator of the Hwaseong serial murders was finally caught—in 2019, thirty–three years after the first murder occurred. Already serving a life sentence for the rape and murder of his sister–in–law in 1994, Lee Chun-jae confessed to and was convicted of fourteen murders during the investigation. Even more unbelievable was the fact that he had seen *Memories of Murder*. What did he think of the movie? "I felt nothing while watching it." It's a shocking answer, and one that makes the end of the movie even more tragic given that final shot's intention. As for Bong's feelings about the case finally being closed: "The film came out in 2003 and so sixteen years later I was finally able to see the face of the murderer. It wasn't just me. All Koreans were able to see, and I don't know if you can say it was fortunate, but fortunately he doesn't have a very normal face. I think if he just had a nice–looking normal face I would have felt more hurt. But thankfully he didn't look that way. Perhaps because I knew he was the murderer."

Bong may describe the real–life detectives as "badass," but his description of the fallout of the investigation, as well as the behavior of Doo-man and his colleagues in the film, makes it clear that the cops aren't exactly supposed to be regarded as heroes, either. Part of their incompetence with the case comes down to what

23.

↖ **Opposite and above** We take the process of crime scene preservation and the exciting nature of forensic science for granted, yet the crime scene depicted in the opening chapter of *Memories of Murder* travels into slapstick territory as key evidence is soiled by apathetic locals, police ineptitude reigns supreme, and any sense of clear hierarchy seems to have gone out the window. Then, at the center of it all, is the macabre image of a trussed and gagged body.

24.

→ **Opposite**
One of the only characters in the film who is legally reprimanded is Doo-man's hotheaded partner Yong-koo (Kim Roi-ha), who starts a brawl with some students. This sequence represents wider antagonisms, as police corruption is a major theme, and student protests have been occurring in the film's backdrop, often sapping vital police manpower to aid with the murder investigation.

25.

↓ **Next Page**
The film ends with no clear answer as to who the murderer is, and the detectives lost in despair. The climax, which takes place on the train tracks, is gloomy and sapped of color, reflecting the emotional states of the characters involved.

little support they have when it comes to forensics and technology, but there's no question that they simply aren't good at their jobs. Hyeon-gyu even says, "Even kids in this town know you torture innocent people."

The degree to which the detectives are ill–equipped is initially a source of humor, as perhaps best illustrated by one of the film's early sequences, a one–shot take that sees the inadvertent destruction of a crime scene. The take begins with Doo-man being shown a footprint that the police believe belongs to the killer. He marks it not with a barrier of tape but simply by scratching a circle into the dirt with a stick. When Sergeant Koo Hee-bong (Byun Hee-bong, whose characters, with the exception of the janitor he plays in *Barking Dogs Never Bite*, always share his given name) arrives on the scene, he promptly falls down a hill. Kids dash through the scene, right by the dead body. A tractor ignores Doo-man's instruction to change course, driving right over and destroying the footprint. Another police officer falls down the same hill. The dialogue constantly overlaps. It's total chaos. It's also hilarious—particularly the repeated falls—even as the destruction of evidence is sure to elicit a cringe.

But that clear inability to exert any control over what's happening is laced with sadness, as the search for the killer continues to hit dead ends, and the cops' methods grow more brutal. The scenes of torture are genuinely harrowing, as the detectives strip their suspects down to their underwear before beating them—and even hang one man upside down from the ceiling. The fallout from their abuses of power culminates in one of the movie's most tragic scenes, as Baek Kwang-ho (Park No-shik), an intellectually disabled young man and former suspect, is killed as a result of the way the investigation has been conducted. When the detectives attempt to question him after discovering that he might have witnessed one of the murders, he flees in fear, having been beaten and even forced to dig his own grave during a previous interrogation. They discover that he did indeed see the killer's face, but, frightened by the sudden appearance of Yong-koo, his main tormentor, Kwang-ho runs again, this time into the path of an oncoming train. (The incident is, unfortunately, based on something that happened during the real investigation, as a factory worker, falsely accused and beaten by the increasingly desperate detectives on the case, committed suicide by jumping in front of a train.) It's the only death that is actually depicted on–screen, as the murderer is only seen abducting his victims, but never killing them.

There's no excuse for the detectives' behavior. They may not necessarily be the villains of the story, but they have precious little moral standing. The historical context of the film also positions the police as morally ambiguous at best. The audience is automatically poised to sympathize with Doo-man, a lovable loser, as he's the film's main character, but the institution he's a part of is hardly painted in a sympathetic light. ("I've never liked cops, maybe because of my student experiences fighting them," Bong has said, though he qualified that thought by adding that his experience speaking to one of the detectives who had been on the case gave him pause. "What struck me most was the purity of his desire to catch the criminal.") In a key scene, Doo-man is left without any support because all available police forces have been summoned to suppress a student demonstration against the authoritarian rule of the time, and another scene involves a news report on a police detective charged with torture and sexual assault (itself a reference to a real–life event). Even Tae-yoon's descent, prompted though it is by the repeated dead ends that they face, is as frightening as it is sad, as his initial by–the–book attitude collapses into a willingness to kill Hyeon-gyu, even though there's no definitive proof that he's the killer, or to beat him as much as necessary to force a confession.

As journalist Ed Park wrote, *Memories of Murder* is "a period piece from which all nostalgia has been eliminated." In emphasizing the importance of the violent period in which the movie takes place, Bong has also related some of his personal experiences of the time, recalling that he was hit by faculty members many times

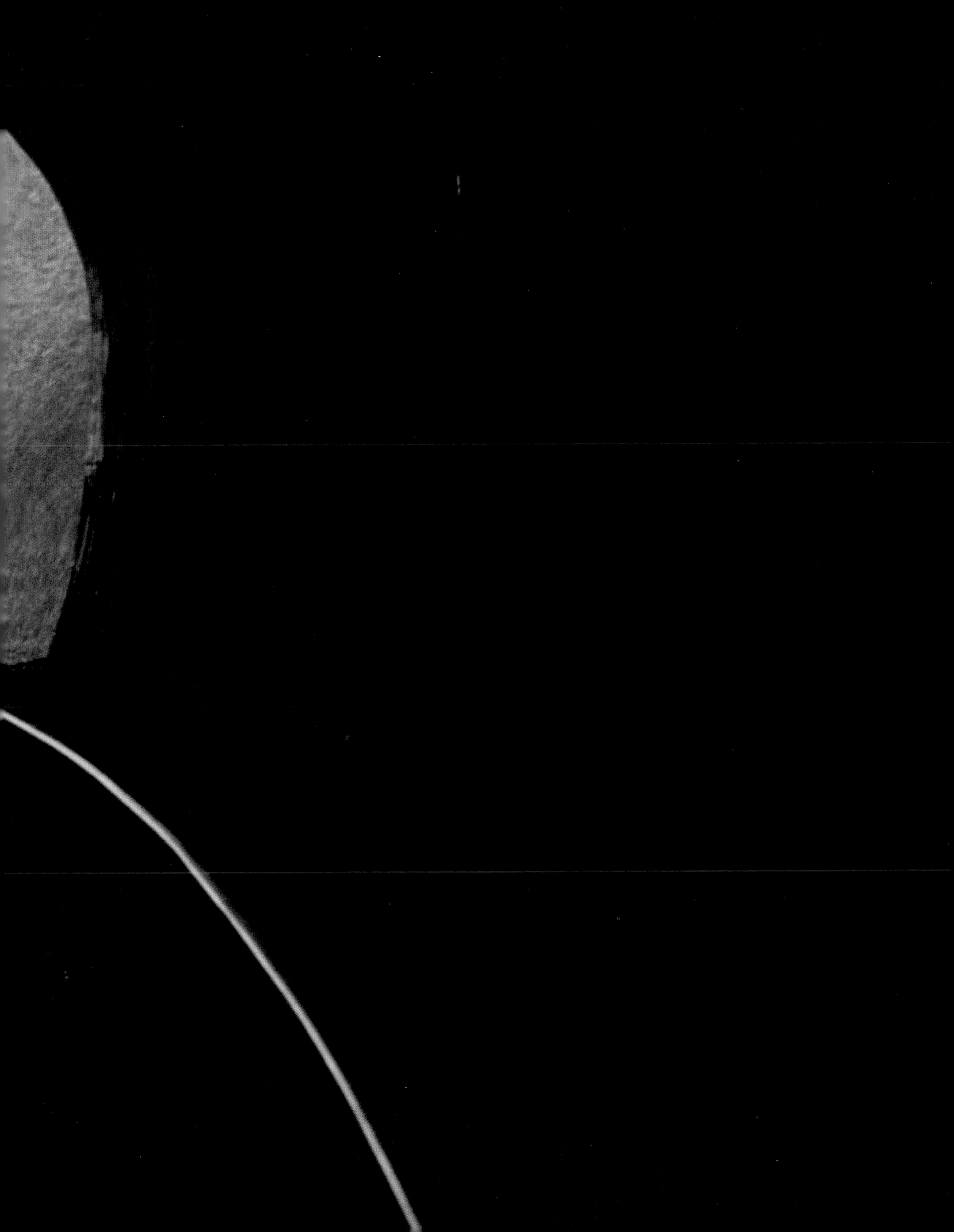

26.

→ Opposite
There are two key occasions where Doo-man believes he has caught the killer: In the first, his swagger is shown to be premature when Tae-yoon humiliates him at a recreation staged for local press; the second hangs on some compelling circumstantial evidence, but any potential glory is quashed when the real murderer stikes again while their man is in custody.

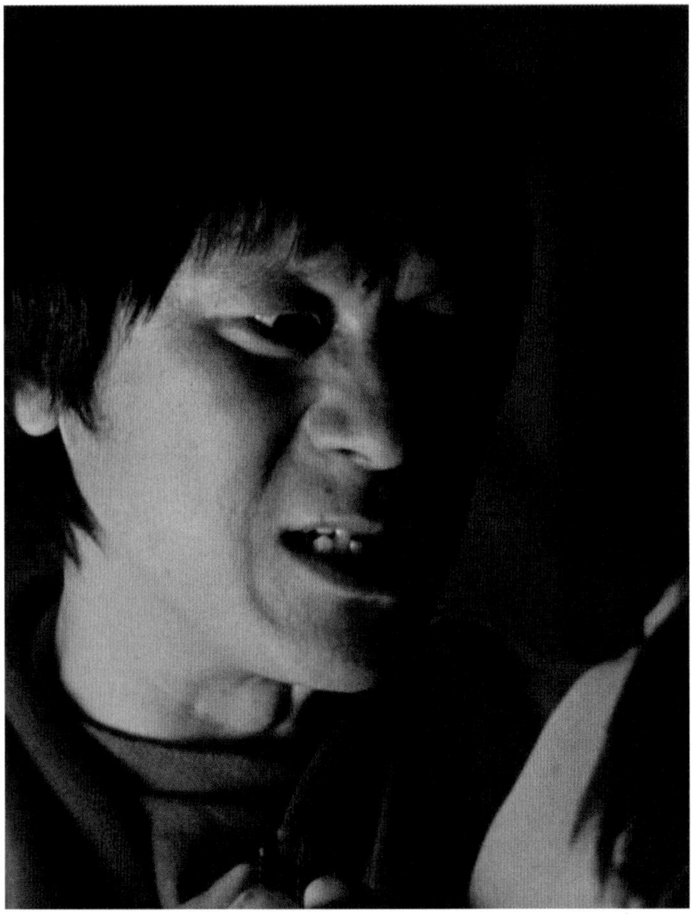

during high school, and that during college, while attending Yonsei University, he would participate in student protests that were so frequent that they were basically part of the students' routines. ("We would go to class for three hours and then maybe protest for two hours. We would go to eat and then go back to protest and then go back to studying. So it was very daily.")

That on-off violence and tumult is reflected clearly in the film—even the police chief, when telling his detectives not to beat the people they bring in to interrogate, smacks them by way of reprimand—and is also still fairly recent history. "The movie came out around ten years after the government changed to democracy, so Korean audiences had a dual reaction," Bong noted. "*We don't live in that time anymore, we've changed, we don't live in that violent society anymore.* But also, the murderer still hadn't been caught, so it was a painful memory, too." The sense of memory—but not nostalgia—is accentuated by the film's color palette, which is deeply desaturated and largely features a mix of browns and sickly greens. Bong and cinematographer Kim Hyung-ku (who also worked with Bong on *The Host*) achieved the film's dreary look through a "bleach bypass" process, skipping the bleaching step common in film processing. The first and last scenes, however, were processed normally—their bright, golden colors are a stark contrast from the rest of the movie—making the "eras" of the movie, as it were, visibly clear. When the movie transitions from that first scene in the fields to the police station, the shift in color tones doesn't seem so drastic, in parallel with the way the detectives have no idea what's waiting for them as they continue to investigate the case. But when the colors become bright and gold again at the end of the film, it's a jarring change after a series of increasingly grim scenes. (Further context on Bong's commitment to a sense of dreariness: For exterior shots, Bong and the crew would even wait for overcast conditions, and played soccer among themselves to pass the time if clouds weren't in place.) There's life before the case, and life after, and the time that the detectives spend on the case itself is quite literally a dark period.

27.

↑↓ Above and below
Yong-koo is able to employ his tried and tested method of stomping on detainees by covering his boots with a soft decorative cover so they don't leave an imprint or get his shoes bloody. Even this brutal note, however, has a wistful payoff.

28.

✓ **Left and below**
A key relationship in the film is between Tae-yoon and the schoolgirl So-hyeon (Woo Go-na); as the movie progresses, they form a rapport, and it is her death—confirmed by the presence of a Band-Aid he'd helped her put on earlier in the film—that finally drives Tae-yoon to nearly abandon his moral code.

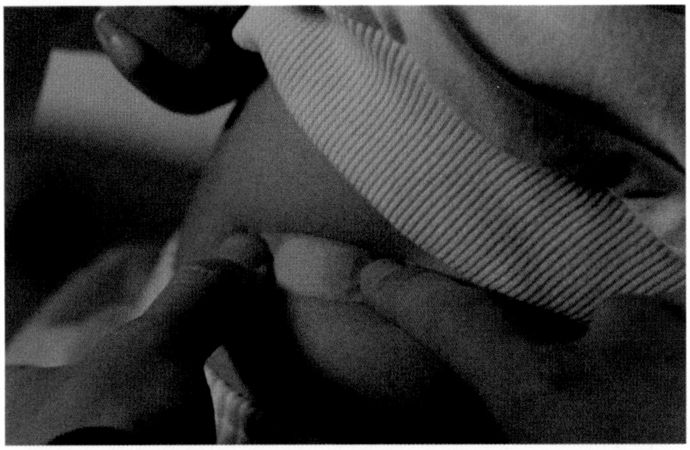

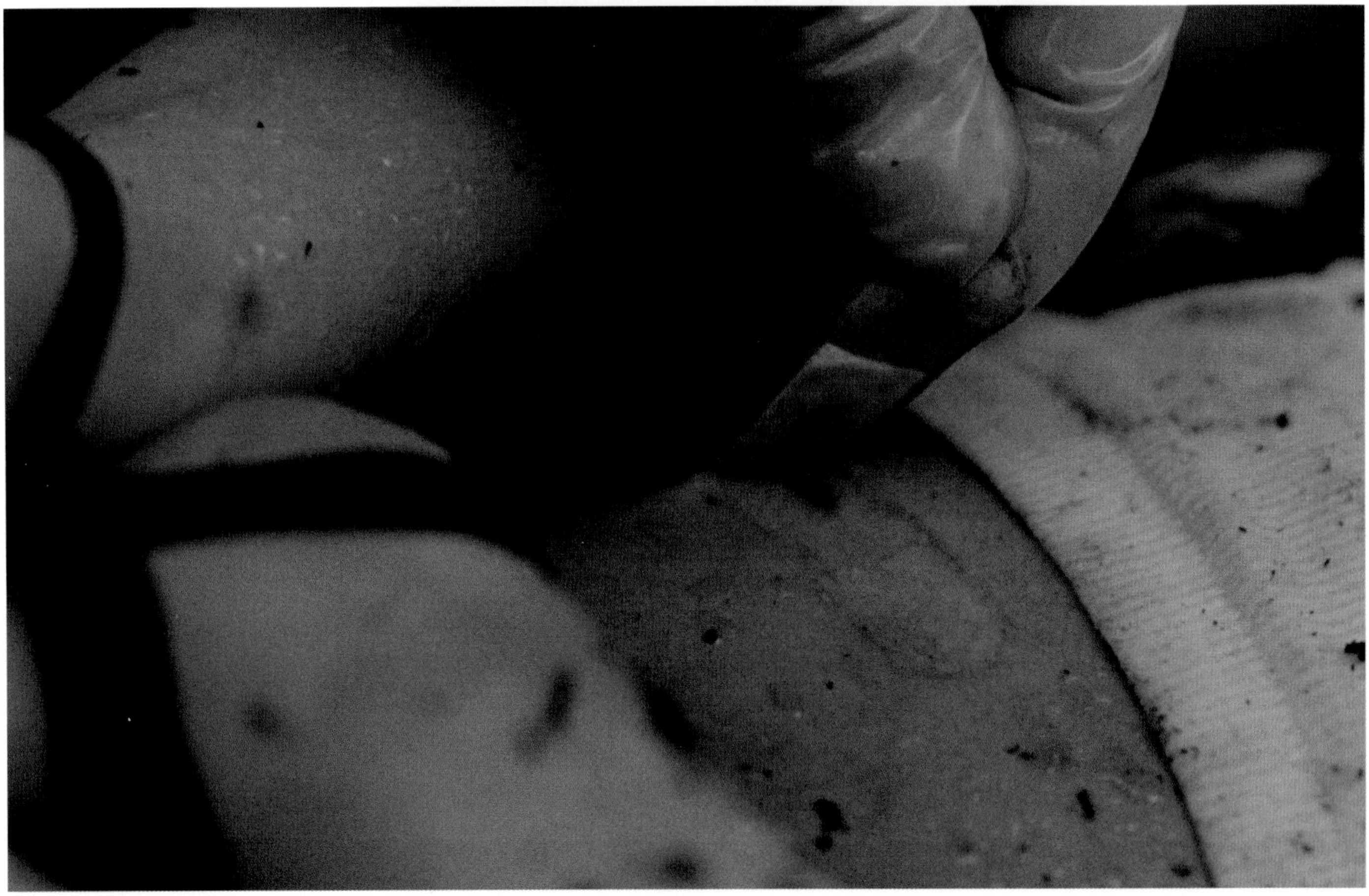

29.

← **Left**
Bong, on the character of So-hyeon and the Band-Aid moment: "The murder of the schoolgirl, for instance, closely follows the most brutal of the real murders—but I added the detail of the Band-Aid. Actually, I filched it from Kubrick's *Lolita*."

"In a straight thriller, death is just a part of a game or a puzzle," reads Bong's director's statement. "But in *Memories of Murder*, death is accompanied by sadness and anger. I am genuinely saddened by the deaths of these women. Not only do I feel rage toward the murderer, but I am also enraged about the circumstances that allowed these women to be killed. I hope that audiences who watch the film will feel as I do."

Of course, it is impossible to talk about the murders without talking about the victims. Most of the women are fairly anonymous—glimpses of their faces are brief, if provided at all—but the way they're shot is, like the shot of the murderer in the rain, deeply affecting. The pallor of death is especially ghostly given the film's palette, and the griminess of those green tones makes the examinations that the bodies then undergo even more unpleasantly tactile. The details of the case—the pieces of peach inserted into some of the victims' bodies, the way their hands and feet have been bound—are horrifying, not least in part because the actual murders all take place off-screen. As always, an imagined monster is scarier than a known one.

The exception to the rule is the schoolgirl whom Tae-yoon befriends while searching for clues. In addition to being the killer's youngest target, she is the only victim introduced to the audience prior to her death. She is also the final victim in the film, as her murder triggers Tae-yoon's decision to confront Hyeon-gyu and either kill him or force him to confess to being the murderer. That she is actually developed as a character—it's implied that she has a crush on the detective, and Bong has said Tae-yoon helping the girl with a Band-Aid, only to later find it on her corpse, was a nod to Stanley Kubrick's *Lolita* (1962)—isn't to say that she's more important than any of the other victims, but adds weight to the idea that her murder is the final straw, in addition to making the case that much more personal for Tae-yoon. Her murder also feels like a particularly heinous crime given her age, as her interactions with the detectives always touch upon the fact that she's just a child, and the feeling that it all could have been prevented is made keener by the fact that the moment of her abduction is actually preceded by a shot from the killer's POV. He feels so close in that moment that the detectives' inability to catch him is infuriating. (Even the real killer later expressed his surprise that he hadn't been caught all those years ago.)

Of Bong Joon Ho's films, *Memories of Murder* is something of an outlier as the only movie that does not, in some way, center on a family. (Even the protagonist of *Barking Dogs Never Bite* is acting in part for the sake of his wife and soon-to-be-born baby.) But it fits perfectly into his catalog as a film that's more complex than it appears to be on the surface. Loglines for the film focus on the serial murders, but the film is so much more than just a murder mystery or thriller.

The movie is also a testament to Bong's clarity of vision as a filmmaker. *Barking Dogs Never Bite* is impressively realized, but *Memories of Murder* immediately distinguishes itself as a more mature work. From the color palette to the layers of the story to the music (the score, by Tarô Iwashiro, is reminiscent of the piano-heavy, contemplative scores written by Studio Ghibli mainstay Joe Hisaishi more than anything else), *Memories of Murder* feels more refined—though that may be a strange word to describe a film that triumphs in how many plates it has spinning in the air at once.

It's an indictment of Korea's past packaged as a look at Korea's most infamous serial killer, and a paragon of the kind of micro–macro storytelling that has become a Bong Joon Ho signature.

30.

↑ **Above**
Memories of Murder's finale jumps forward to 2003, as Doo-man, now a traveling salesman, finds himself back where it all began. The film ends with Doo-man looking directly into the camera after discovering that the killer, too, has recently revisited this spot. The shot is striking, not just because it breaks the fourth wall, but because, as a result, it confronts both the audience and the killer.

2003
Memories of Murder
2h 11m

Director	Bong Joon Ho
Writers	Bong Joon Ho Shim Sung-bo
Key Cast	Song Kang-ho Kim Sang-kyung Kim Roi-ha Park Hae-il Byun Hee-bong
Budget	$2.8 million *Estimated*
Producer	Cha Seung-jae
Music	Tarô Iwashiro
Cinematography	Kim Hyung-koo
Film Editing	Kim Sun-min
Production Design	Ryu Seong-hie
Art Direction	Ryu Seong-hie

INFLUENCES
CURE (1997)

Japanese director Kiyoshi Kurosawa has long been known as a horror master (his unofficial nickname is "the David Cronenberg of Japan"), with arguably the most famous and influential of his works being the 1997 psychological horror film *Cure*. Though it is less well-known than some of its "J-horror" contemporaries—1998's *Ring* and 2002's *Ju-On: The Grudge*, for example—it also stands apart from them in how much of a slow burn it is, resisting typical jump scares in favor of a much more unsettling, eerie approach.

Koji Yakusho—in the first of many collaborations with Kurosawa—plays Takabe, a police detective who struggles to unravel a strange series of murders. All of the victims are killed in the same way, with an X carved into their neck. However, the killer is different each time, and in each case, can't explain what they've done. As Takabe's investigation continues, he is drawn into the orbit of a mysterious young man named Mamiya (Masato Hagiwara) and is pulled into the world of hypnosis and mesmerism—and, of course, danger.

There's no question, especially given its use of mesmerism as a gimmick, that *Cure* is a genre film, but it almost doesn't feel like one—the *Little White Lies* review of the film describes it as "unnervingly plain, unfussy and aloof." *Cure* also doesn't answer all of the questions that it poses, ending on a relatively open note, and the central mystery demands investigation beyond face value. What's integral about these murders is not who's perpetrating them, but why they're happening, and the social commentary they represent—the suggestion the movie invites is that this hypnosis frees people from the societal and cultural norms they've been following, revealing the anger and aggression that's been allowed to fester underneath. It's no accident that Takabe, who seems to be the only person capable of resisting the sinister influence driving these murders, is also the only person who doesn't bother with such pretenses.

As such, it's easy to see just how *Cure* serves as an inspiration for Bong, who once called it his "all-time favorite film" and wrote that it was among a handful of films to have had the biggest impact on his personal view of film. Bong is, after all, a master at subverting genre conventions—*The Host* (2006) is a monster movie to which the monster is almost incidental. Of his work, *Cure* is perhaps most comparable to *Memories of Murder* (2003), as the investigation in *Memories of Murder* is similarly less hinged on whether or not the murderer is caught and more the circumstances that allowed such events to occur. The films are even stylistically similar, with relatively muted color palettes and careful shots and staging that stay firmly away from typical action or thriller territory, allowing the viewer to parse the clues on their own rather than holding their hand the entire way.

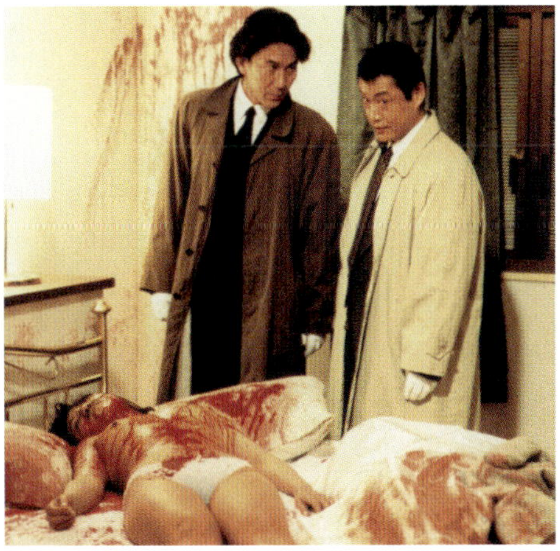

괴물

THE HOST

31.

→ **Opposite**
The seriocomic prologue to *The Host* encapsulates much of the film: not only does it tease the inevitable environmental blowback of dumping toxins in Seoul's Han River, but also the paradox of professional power structures and the malign influence of the West.

The opening of 2006's *The Host* practically screams "monster movie." Its first scene, in which an American military pathologist at a Seoul base orders his reluctant assistant to pour two hundred bottles of formaldehyde down the drain and into the Han River, is saturated in an oppressive, eerie blue. The scenes that follow, which jump forward in time, are similarly gloomy in palette, feeding a sense of impending doom. Two fishermen encounter a mutated fish. A man commits suicide by jumping from a bridge—but before he does, he sees a shadow swimming beneath him in the water. *Something* is clearly brewing. But this perfectly disquieting prelude is one that Bong immediately shatters with a bright, colorful introduction to the movie's main character, Park Gang-du (Song Kang-ho), who is sound asleep, his head resting on a pile of snacks. There is a monster in *The Host*, yes—a bus-sized creature with a long, prehensile tail and a mouth that opens like a toothy flower—but it's ultimately a monster movie in the same way that *Memories of Murder* (2003) is a crime drama. That is to say, it almost isn't.

The opening scenes do more than just set up the monster—they set up the themes present throughout the entire film. The incident with the formaldehyde (depressingly based on a true story, the McFarland case, in which a mortician at a US military morgue in Korea ordered one hundred and twenty liters of embalming fluid to be dumped down the drain) sets up the deleterious presence of the American military; the fisherman noting that his daughter gave him the cup in which he scoops up the fish foreshadows the importance of the bond between father and daughter pair Gang-du and Hyun-seo (Go Ah-sung); and the way the suicidal man is the only one who notices the monster ("Morons, to the very end," he says, of the people around him) echoes the way Gang-du's protests are ignored again and again by the very government officials who are supposed to be helping him, to disastrous effect.

Of the themes presented, however, it's family relationships that are the most pivotal to the film. From the lengths people are willing to go to for their loved ones to knowing someone so well that the sound of their farts becomes a clear indicator of how well they're doing on any given day, it all comes back to the bonds of family. When the teenage Hyun-seo is taken by a monster that appears from the Han River, her family bands together to try to find her, eventually becoming fugitives as, concurrently, government officials search for a virus they believe the monster to be carrying. But, as proven in *Barking Dogs Never Bite* (2000) and *Memories of Murder*, this relatively straightforward premise is but a cover for the myriad layers that Bong has constructed.

The subverting of expectations, both big and small, is a constant throughout the film—in an early scene, the monster charges, but the scream that rings out as it does is one of joy rather than fear as, oblivious, two characters cheer on an archery match that's happening at the same time. The resulting sensation is less whiplash and more the butterflies-inducing experience of riding a particularly thrilling roller coaster, the innate fear of the heights and precarious angles the ride climbs to competing with the rush of flying through the air. That *The Host* became such a phenomenon, serving as Bong's big breakout for most Western movie goers and becoming, at the time of its release, the highest-grossing South Korean film of all time, comes as no surprise.

The monster in *The Host* first appears less than fifteen minutes into the movie, and in broad daylight no less. It's a bold subversion of monster movie norms—most keep their monsters confined to the shadows for as long as possible so that a late reveal will feel more significant, as well as make the monster more mysterious and more frightening up to that point—and speaks to Bong's confidence as a storyteller. (To that end, Bong himself has pushed back against the label of "monster movie" with regard to *The Host*, and on multiple occasions professed his hatred for the convention of hiding monsters.) In this case, however, the reveal is

32.

← Left
Bong introduces his lovable loafer hero Park Gang-du (Song Kang-ho) wreathed in snack food and happy to be momentarily disconnected from worldly responsibility by manning the family concession stand.

33.

→ Opposite
By revealing its monster at the very top of the film, *The Host* both announces itself as the anti-*Jaws* and delivers a sudden and shocking rampage of bloody destruction, climaxing in the shallow-focus kidnapping of Gang-du's daughter Hyun-seo (Go Ah-sung).

necessary so as to get to the meat of the story, that is, the Park family's efforts to rescue Hyun-seo and the government's campaign to find, and eventually fabricate, a virus. But the fact that the scene is crucial to the story's structure doesn't mean that it feels in any way rote or prescriptive—it's still utterly terrifying. The monster's first rampage even includes a sequence ripped straight from many zombie movies, as it chases a group of victims into a shipping container, the other side of which is held shut with a chain. The hands of the people inside claw fruitlessly through the slender gap left in the door as blood seeps out below. Soon afterward, the heat of the moment causes Gang-du to grab another young girl's hand as they dash to safety, leaving Hyun-seo behind. When he realizes his error, both he and the audience are instantly aware of what's at stake. As Hyun-seo, in slow motion, recovers from a fall, the monster looms behind her—it seems as though we're about to watch her get torn apart. That it grabs her instead only provides minimal relief.

Gang-du's mistake is both horrifying and painfully funny, and that alchemical mix of the comic and the tragic is a Bong trademark. At first, neither Gang-du nor the audience realize that our slovenly hero is pulling along the wrong teenager. It's only as the camera pans back in slow motion that the awful truth dawns. The mass funeral that's held for the victims in the wake of the monster's attack unfolds in much the same way. The Parks collapse onto the floor in grief, wailing and clutching at each other, only to be immediately mobbed by news photographers. In the chaos, patriarch Hee-bong (Byun Hee-bong), who owns the snack stall that Gang-du works at, still has the presence of mind to pull down the shirt of Gang-du's sister Nam-joo (Bae Doona), a competitive archer, so that she's not showing too much skin. But that hint of tenderness is quickly drowned out by the sound, in the background, of a woman being called to move her car, and the way the photographers fade away as the Parks begin bickering once again, shattering the illusion of a truly united family. In any other movie, those distractions and sidebars wouldn't exist—the scene would be played straight with the intention of tugging on viewer heartstrings as much as possible. What is remarkable about Bong's execution of the scene, which takes the family's tragedy no less seriously, is that the background annoyances, comedic though they are, only serve to amplify the sense of devastation rather than detracting from it. The scene feels more truthful in that respect—real-life misfortune doesn't preclude an element of absurdity, so neither does this fictional telling.

These beats grow less frequent—or at least smaller in scale—as the movie progresses, and *The Host* uses a trick to convey the shift in its overarching tone that is similar to the one used in *Memories of Murder*. As the story becomes increasingly bleak, the color palette evolves from bright hues to increasingly desaturated tones, emphasizing this change. The dull feel of the film's opening returns as it reaches its conclusion (by the finale, the grayness that dominates the screen is reminiscent of *Memories of Murder*'s muted colors), and the final scene, though peaceful, takes place at night. The interior of the snack bar is cozy and warmly lit, but the darkness outside is menacing, even with specks of falling snow in the air. For Gang-du, the world has fundamentally changed, a fact that Bong conveys with all of the sensory stimuli in his arsenal.

What we hear and how we hear it (the fruit of Bong's long-standing collaboration with sound editor/supervisor Choi Tae-young, who has worked on all of Bong's films) is also vital in being able to make sure the overall "arc" remains robust. For instance, the moment of Hyun-seo's abduction plays out in total silence, as does the death of Hee-bong in an act of selfless family preservation, as well as the final moments of the monster itself. Again, Bong's deftness with tone isn't winking or ironic—every choice he makes as a director has an underlying earnestness. When scenes play with both humor and tragedy, it's because the circumstances are so outlandish or worth some small ridicule—they are as they would be in real life. So it goes with the pivotal moments in *The Host*, which aim straight for the heart.

All three of Park Hee-bong's children are losers to some extent. From the moment he's introduced, Gang-du is almost cartoonish in how clumsy and lazy he is, falling asleep at the concession stand he's supposed to be running and getting coins stuck to his face, and tripping over thin air in his excitement to see his daughter. Even his hair—subjected to a halfhearted bleach job that has left it more orange than blond, with his roots growing out—was a deliberate choice in order to make him seem listless and dull-witted. He's the human equivalent of a golden retriever—it often seems as though he doesn't totally understand the gravity of the situation he's in, as he responds to a news bulletin decrying the family as wanted fugitives by saying they should record it to show Hyun-seo ("Daddy's on TV!").

But at the same time, he's the most uncomplicatedly earnest member of the family. All he wants is for Hyun-seo to be happy—he has no unfulfilled ambitions for himself—and almost every scene reflects that, from the ramen bowl full of coins he's saving to buy her a new phone, to his decision to jog in the chemical trail of a stolen fumigation truck in order to make sure he won't pass the supposed virus on to her when they're finally reunited. The superhuman love he bears for his daughter only makes the story more tragic as, after essentially being held hostage and having a lobotomy performed upon him by unheeding government officials, desperation transforms his naïveté into anger and violence.

For the most part, however, he's at the bottom of the family totem pole, as Hee-bong has to constantly tell his other two children to dial back their derision toward him. Nam-il (Park Hae-il, whose supposedly innocent-looking face Bong once again uses for a sour character, as he did in *Memories of Murder*) is a burnout. A university graduate and former student protester, he's a budding (if not full) alcoholic who can't seem to find a job. His frustration makes him volatile and, of his family, the quickest to turn a conversation into an argument or resort to violence. Of the three siblings, Nam-joo seems the most levelheaded, given her national profile, but she's fragile when under pressure. We see her choke while competing in an archery contest

34.

← **Left**
The death of Park family patriarch Hee-bong (Byun Hee-bong) is among the most heartbreaking scenes in the film, intertwining terrible tragedy with the selflessness of a father's love.

35.

↖ **Opposite top**
Bong's tactic of subtly seeding eccentric character traits that will return as major plot points is exemplified by Gang-du's taciturn sister, Nam-joo (Bae Doona). Early on, we learn that she is a nationally-competing archer whose matches are broadcast on live TV; later on, her talents become crucial to the family's triumph over the monster.

on TV, losing her shot at placing first and bringing home a bronze medal instead of gold. But the two siblings' introductions, as they arrive at the mass funeral to grieve for Hyun-seo, are nearly the same, with close-ups on Nam-il's hand clutching a soju bottle, then Nam-joo's hand clutching the strap of her medal, neatly physicalizing each character's sense of and obsession with their failures. It's worth mentioning that the adult members of the family—Byun Hee-bong, Song Kang-ho, Bae Doona, Park Hae-il—had all worked with Bong before, and their casting in this movie was decided upon before the script was even written. Of the Parks, only Go Ah-sung, who would later appear in *Snowpiercer* (2013), got her role through auditioning, making this her feature film debut. In a film about a family desperately trying to pull together despite the odds stacked against them, Bong's attitude toward close-knit casting feels strangely resonant.

None of his protagonists really fit the bill of the kind of "action hero" that you might expect in a run-of-the-mill monster movie, but then again, none of Bong's protagonists are anything other than ordinary. The detectives in *Memories of Murder* are well-meaning but ethically and intellectually ill-equipped; the title character of 2009's *Mother* is an old woman; and even Chris Evans's character in *Snowpiercer*, who, of all of Bong's characters, is the closest thing to a typical alpha leading man, is hardly squeaky clean in the morality stakes. But it's the fact that Gang-du and his siblings are "lovable losers," in Bong's own words, that makes the film that much more compelling. When it comes to defeating this monster and foiling the corrupt government, they don't seem to stand a chance, and the disadvantage they're at makes their efforts more herculean, their successes more heartwarming, and their losses more devastating. They're only human.

Even their "heroic" moments fall within reasonable limits. A Molotov cocktail thrown by Nam-il is crucial to the monster's demise, but he fumbles it—he drops his last bottle. It only "hits" the monster by the grace of Nam-joo, who lights an arrow from the debris it leaves and fires it directly into the monster's eye, setting it ablaze. And, most tragically, everything they do isn't ultimately enough to save Hyun-seo, who dies just moments before the family are finally reunited.

In fact, the two casualties the Parks suffer are also the two most resourceful members of the family, and the most separated from the main action. Hee-bong, who spends most of his screen time preoccupied with corralling his kids to safety, dies halfway through the film. In a wrenching sequence, Gang-du hands him a gun with which to face off against the monster but miscounts the number of bullets he left in the chamber. Hee-bong faces the monster dead-on, and when he realizes he has no ammo left, instead of panicking, turns calmly back to his children and waves at them to keep running as the monster closes in on him. His acceptance of death is perfectly in character, but the matter-of-fact staging is still incredibly chilling and affecting, not least because it immediately follows a scene in which Hee-bong expresses his regret at not having been a better father to Gang-du. Gang-du, by contrast, is reduced to a mess by his father's death, covering Hee-bong's face with a newspaper and trying—and failing, in his grief—to run away from approaching government forces. Hyun-seo doesn't depart so early in the movie, but she spends most of the film in the sewer, separated from the main cast. Her death—she dies in the monster's maw, protecting another child, an orphan named Se-joo (Lee Dong-ho), from being devoured by shielding him with her body—is also somewhat ambiguous. In the same way that *Parasite* (2019) doesn't clarify who lives and who dies until its final scene, it's not totally clear that Hyun-seo is dead until it's confirmed in the film's epilogue.

As to the decision to kill Hyun-seo at the end of the film, her death was in the script from the very beginning—a decision that producers and financers hated. (That ending, at least in part, was inspired by the 1983 film *Uncommon Valor*, which Bong saw on his own while in middle school. The movie stars Gene Hackman as a man who goes to Vietnam to try to rescue his son, who has been a prisoner of war for the last decade.

When he finally arrives at the prison camp, it turns out that his son is already dead.) But Hyun-seo's death ties neatly into the big themes of the film: How much does the government actually protect its citizens? Throughout the movie, the government turns out to be an active roadblock if not an outright negative force. In the end, the weak must help the weak.

The hapless Parks do their utmost to save Hyun-seo, and Hyun-seo, in turn, does her utmost to save Se-joo, who is even younger than she is. Even the concept of *seori* (stealing), which Se-joo's older brother (Lee Jae-eung) claims isn't truly a crime when stealing what is necessary to survive, ties into this idea. But though Hyun-seo tells Se-joo that she's going to bring the police, doctors, and the military to help save him, none of those forces mobilize on their behalf. The only person who helps in the fight against the monster is a homeless man (Yoon Je-moon). Bong has said he regrets the choice to include the character, as the inclusion of a "crazy" character to solve a plot problem—the homeless man's role is to rescue Nam-il, and then pour gasoline all over the monster—seems like a cheat, comparing the character to Telly Savalas's role in the 1977 film *Capricorn One*, but, nevertheless, the moment doesn't seem at all out of place.

And there's no question that the finale is bittersweet. "The positive epilogue in *The Host* is deliberately pretentious," Bong said of the ending. "Just consider that the Park family is slaughtered before the final victory against the monster." The monster has been vanquished, but when thinking of *The Host* as a family story, that's hardly a win. Gang-du's father and daughter have both been killed, and though there's a new Park family member (the epilogue reveals that Gang-du has adopted Se-joo, whose brother has fallen prey to the monster), it's apparent that Gang-du still fears what could come out of the river.

What's notable about the river creature is that, despite the fact that humans are its primary prey, it's not really a villain. In directing the animators, Bong told them to think of the monster as an unstable teenager, and even went so far as to give the animators a picture of an actor and tell them to work with him in mind. That actor? Steve Buscemi in *Fargo* (1996). The character of the "kinda funny lookin'" Carl Showalter struck Bong as a kindred spirit, given his impatience and the way there always seemed to be something wrong with his body. The monster who, in Bong's words, "didn't ask to be born this way," is in a similar position, always in pain due to being a result of chemicals and pollutants. It has no imperative to destroy all humans, nor does it take Hyun-seo with any sense of intention beyond survival. It eats to live, as everything else around it does. It's a monster only in that it's a kind of creature that we haven't seen before—at the end of the day, it's just an animal. The blame for the destruction it causes rests solely with the American government employee who saw fit to pour chemicals into the Han River. Later, when the government drops the toxic chemical Agent Yellow (a barely veiled reference to Agent Orange, the defoliant chemical most widely known for its use during the Vietnam War) on the creature and the people who have gathered to protest its use, the shape of the pod used to disperse the chemical deliberately recalls the shape of the monster when it's first seen dropping into the Han River. The chemical cloud causes the protesters caught in it to bleed from the eyes, ears, and nose, in a way that makes it abundantly clear it shouldn't be being used, especially in an urban space.

36.

← **Left**
Telly Savalas appears as an unhinged crop-dusting pilot and deus ex machina in Peter Hyams's 1977 film *Capricorn One.* A similar character appears in the fiery climax to *The Host*—one that Bong wishes he'd fleshed out further to make him feel less purely functional.

37.

↖ **Above and left**
Bong juxtaposes the terror of a monster simply looking to feed against a state apparatus that is corrupt to its core. Scenes of protest are met with brutality as those who stand up to corruption are battered, bruised, and worse.

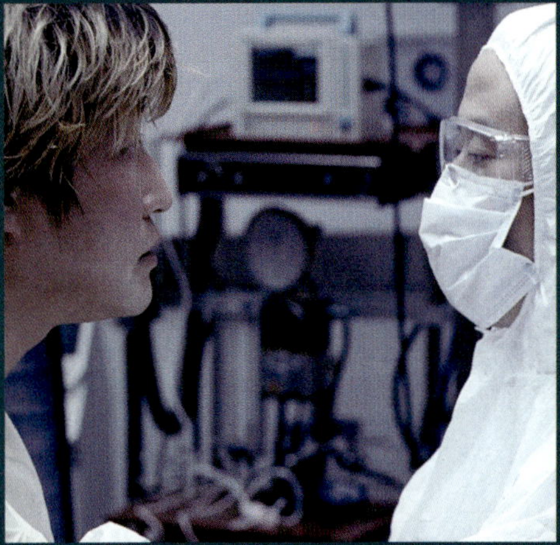
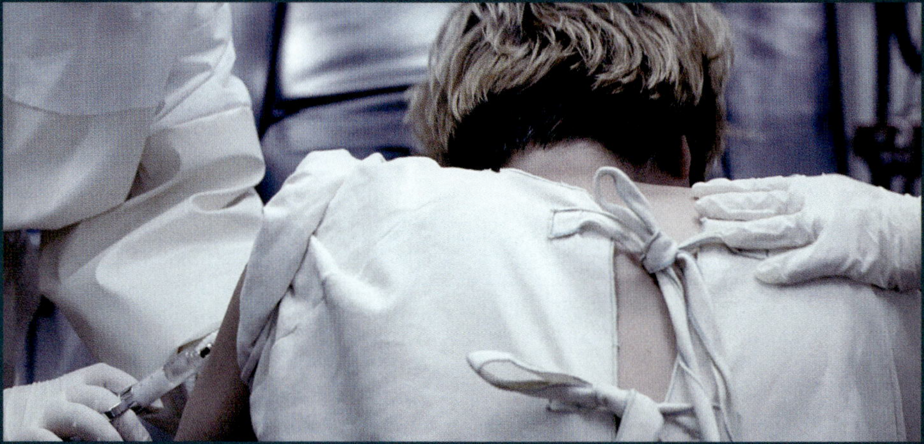
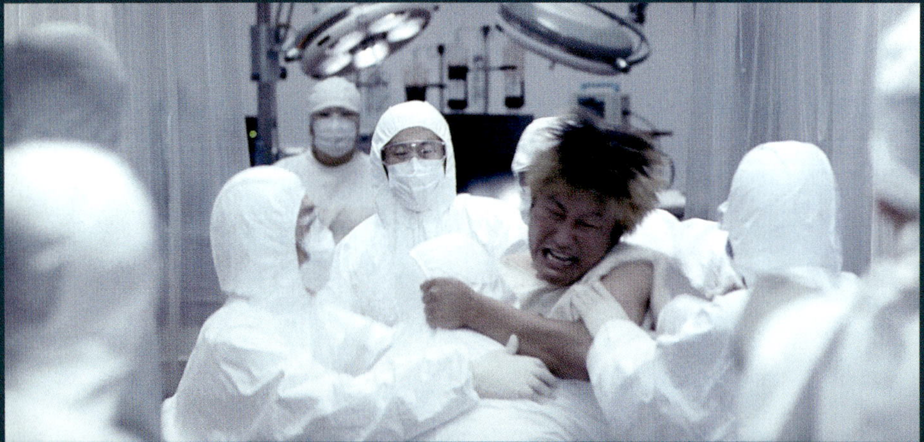
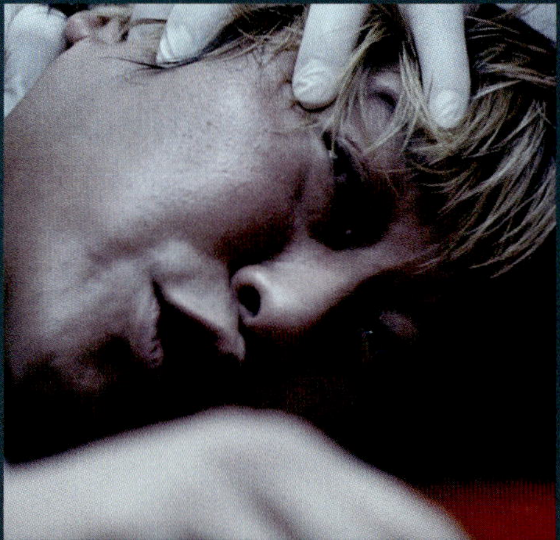

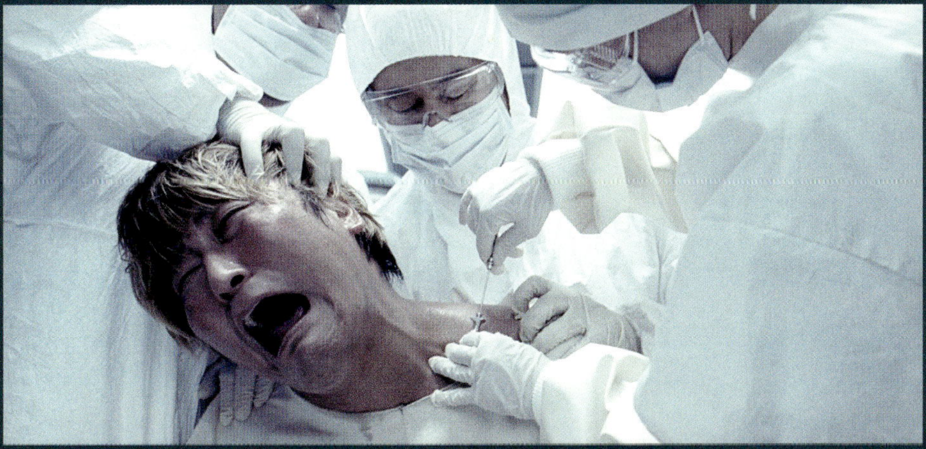

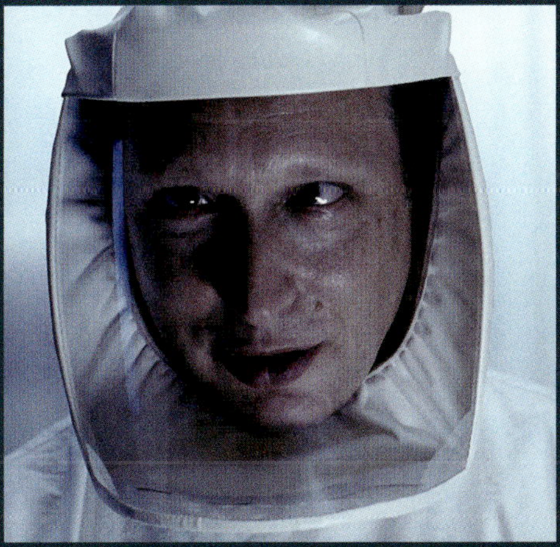

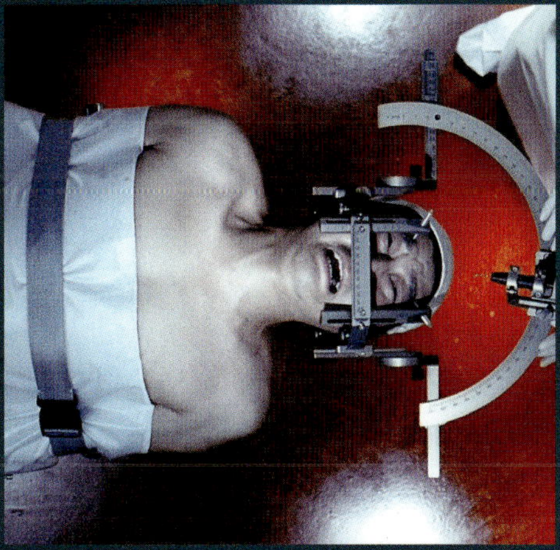

38.

↖ **Opposite and above**
An early example of government disinformation costing lives sees Gang-du co-opted as a lobotomy subject for a cooked-up conspiracy about the monster spreading a deadly virus. The sequence uneasily melds physical comedy with chilling medical horror and serves as an example of Bong's tonal mix-and-match MO.

Both the government and the monster are destructive forces of equal magnitude.

And it's not just *The Host*'s monster—all of Bong Joon Ho's monsters tend to fall into a similar category. Often, the antagonists of any given film are antagonists purely because what they want is at odds with the protagonist's goals. It's not necessarily that they're inherently malicious—the unseen killer in *Memories of Murder* being the large exception—and, more often than not, they're not difficult to understand. For instance, the closest thing *Barking Dogs Never Bite* has to a villain is the barking dog of the title, and it's only doing what's in its nature. *Okja*'s Lucy Mirando may be grotesque, but she's not outright evil; she's simply desperate for approval. Even her sister Nancy isn't truly evil—rather, she's a staunch capitalist who knows how to work the system. Granted, the latter trait is generally a sin in Bong's view (if his movies are any indication, at least), but her concern for profit doesn't make her unnecessarily cruel. Even in *Mother*, the most monstrous acts are committed by those for whom we feel the most sympathy and pain. Circumstances can make a monster out of almost anyone.

The real "villains," as such, are the societal ills that lead to such strained circumstances—the ravages of capitalism, useless bureaucratic structures—and manifest in multiple, usually nameless characters who appear for a scene or two each. In *The Host*, these manifestations arrive in the form of the various doctors and government stooges that the Park family run into, who alternately seem completely disinterested in what's going on around them and overinvested in results concerning the good of the people they're supposed to be serving. At every turn, Gang-du's protestations that Hyun-seo is still alive aren't taken seriously, and the pain he and the rest of the Parks are put through turns out to be in pursuit of a "virus" that doesn't even exist. Even as Gang-du weeps that nobody listens to him, he continues to be talked over and ignored, despite the fact that taking him seriously would have led to a speedier capture or killing of the monster, and perhaps even prevented Hyun-seo's untimely death. Toward

39.

↓ Below
The incompetence of government officials—and the folly of the social caste system—is expressed through masterfully executed incidental touches, such as a random moment where a stooge in a hazmat suit (Kim Roi-ha) slips on the floor, then tries and fails to keep the crowd under control.

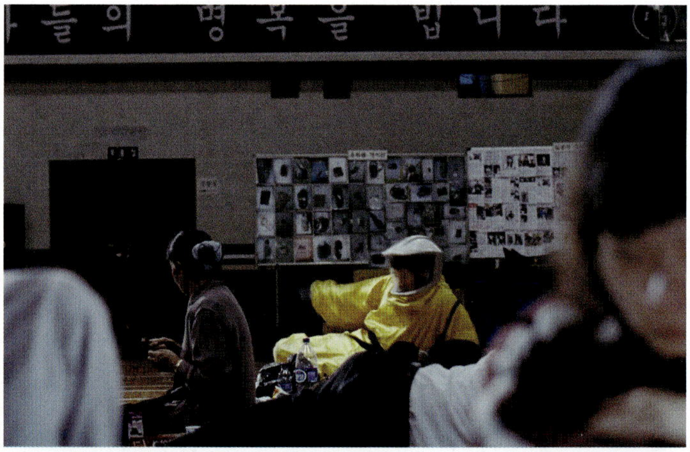

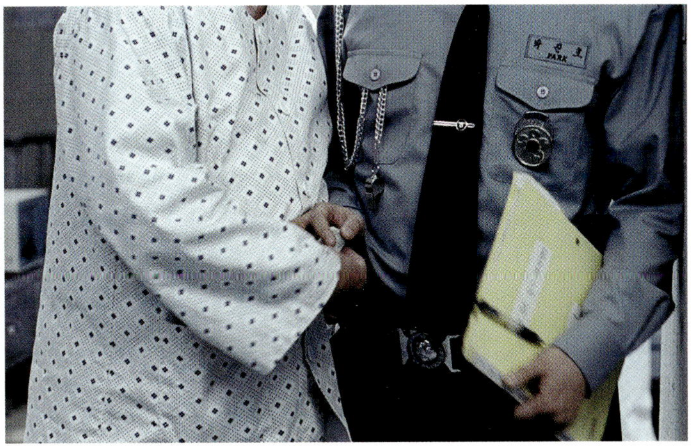

the beginning of the film, government incompetence is a source of humor—a government worker (played by Kim Roi-ha, leaving the violent detective he played in *Memories of Murder* far behind) enters a room of grieving people in a yellow hazmat suit, promptly trips, recovers, and awkwardly tries to play it off as if nothing had happened. As the people around him start to ask what's going on, he directs their attention to a TV, saying that there should be a news report explaining the situation. As he flips through channels, it becomes apparent that isn't the case, and the chaos only spirals from there. Even the former classmate who ends up betraying Nam-il to the police is a mixed bag, as he sets him up for the reward money but eventually raises a fist in solidarity as Nam-il manages to make his escape.

Through their incompetence and willingness to cause collateral damage, the American and Korean governments play a major part in the film. So too does a much simpler force: money. Money, or the lack of it, is an obstacle at nearly every turn, from the forfeit of Gang-du's aforementioned phone fund to how Hee-bong is fleeced into paying for the release of his family from the hospital. Even Nam-il's friend sells him out purely for the cash reward. There's no line between the haves and have-nots in the way that there is in *Barking Dogs Never Bite*, but the underlying preoccupation of having to pay for everything—that everything has a cost as well as a value—mirrors the more prominent role that class and social division plays across Bong's filmography.

Here, the fact that all of the characters are struggling to get by adds to the absurdity of the government's quest to find a virus, itself an allusion to the Iraq War and the fact that the theoretical reason for invasion (weapons of mass destruction) never existed. It's revealed toward the end of the film that the virus is an invention—the American who supposedly succumbed to it simply died of shock during an operation, and none of the quarantined people have shown any traces of illness. An American government official outright says, "There is no virus whatsoever." But the lie has proliferated too far to be walked back without admitting fault, and so it's taken

40.

↑ Above
Cash still rules when it comes to greasing the crooked wheels of government. Before doing the right thing, everyone is eager for their thirteen pieces of silver.

41.

↓ Next Page
The Host's centerpiece scene is a moment of tonal respite in which the promise and possibility of the family unit is rekindled. A magical realist flourish sees the kidnapped Hyun-seo appear as the Parks scarf down junk food—an apparition of hope sparked by the need for regeneration and self-care, and a reminder of why the Parks are doing all this to begin with.

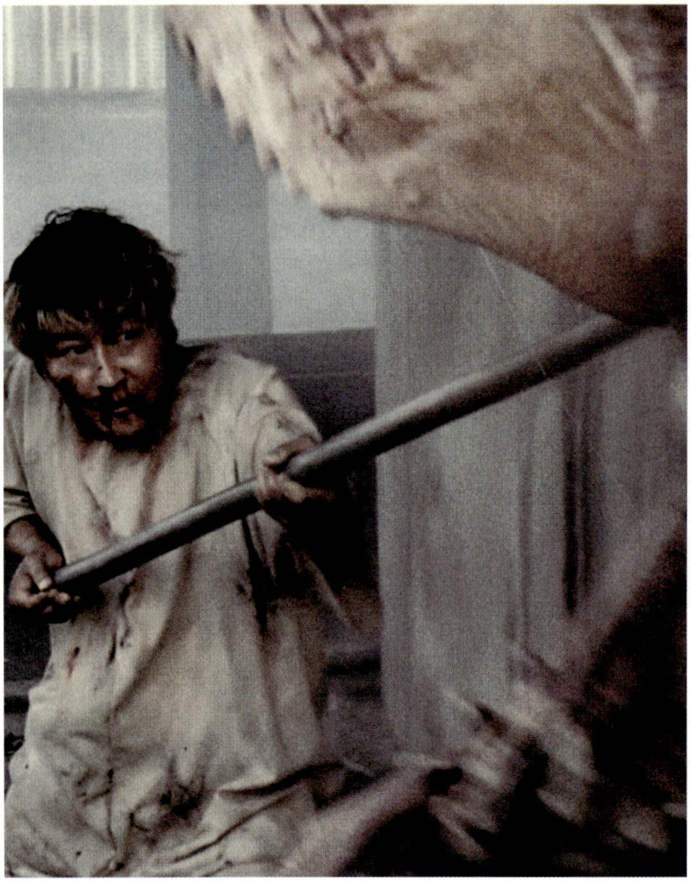

42.

↑ Above
The Host is a family affair until the last, with the beast finally vanquished via a handy tag-team effort between the three Park siblings. Bong is careful to frame this explosion of violence as sincerely retributive—as well as, to a certain extent, reluctantly executed—rather than just the necessary climax of a fun genre film.

to the extreme of strapping Gang-du to the operating table for invasive cranial surgery. That fabrication is even sort of alluded to in the film's title; like *Barking Dogs Never Bite*, *The Host*'s title differs in English and Korean. Its Korean title, 괴물, or *Gwoemul*, translates to "monster." Speaking as to why the title was changed (*Memories of Murder*, for instance, retains the same title in both languages) at a New York Film Festival screening of the film, Bong said that he wanted to avoid a John Carpenter-esque title like *The Thing*. More interestingly, however, he noted that the word "host" is the opposite of "parasite," unintentionally foreshadowing his Oscar-winning hit in describing both the way the monster is meant to play host to a virus and the way that the title is almost misleading, given the discovery that a virus has been entirely made up.

That said, the negative portrayal of the government—and, in particular, American bureaucracy—is worked naturally into the flow of the film. "It's fun for me to bury my political comments here and there in a film, but this is also part of the tradition of the monster or sci-fi genre," Bong said of the film's social commentary. Like *Memories of Murder*, which uses the lens of an infamous serial murder case as a window into Korea's turbulent past, *The Host* is operating on multiple levels, to the point that the monster could almost be called incidental. In fact, the monster doesn't actually appear all that frequently in the movie—generally, we see the Park family in search of it, and Hyun-seo braving the sewer while the monster is away. "[*The Host*] is more of a kidnapping movie," Bong has said. "The kidnapper just happens to be a creature."

In the end, the creature also feels like it isn't totally alien to the people pursuing it. It isn't particularly cool or awe-inspiring in the way that Godzilla is—in fact, Bong's desire to create a believable monster contained it in scale, as his marker for what was and wasn't going to convince audiences came partially down to size. ("The bigger the creature is, the less realistic he becomes. If the creature can hide behind a bus or truck it is more realistic.") But there is ultimately one thing that ties *The Host*'s monster to the kaiju who have preceded it in films like *Godzilla* (1954): Though it may be wreaking destruction, it's also deserving of a little sympathy. In the film's climax, Gang-du deals the finishing blow to the monster by thrusting a metal pole directly into its mouth. Initially, his expression is one of rage, but it slowly shifts into something else. "[It's] as if he is thinking, *You're sort of in the same situation as I am in*," Bong said of that close-up. "It wasn't something that came as an accident. It was something that the actor and I discussed, that at this moment we should show some pity for the monster." The parallels between Gang-du and the monster he's pursuing are actually present throughout the film; for example, there's the way they both keep tripping and falling during the initial reveal on the riverbank, underlining the fact that both are (clumsy) victims of circumstance rather than enemies.

At this point, the seamless melding of genres is de rigueur for Bong, but following on the heels of *Barking Dogs Never Bite* and *Memories of Murder*, *The Host* represents an exciting leap forward. The mutated monster at its center—as well as the ghostly dinner scene that serves as one of the film's most poignant moments—sets it worlds apart from a story about a man with a vendetta against yapping dogs in his apartment complex, or the retelling of a real-life serial murder case. But, as with all of Bong's films, the elements that

43.

← Left
Ishirō Honda's 1954 *Godzilla* is a cornerstone of the "kaiju" cycle, but the metaphorical monster's gigantic frame actually inspired Bong to go for something a little more compact and refined with the creature in *The Host*.

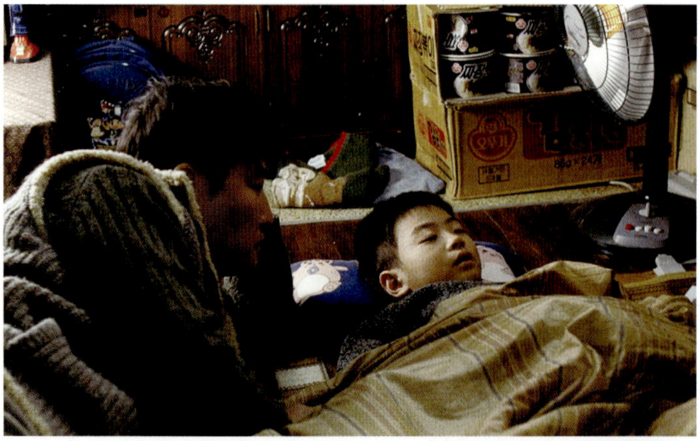

verge on science fiction or fantasy are grounded in, or serve to emphasize, reality.

The dinner scene serves as a prime example of this—the film is all about family, but the one moment we actually see all of them together takes place in a fantasy. After a long day of searching for Hyun-seo in the sewers, Gang-du, Nam-il, Nam-joo, and Hee-bong retreat to the riverside snack bar to rest and recharge. In near darkness, they eat in silence, in sharp contrast to the constant bickering that otherwise seems to characterize their family dynamic. Suddenly, Hyun-seo rises up behind them as if waking from a nap. Without a word, each member of the family picks out food for her as they continue to eat. They dote on her without question, and the love between them is palpable, making the ensuing cut all the more heartbreaking as we see Hyun-seo, still captive, drinking rainwater from her cupped hands at the bottom of the sewer. The scene is clearly a dream—a hallucination, a fabrication, something of the sort—but it's both necessary and totally seamless within the tonal structure of the film as a whole. It's crucial to have at least one scene of the Parks all together, even if it isn't real, and the naturalism with which it's executed makes it feel all the more poignant.

Though Hyun-seo's part in the story isn't as active and eventful as that of her screwball father, everything that happens in the plot comes back to her. Early in the film, she tells Gang-du that she hates the bitter taste of beer after he hands her a can, despite the fact that she's under legal age. Later, stuck in the sewer and prompted by Se-joo to think of what she'd like to eat or drink after they're rescued, she sighs and says, "A cold beer." Even when she's not on screen, there are constant reminders of her, not just because Gang-du can think of nothing else, but because symbolic associations with random objects spark memories of her character, such as the bowl of coins Gang-du's been saving for her, which Hee-bong ends up giving away as a bribe. That isn't to say that the ending of *The Host* is totally bleak. The cozy scene painted by Gang-du and Se-joo, which frames Se-joo as essentially a miniature version

44.

↑ Above
Bong's unabashed sentimental streak plays out in the film's moving coda in which the newly responsible Gang-du has, in the wake of tragedy, transferred his fatherly love to the now-orphaned street urchin, Se-joo (Lee Dong-ho).

45.

→ Opposite
The Host shows Bong as a master of the conciliatory grace note, where small details suddenly resurface to bittersweet effect. Early on, Hyun-seo expresses her distaste for the beer her father offers her; later, it becomes a reminder of family, and in fact something she dearly misses.

of Gang-du, makes for a relatively happy finale despite the cold of the night. They've both lost family, but they've found family in each other, too, and the ease with which they sit down for dinner with each other mirrors, if at a smaller scale, the earlier scene with Hyun-seo at the table. On TV, a news program calls out the misinformation spread about the monster and the virus, but it's hardly of concern to either of them. And though that epilogue begins with Gang-du looking suspiciously out into the night, perhaps wondering what else might come clambering out of the Han, it ends with the pair quietly eating together, with the TV and all those old troubles out of mind. For all of his cynicism toward society, truly hopeless and nihilistic endings are a rarity in Bong's work. (*Memories of Murder* ends with the case still unsolved, but Song's detective is happily married with two children. By contrast, it's the hopelessness and loneliness of *Mother*'s ending that makes it stand out from the rest of Bong's films.) These characters have at least partially managed to move on with their lives, and made the best of what they've been left with. Even if Gang-du and Se-joo are to be considered the weakest of the weak, they now have each other to depend on. Though tragic on the surface of it, the film begins and ends as a sincere and poignant celebration of family. ****

46.

↓ Below
Where Bong always tries to dash hope with tragedy and vice versa, he's certainly no fan of the cheap trick or rug-pull, as this sober final shot suggests that Hyun-seo—one of the film's main characters, and a plucky heroine to boot—is truly gone, not to be resurrected in a cash-grab sequel or spin-off.

2006
The Host
1h 59m

Director	Bong Joon Ho
Writers	Bong Joon Ho Ha Won-jun Baek Chul-hyun
Key Cast	Song Kang-ho Byun Hee-bong Park Hae-il Bae Doona Go Ah-sung
Budget	$40 million *Estimated*
Producer	Choi Yong-bae
Music	Lee Byung-woo
Cinematography	Kim Hyung-koo
Film Editing	Kim Sun-min
Production Design	Ryu Seong-hie
Art Direction	Ryu Seong-hie

Case Study: Making a Monster

1.

2.

1. Sketch of the monster consuming one of its human prey.
2. Shimmering skin texture samples of the creature.
3. Graphic details of the creature's eye and mouth.
4. Physical model of the creature, attack stance.
5. Sketch of Gang-du attempting to save his daughter from the creature.
6. Physical model of the creature.

3.

4.

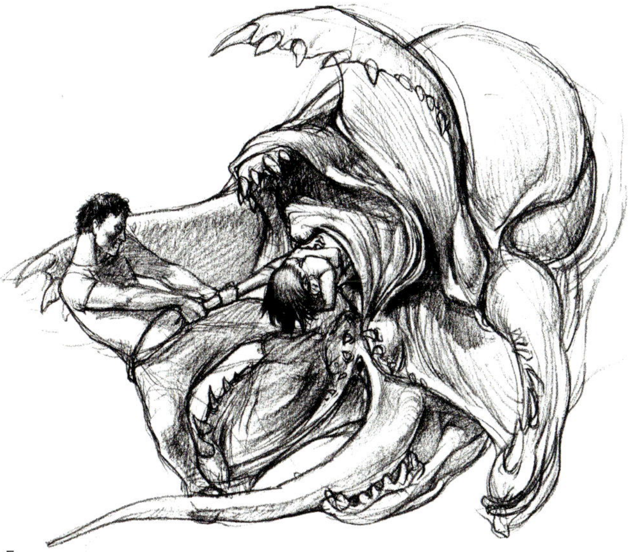

5.

6.

INFLUENCES
SIGNS (2002)

On the occasion of *The Host*'s release in 2006, popular impulse was to compare it to *Jaws* (1975). In fairness, Bong has said that Steven Spielberg's vaunted creature feature—especially its first half, with its depiction of a community spiraling into panic—did serve as an inspiration, but with a caveat: "If you think a shark is a monster, you can say Steven Spielberg's *Jaws* was a sort of influence [. . .] but I have to say, M. Night Shyamalan's *Signs* was a bigger influence."

Though Shyamalan, whose other works include *The Sixth Sense* (1999), *Unbreakable* (2000) and, more recently, *Old* (2021), is probably best known now for his hair-raising plot twists, he is also a filmmaker whose stories, while fantastical, generally center on very normal characters and families. *Signs*, for instance, is a science fiction thriller involving a visitation by malevolent extraterrestrial creatures that uses those genre trappings to explore family relationships, media hysteria, grief, and faith. And though the star of *Signs*, Mel Gibson, was at the time considered an action hero and star (and thereby projects a very different image from Song Kang-ho's goofy Gang-du), he and the other characters in the film don't fall into that typical heroic archetype, and it is the bond between them, as in *The Host*, that is most crucial to the movie's narrative. Even as the protagonists deal with the appearance of mysterious crop circles and, subsequently, alien invaders, they struggle with things as quotidian as managing a child's asthma and the pain of losing a loved one. Shyamalan's other films—*Unbreakable* in particular, as well as *The Sixth Sense* and even *Lady in the Water* (2006)—also bear similarities to Bong's work (or is it the other way around?) in that respect; what makes these stories compelling is the fact that these incredibly ordinary people are managing to cope with extraordinary circumstances.

Even the ways in which Shyamalan builds up tension are mundane, whether it's through the sound of a dog barking, an ominous breeze, or the eerie crackle of a baby monitor—or sometimes even just simple silence. There's no need for the supernatural elements themselves to create a scary atmosphere (though, as the film progresses, Shyamalan does allow for some big reveals), and Bong seems to have taken a page out of Shyamalan's book in constructing some of the tensest and scariest moments in his oeuvre. *The Host*'s monster is hardly hidden, and much of what is actually frightening in the film isn't the creature itself, but the manmade chaos occurring around it.

On top of it all, *Signs* also resists a surfeit of plot exposition, and ends without any clear answers as to what is, on paper, its central mystery. Rather, the denouement hangs upon the characters affirming their bonds—and their faith—to the point that it's almost easier to describe *Signs* as a film about a family than it is a film about an alien invasion. Bong's description of *The Host* (and its link to *Signs*) follows in a similar vein:

> *There won't be any feel of comic science fiction. The nature of the catastrophe is supernatural, but the setting is present on the Han River. The characters are from the working class. Except for the huge catastrophe, everything else is ordinary. M. Night Shyamalan's* Signs *is an example. The film takes place within the territory of a cornfield in the countryside, but that is also where an alien appears. It makes the incident look very real. That's what* The Host *feels like.*

마더

MOTHER

47.

→ Opposite
Beginning at the end: Bong subverts the hackneyed narrative trope of presenting the end of a film first and then orchestrating the narrative as a giant flashback. Here, all we have is an enigmatic dance in a field by the film's monomaniacal heroine, the unnamed title character brilliantly played by Kim Hye-ja.

In most of Bong Joon Ho's movies, family is a source of empowerment. The love and support that families—natural, found, or otherwise—offer each other is a safe haven and, more importantly, a conduit for hope. For his fourth and bleakest feature, *Mother* (2009), Bong takes that dynamic a step further, into the realm of obsession. Familial love is still an all-powerful force, but here it warps into something dangerous and destructive.

Where maternal figures were absent from the piecemeal family at the center of *The Host* (2006), they are front and center in *Mother*. The film stars Kim Hye-ja as a widow who is never given a name, as if playing up her role as the archetypal mother to end all mothers, and whose sole care in the world is to tend to her son Do-joon (Won Bin), whose learning disability also makes him something of an outcast in their community. When Do-joon is accused of murdering a local schoolgirl, she embarks upon a quest to prove him innocent. As she becomes more and more desperate, so too does the film become increasingly grim and bloody, culminating in perhaps the most wrenching—and certainly the darkest—ending of any of Bong's movies. Yes, his films avoid straightforward happily ever afters—even the 2017 satire *Okja*, the closest thing he has to a family-friendly movie, ends by stressing that not everyone can be saved—but *Mother* forgoes even the faintest glimmer of light.

It's not just that darkness, however, that makes *Mother* stand out. The film is also the most streamlined of Bong's works, largely forgoing the heavier, more explicit social commentary present in *The Host* and *Memories of Murder* (2003) by focusing on a single main character rather than an ensemble. Though other characters occasionally share the spotlight, notably Do-joon and his ne'er-do-well friend Jin-tae (Jin Goo), the mother is the movie's driving force. Everyone else is a passive presence.

Mother begins and ends with a dance. A woman, alone, dances in a field, her arms waving over her head, her hands occasionally covering her face as her expression shifts, intense in a way that's at odds with her unfocused gaze. At first, she dances in silence. Soon, drumbeats materialize out of the quiet, followed by the strains of a guitar, giving shape to a song, composed by Lee Byung-woo, that's evocative of Spanish guitar music. As a chorus of strings also join the orchestration, the melody becomes increasingly tense, in concert with the way the woman's features twist. Is she happy? Is she in pain? It's not immediately clear, though the minor key of the music and her unmoored manner suggest the latter.

The image is immediately arresting for how many questions it raises, serving almost as an overture or an omen of what's to come. The details—for instance, the old Korean stereotype that a woman wearing a flower in her hair is unstable is referenced through the floral pattern on the widow's jacket—hint at why she is where she is. (On a slightly sweeter note, Kim was apparently embarrassed at having to perform the dance, and so—as can be seen in some of the film's behind-the-scenes footage—Bong and the crew all danced with her, albeit behind the camera.) Late into the film, the context for the scene is revealed: Having killed the junk collector (Lee Young-suk) who witnessed Do-joon in the act of murdering the schoolgirl Ah-jung (Moon Hee-ra)—and then burned down his shack so as to get rid of any evidence—the widow wanders through the neighboring fields in a daze. But the actual dance doesn't return until the movie's finale a few beats later. The two reprises, as it were, mark two climaxes: the first, the death of the junk collector, is the film's climax when it comes to immediate intensity; but the second, as the mother dances, this time on a bus full of other middle-aged women, marks the true emotional peak.

Kim Hye-ja's performance is peerless throughout, but is at its most arresting during these final scenes. The very light in her eyes seems to change as she passes in and out of control of her actions. She is vital as she protests Do-joon's innocence, then blank as she beats the junk collector to death. Even in her protestations to the junk collector that Do-joon is innocent, her emotions get the better of her, causing her to switch between

48.

↓ **Below**
An acupuncture kit is initially introduced as the mother's key to unlocking otherwise unbreachable social circles, and returns later in the film as a vital plot point.

49.

→ **Opposite**
The film's tragic denouement sees the protagonist—who previously has gone to extremes in her attempt to absolve her son from the crime of murder—use acupuncture on herself as a sign of her wish to forget. Though, afterward, she rises to dance, it's not clear if there's any true way of moving on from such trauma.

formal and informal speech. As the realization of what she's done finally comes crashing down, her screams of horror feel born of both the simple act of discovering a corpse and the realization of the fact that she's the one responsible for creating it. A similar back-and-forth occurs as she attempts to cover up her crime. She futilely tries to mop up blood on the dirt floor, though even she, the paragon of motherhood, sobs and says, heartbreakingly, "What do I do, Mom?" Then, when she decides to burn the place down, she is impassive once more. She methodically finds flammable objects in the house and sets them all alight.

The final act of the movie plays like a reckoning between those two states. When the widow is eventually confronted with Do-joon's indirect confession, she visits the young man framed for Ah-jung's murder in prison, and each passing moment levels a tangible, visible weight upon her. Afterward, when Do-joon tells her he found her acupuncture set in the remains of the junk collector's house, just as she's about to embark upon a bus trip with a group of other middle-aged women, it's the straw that breaks the camel's back. She rushes to the bus, no longer able to look Do-joon in the eye. Her expression of anguish shifts into a forced, polite smile as the women board the bus. Once the trip is underway, she performs acupuncture on herself, pricking the meridian point that she claims will "loosen the knots in your heart and clear all the horrible memories in your mind." For a long moment, there's total silence. Her silhouette, caught through the bus window, remains still. Then, as in the film's opening, the music begins. She rises from her seat and begins to dance. Rather than living with the weight of what she's done—and the knowledge that her son is indeed a killer—the widow has chosen to forget.

That final scene was one Bong had in mind from the get-go—it was even included in his initial two-page treatment of the story. The idea to foreshadow it in the film's introduction came along later, toward the end of shooting. The image, Bong has said, struck him as "very Korean," as he'd seen similar scenes (albeit without the same context) as a child, as bus tours like the one

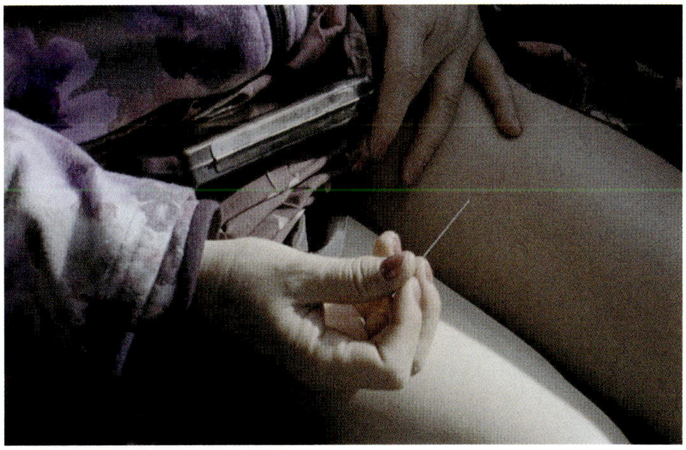

depicted here were and remain relatively popular. But the scene proved challenging to shoot—the window to get it right was half an hour in the morning and half an hour at sunset, as the sun needed to be shining through the bus horizontally, and on top of that, the crew had to account for the position of the sun in relation to the position and speed of the bus. But once it was done, "It was as if I was yanking out a decade-old tumor from my heart," Bong felt. Strangely, the effect of the scene is similar for the viewer—the dance borders on cathartic, as the swell of guitar and the strings on the soundtrack almost take on a triumphant tone. However, that feeling is quick to ebb away as the music maintains its original minor key. If the initial dance scene is anything to go by, she will never truly be free of what has transpired, and there's a sadness to the way she dances—initially, her silhouette is unsmiling, and the farther she gets through the bus, the more frantic her motions become—that keeps even this tragic choice from feeling like a freeing one.

The first time the idea of a near-magical meridian point comes up in the film, the widow offers to use it on Do-joon when he recalls that, when he was a child, she attempted to kill him by feeding him pesticide disguised in a Bacchus (a popular Korean energy drink) bottle. The revelation that follows—that she planned on killing them both because their circumstances had been so difficult—is an awful one, more so because of Do-joon's reaction. He argues that she still made him take the poison first, and asks if she plans to try to kill him again when she offers to erase those memories via acupuncture. It marks a significant rift between this pair who are supposed to be as close to each other as it is possible to be. Even the mother says, as a prison guard attempts to calm her, "You and I are one. We've only got each other." (Worse, she later laments that she should have used a stronger pesticide, and not gone with a cheap brand. The moment stings—her economic status, which drove her to such desperate

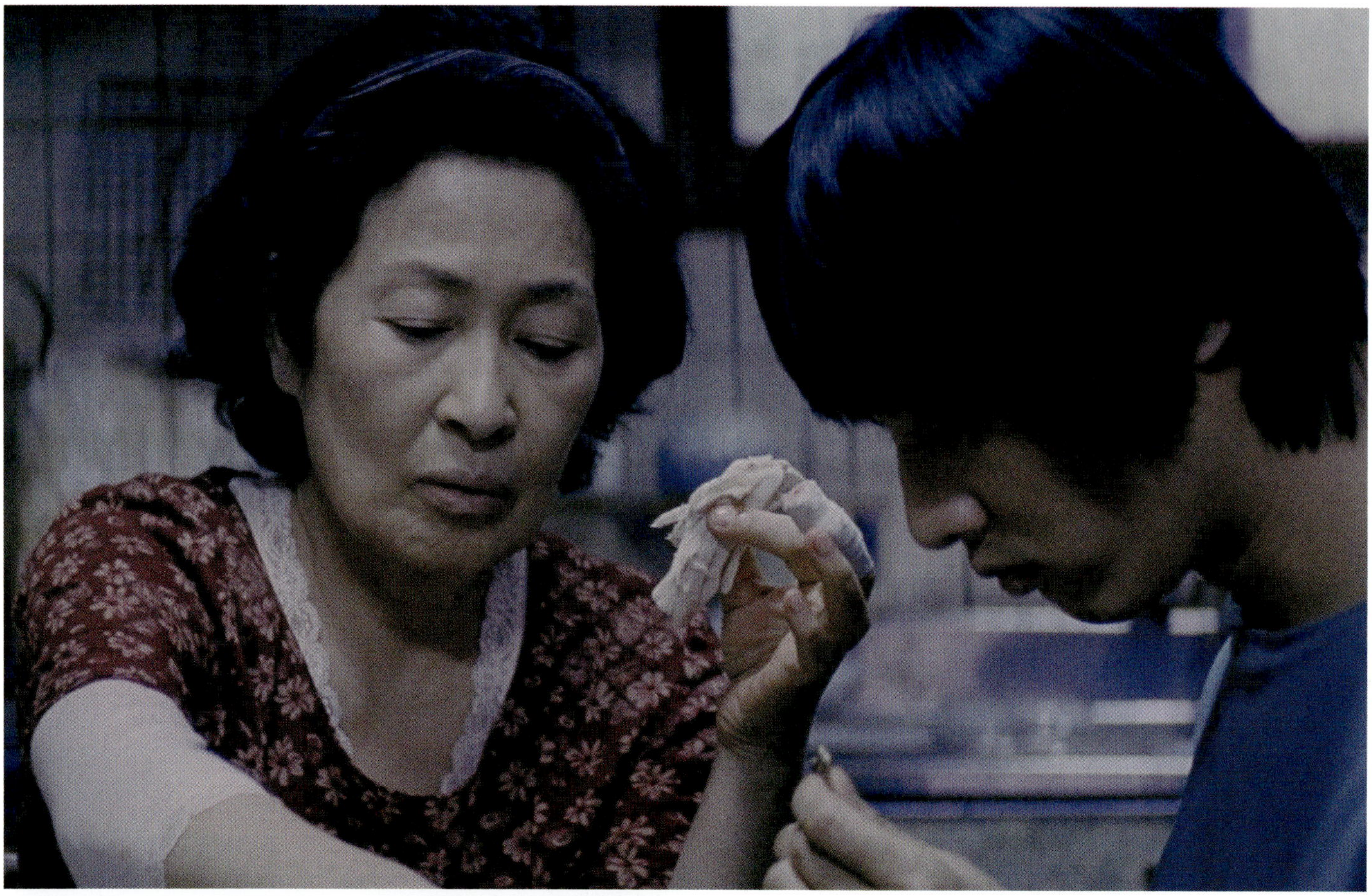

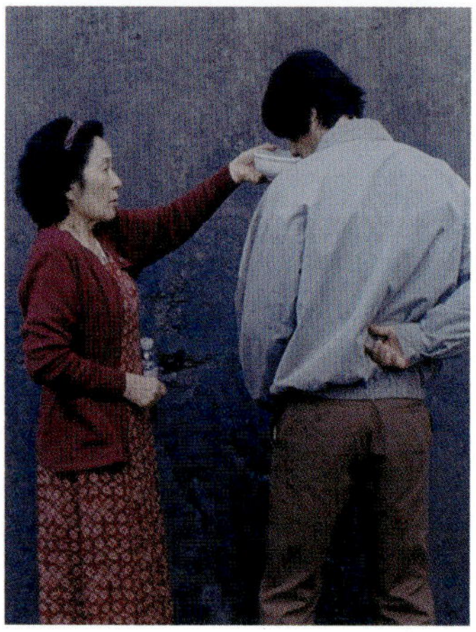

50.

↗ **Above and right**
A mother coddles her son, giving him the best food, watching on as he urinates in the street and—in the film's most overtly Freudian sequence—allowing him to sleep in the same bed. More than just a character tic, Bong takes great care to flesh out the context to her obsessive maternal love.

measures in the first place, even prevents her from committing suicide.)

Their relationship forms the movie's core, and it's established even before any of the characters are properly introduced. Right after that initial dance sequence, we see the widow chopping herbs in a small shop, constantly looking out onto the street as, outside, Do-joon plays with a neighbor's dog. The scene is immediately tense, as we watch as the bundle of herbs gets shorter and shorter, her fingers creeping closer to the blade as her focus is clearly elsewhere. The situation is an accident waiting to happen—the moment Do-joon gets hit by a car, the mother cuts her finger on the blade—and also a clear illustration of the fact that she's more than willing to put herself in harm's way in order to keep her son safe. She loves him, but it's immediately evident that there's tragedy lurking on the horizon—love and obsession aren't mutually exclusive emotions, and her overprotectiveness, already obviously annoying to him, could not only be a hindrance to him, but a source of harm.

That idea is even metaphorically communicated in the mother's medicine of choice: She illegally practices acupuncture, a system of medicine that, while meant to alleviate pain and, in this case, is given out of tenderness, still boasts violent, invasive trappings. It's also a side job that threatens to land her in trouble—one of her customers, a snooty woman (Park Myung-shin) whose husband is a public official, reminds her that it was a hassle trying to cover up for her previously—and is, in Bong's own words, "very scary and off-putting." The act of piercing skin and flesh with a needle is inherently a little frightening, and, despite being meant to promote a patient's wellness, could cause injury or even leave a scar.

There's a similar kind of dissonance to the way we see Do-joon and his mother interact at home. They seem too close—they sleep in the same bed, often embracing (in one scene, Do-joon actually grabs his mother's breast), and she has no qualms about watching him urinate right next to him. (Bong has drawn comparisons between their relationship to that between Norman Bates and his mother in Alfred Hitchcock's *Psycho* [1960]—"If [Norman's mother] was still alive, wouldn't their relationship be similar?") It's a closeness born out of necessity, as they're both outcasts to a certain extent, but it also comes across as suffocating. Do-joon constantly pulls away from his mother, protesting when she tries to feed him or otherwise baby him in an attempt to assert his manhood and independence. That dynamic is central to the film's events—even though they are so tightly bound to each other, she still can't fully control or understand him. Later, after Do-joon is cleared of suspicion, we see the split between them more literally. Though they still sleep in the same bed, they now lie apart from each other, rather than together.

In speaking about the movie, Bong has made one thing abundantly clear: There would be no movie without Kim Hye-ja.

"I made this movie for her," he said, explaining that the movie was born out of his fascination with the warm, maternal image she'd cultivated through decades of work in TV dramas—such as *Country Diaries* (on which she appeared from 1980 to 2002), 1991's *What Is Love?*, and 1999's *Roses and Bean Sprouts*. In contrast, *Mother* would explore the "psychotic" side of that personality, pushing the innate comfort and safety usually associated with motherhood to a new extreme. And if Kim turned the film down? Bong would scrap

51.

← **Left**
Bong has suggested that the uncomfortably close relationship between mother and son in the film contains echoes of Norman Bates's relationship with his (deceased) mother in Alfred Hitchcock's *Psycho* (1960).

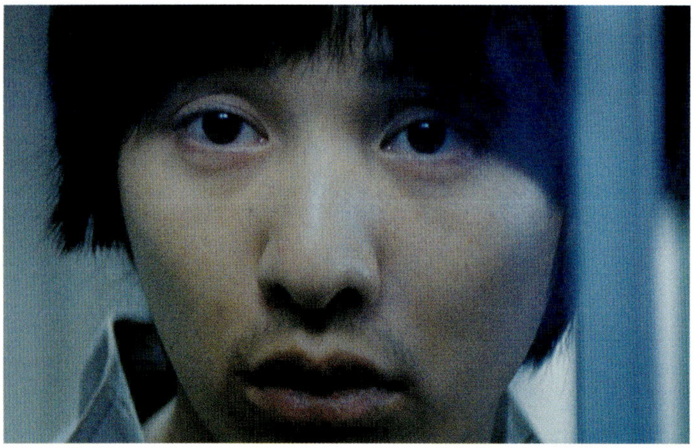

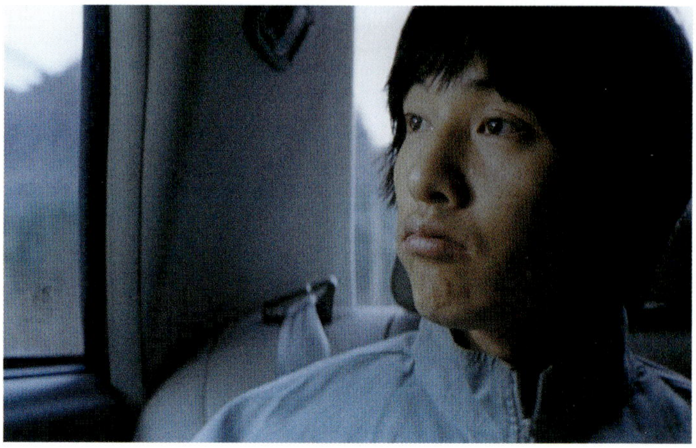

the entire idea—no one else could play the part. Luckily, Kim herself wanted to try something more extreme, and agreed to star. (In the storyboards and in the script, the character is referred to as "Hye-ja.")

The subversion of expectations is something that has remained consistent in Bong's casting—as previously mentioned, he cast Park Hae-il as the potential killer in *Memories of Murder* because of his sweet, doe-like eyes, and then cast him as a bitter alcoholic in *The Host*, and Chris Evans's grimy role in *Snowpiercer* (2013) is a sharp one-eighty from being Captain America. But Kim's turn in *Mother* is, at time of writing, still the apex of that penchant. Though Kim's reputation as the "mother of the nation," as Bong puts it, will likely be lost on Western audiences, her skill as an actress is enough to get the point across. Even aside from her helicopter behavior around Do-joon, her emotions and care for her son are clearly legible in her wide, expressive eyes. As a middle-aged woman, she is already not a typical lead, especially not for a thriller revolving around attempted vigilante justice. Where a usual action hero might show no remorse, Kim hardly has any poker face—everything she feels is written clearly on her features.

Won Bin as Do-joon, by contrast, seems almost like a blank slate. His expression is almost always impassive or a little dazed. His shaggy, bowl-ish haircut adds to his aura of cluelessness and childishness. It's a far cry from his image up to that point—and since—as a major celebrity and a heartthrob, so much so that Bong didn't initially see him as a strong candidate for the role. But a meeting with the actor changed his mind; face to face, he fit with Bong's idea of the character, and on top of that, his eyes reminded him of Kim Hye-ja's. The line "His eyes are like a work of art, like a deer's" was added to the script after Won Bin was cast.

Like Kim, Won Bin's reputation might not precede him for Western viewers, but his angelic features are still imperative like Park's casting in *Memories of Murder*, in making the eventual realization that he is indeed responsible for Ah-jung's death all the more chilling. When he attempts to explain his reasoning for

52.

↑ Above
In his performance as Do-joon, Won Bin reacts to the tumult in his life with sublime apathy—the actor often strikes a surprisingly neutral expression at times of danger, conflict, and high emotion.

53.

→ Right
Mother is perhaps the most violent of Bong's films, or at least the most explicit in its gore. As the protagonist attempts to uncover what truly happened to schoolgirl Moon Ah-jung (Moon Hee-ra), she winds up traveling down a bloody road.

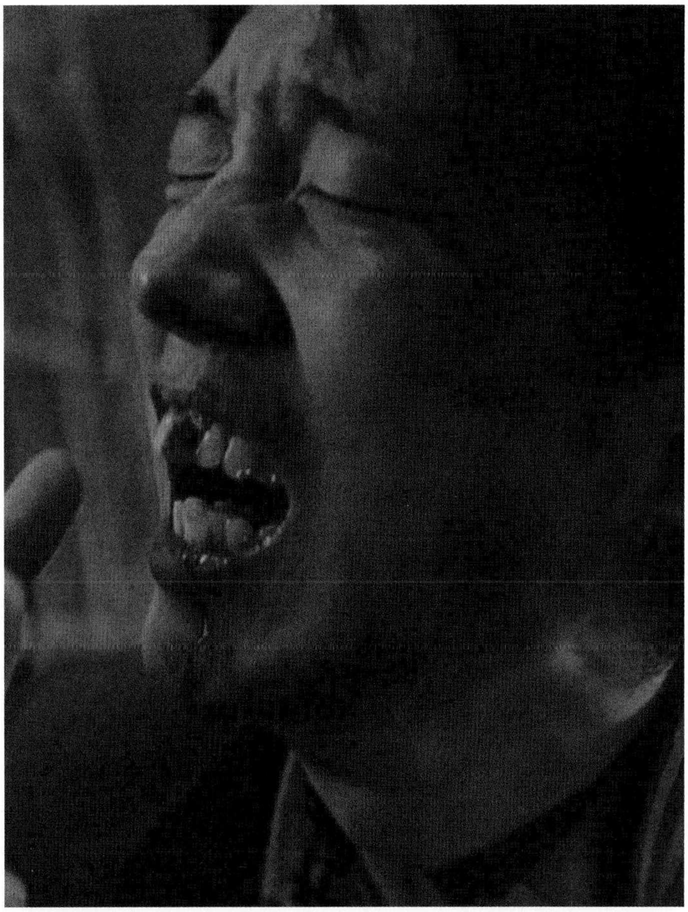

leaving the dead girl on the roof, saying that she must have been left there so that she'd be quickly spotted and brought aid, there's no doubt as to the fact that he means it. He isn't inherently cruel or evil—none of the characters are.

Bong's movies don't shy away from brutality, but the violence in *Mother* feels particularly harsh in light of the film's relative absence of humor. Where all of Bong's other films manage a deft balance of tone, bringing humor to horrible situations and vice versa, *Mother* sinks into desperation and despair, and the few amusing moments are diffused by their context. In an early scene, Do-joon attempts to perform a flying kick at a car's side mirror after seeing Jin-tae do the same thing, and essentially ends up flinging himself to the ground. Whatever laughs the moment prompts are rendered bitter by how easy it is for Jin-tae to later manipulate him into taking the fall, pinning the broken mirror on Do-joon even though his kick was unsuccessful. The lawyer that the mother hires to defend her son is also funny in the immediate moment—he's a classic blowhard—but given how quickly it becomes clear that he doesn't really intend to take her seriously, it's difficult to laugh.

Those already compromised elements don't balance out the shock of the bloodier scenes that play out as the movie progresses. Later in the film, as the widow and Jin-tae team up to try to prove Do-joon innocent, they come across a pair of schoolboys attacking one of Ah-jung's former friends, and then torture the boys to get more information about Ah-jung out of them. The sequence, which takes place on a defunct Ferris wheel, is incredibly cruel—Jin-tae beats them within a hairsbreadth of consciousness, even going so far as to knock out one of the boy's front teeth. The cuts, which are sharp, sudden, and jarring, jostling the viewer as much as the victims, only make the scene more upsetting.

There are ultimately two murders that take place during the film: Do-joon's murder of Ah-jung; and his mother's murder of the junk collector. Both are difficult to

54.

↖ **Opposite and above**
Although *Mother* is, in true Bong fashion, a fusion of tones and themes, at its core it is a classical murder mystery in which the pivotal moment—Do-joon returning home drunk from a bar as the soon-to-be-victim walks just in front of him—is repeated from different vantages, with new, vital details revealed each time. In this chilling sequence, Bong is keenly aware that every inch of every frame counts as evidence for the audience.

55.

← **Opposite**
Bong seldom deals in moral absolutes; his characters are never one-dimensional and are always freighted with hidden depths. Here, Ah-jung's hidden life of abuse and masochistic sexual encounters—all filmed on a camera phone—is revealed, lending tragic context to her murder as well as the events directly preceding it.

56.

↓ **Next Page**
The fresh crime scene, in which Ah-jung is seen hanging over a concrete balustrade in the crisp morning light, is one of the most shocking and baroque images in Bong's entire oeuvre, which in turn massively raises the dramatic stakes and spurs the race to discover the true culprit of this heinous crime.

watch, in equal parts because they're both preventable, and because they are, for Bong, shockingly violent. The murders in *Memories of Murder* are always committed off-screen. The violence in *The Host*, by contrast, is on full view, but diluted in effect by the slightly more cartoonish tenor of the film, in addition to the fact that the monster is not an intentionally malicious force. Granted, both of the murders committed in *Mother* could be described as accidents, as they both occur in fits of pique and desperation. In the moment, the characters lose control. The way the scenes play out—the uncomfortable sound effects that accompany the crushing of a skull, the pools and spurts of blood—are all the more horrible to watch for it, as, in both instances, the killer immediately feels remorse.

Bong intercuts the two scenes just enough to make the parallel clear. Most of the flashback with Do-joon and Ah-jung plays out right before the widow murders the junk collector, save for a single beat: As the mother realizes what she's done, Bong briefly cuts to Do-joon flailing, gesturing as if to direct help toward Ah-jung's prone form. The flashback, as told by the junk collector, previously felt like a separate timeline, but now feels intertwined, as the mother's screams of horror bellow out over the footage of Do-joon waving his arms in panic.

There's no question that Bong feels for the characters he's showing us—the film wouldn't be nearly so affecting if it adopted a stance of condemnation. When the widow kills the junk collector, it's a hell of her own making. As she refuses to accept his recounting of Ah-jung's murder, she becomes almost hysterical, telling the junk collector that Do-joon has been found innocent and will soon be set free. It's only because he hears this that the junk collector attempts to call the police, thereby prompting the widow to take drastic action. Do-joon kills Ah-jung because she calls him an idiot, a term that we've already seen triggers him to violence. (What's worse, we've also seen his mother tell him to fight back when people call him names.) And it's hardly as if Ah-jung isn't suffering, too. The details of her life that come to light—the fact that she performed sex work in exchange for rice, becoming known as the "rice cake girl," and how much she came to hate men as a result—highlight the way that those with even a modicum of power will prey on those without.

Where *The Host* placed emphasis on the idea of the "weakest" members of society banding together in order to overcome the obstacles set before them, *Mother* turns people against one another. It's the degree to which the teenage Ah-jung's poverty is exploited by the men around her that makes her bitter, in turn causing her to lash out at Do-joon, who refuses to let anyone get away with verbally abusing him. The police exploit Do-joon's lack of mental facility to trick him into signing a confession. They even come precariously close to physically coercing it out of him, à la *Memories of Murder*. The pricey lawyer the widow briefly recruits to help with Do-joon's case is exploiting her desperation. Even the widow, when she burns down the junk collector's house, is arguably assuming that no one will care enough to investigate his death thoroughly. And Jong-pal (Kim Hong-jib), Ah-jung's boyfriend, who is ultimately jailed for her murder, is revealed to be a young man whose intellectual disability is more severe than Do-joon's. Unlike Do-joon, he is actually innocent, but lacks any family or friends to help him prove it. When the widow, who visits him in prison, realizes that he is all alone, she begins to weep. In perhaps the only uncomplicatedly kind gesture in the entire film, Jong-pal tells her, "Don't cry."

Given the idea that a person's true character is reflected in how they treat those less fortunate than them, Jin-tae is the other character in the film that really stands out. He's fairly ruthless—again, he's brutal with the schoolboys, and has no qualms about squeezing the widow for money—but he's the only character besides the widow who treats Do-joon with a measure of kindness. He prods Do-joon into taking the fall for an early offense, but he seems to be Do-joon's only friend, and agrees, even if it is for a fee, to try to help the widow prove him innocent. He also appears to be the most well-adjusted of the film's cast, as his relatively poor social status doesn't seem to have made him particularly bitter against anyone except the kind of people who think they can get away with hit-and-runs or otherwise look down upon the less well-off. He's also, despite the fairly prominent role that sex plays in the film, the only character actually seen in the act. The closeness of Do-joon and his mother, while meant to provoke questions, isn't explicitly sexual, and despite Do-joon's flirting with the local girls, he is never seen as a serious suitor due to his disability. And Ah-jung,

9-1

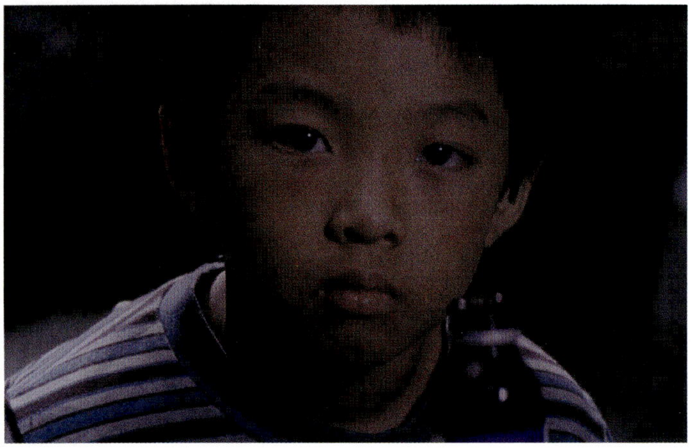

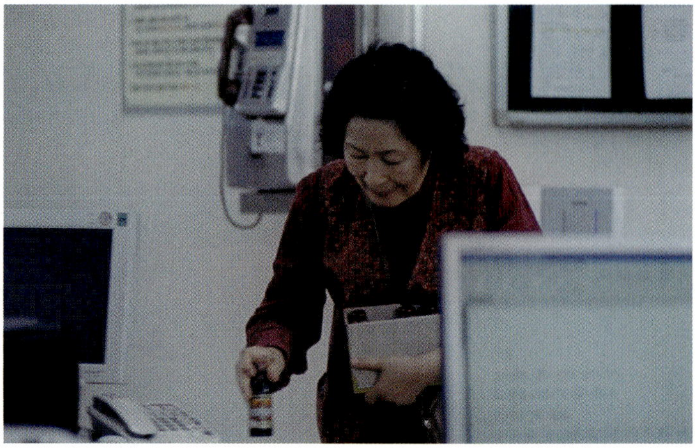

who turns to sex work to survive, hates it. By contrast, Jin-tae's relationship with his girlfriend Mi-na (Chun Woo-hee)—which, from the brief glimpses we get of them, seems playful and stable—is a healthy one.

The softer moments in the film are either incidental or border upon fantasy. In the former category are the majority of the widow's interactions with her son—she is always warmer to him and, when not trying to impress other people, he's sweet to her in turn, doing his best to look after her, e.g., buying her snacks for a bus ride.

But it's only her love for him—partially because the narrative adopts her perspective—and not the other way around that results in phantom images. Almost halfway through the film, there are two visions that play almost back-to-back. The first occurs after the mother fails to convince the lawyer she's hired that Do-joon is innocent. Bong cuts to an image of a young boy looking directly into the camera as a Bacchus bottle is held out to him. It's a mystery in the moment, and an ominous one given how its abruptness immediately sets it apart from the rest of the film (though it's also seeded early on, as, when Do-joon and Jin-tae are initially brought into the police station for confronting the men who hit Do-joon with their car, Do-joon appears somehow transfixed by the drinks, cased in similar bottles to Bacchus, that his mother brings to appease the detectives). Its later explanation—yet another illustration of the way that the love the widow bears for her son can be deadly—makes the shot's significance clear: The memory is one that still tortures her, and is also a trauma that Do-joon has largely suppressed.

In the scene that follows, the widow returns home and vomits into the toilet. (In a rare instance of comedy, the seat falls on her head as she bends over the bowl, an unplanned moment that made it into the finished film.) As she gets up and goes to bed, she senses something in another room. As she cautiously opens the door, she sees Do-joon sitting at a computer. The shot reverses to her as she calls his name. When we see inside the

57.

↑ Above
At first, the unnamed widow's act of distributing energy drinks to members of the local constabulary seems innocuous enough, but, through this act, and Do-joon's fixation upon it, Bong sets up one of the most crucial reveals in the film: that, years ago, the widow had attempted to kill Do-joon by filling a Bacchus bottle with pesticide, intending to commit suicide the same way immediately afterward.

58.

→ Opposite
Even in one of his most realistic works, Bong includes a few moments of fantasy that shed warmth on seemingly cold characters. In the depths of despair, the widow imagines that Do-joon is back home, only to realize that it's Jin-tae (Jin Goo) who's broken into her house. And, as one of the schoolboys who'd known Ah-jung recalls a conversation they'd had, she materializes in front of him.

59.

↑ **Above**
Ah-jung's funeral is wrenching—even in death, she can't seem to find peace. As the widow protests her son's innocence, Ah-jung's family members descend upon her, prompting Ah-jung's grandmother (Kim Jin-goo)—who hardly seems to comprehend that she's at a funeral at all—to spray makgeolli all over the crowd in an attempt to get them to shut up.

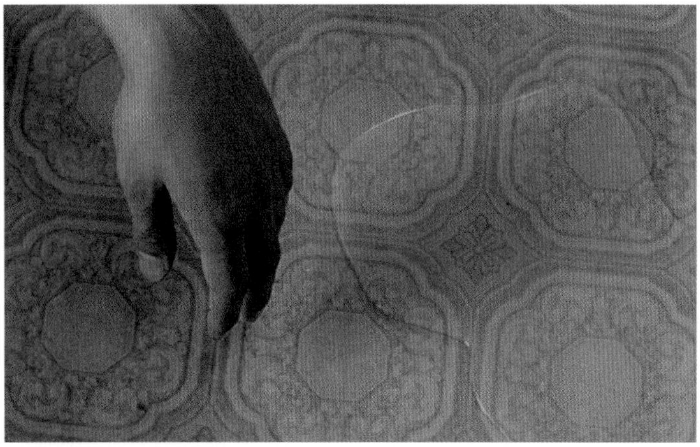

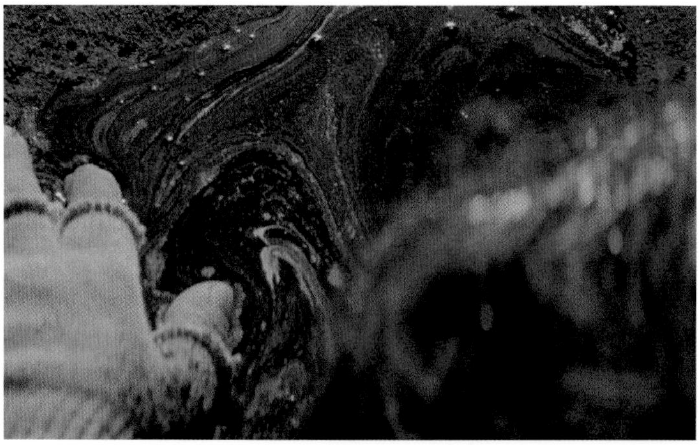

room again, it's no longer Do–joon—rather, it's Jin–tae, who has snuck into the house—but the message is obvious. She only has eyes for her son.

The other quasi–fantasy scene in *Mother* is almost reminiscent of *The Host*'s dinner scene. As Jin–tae interrogates one of the schoolboys about his relationship with Ah–jung, the boy recounts an old memory. The camera pans down from his face to reveal Ah–jung lying with her head in his lap, the conversation playing out as if it were happening right then and there, and not in the past. It's oddly tender—the boy tells Jin–tae that, although he wasn't among those who paid her for sex, he was close with her "spiritually"—as he idly touches her hair and, despite clearly not understanding just how embittered she's become, tries to connect with her.

Besides the flashback to her murder, this is the only real time that the movie spends with Ah–jung, and paints her, even with her cynical streak, as perhaps the film's most sympathetic character. Again, one of the movie's major themes is the way that people will exploit each other, and Ah–jung is, without a doubt, close to the most downtrodden character in the entire story. Being able to see her face only drives home just how young she is, a fact that's hard to stomach given how old we see that some of her clients (for lack of a better word) are, and how much she's suffered in order to become so cold so quickly. In her fateful encounter with Do–joon, it's evident that she's been pushed to her limit. That she behaves cruelly toward him is partially out of larger frustration, but also because the way he talks to and stalks her—asking if she doesn't like men because she won't acknowledge him, in a classic street harassment move—is exactly what she's grown sick and tired of. The previous memory, forced out of the boy though it is, at least offers her a moment of respite.

These more fanciful moments comprise just a couple of the details that make *Mother* so special. For one, despite an arc that feels inexorable, at least in retrospect, *Mother* sees Bong going all–out when it comes to ramping up tension. The film is both a thriller and, to a certain extent, a murder mystery, and Bong treats it as such, with elements like the slow movement of liquid—the spilled water that creeps toward the sleeping Jin–tae's hand as the widow attempts to escape unnoticed from his house, the pool of the junk collector's blood spreading across the dirt—manufacturing an aura of anxiousness.

The cinematography (the work of Hong Kyung Pyo, who would collaborate with Bong again on *Snowpiercer* and *Parasite*) also plays a key role in contributing to the overall unease—*Mother* utilizes handheld camerawork and extreme close–ups to create a sense of instability and discomfort. The shakiness of the handheld camera increases the sense of desperation and confusion, especially in scenes where action is involved—when the widow visits Ah–jung's funeral, it's total chaos, with hidden cuts enhancing the effect—making it all the more of a contrast when a shot is completely still. Ah–jung's murder, for instance, plays out in a chillingly sedate manner. Observed from the junk collector's vantage point—through the hazy windows of an abandoned house—there's never any confusion about the unfolding events. It's also almost alarming to watch, as the truth coming out is a pivotal moment in the film, yet shown from an arm's length.

The close–ups—the film's aspect ratio of 2:39:1 cinemascope was chosen specifically so that close shots would crop to the forehead and chin—serve the dual sense of making the audience feel too close to the characters and making it impossible not to clock the emotions at play, especially upon Kim's face. Interestingly, however, close–ups aren't just reserved for faces, but for Kim's hands as well. Often, her hands tell just as much of a story, whether it's how they creep closer and closer to the blade when she's chopping herbs at the beginning of the film, or how her fingers uncomfortably flex by her side as she walks away from the debris of the junk collector's house. Even at the beginning, though not in close–up, her hands serve as a sort of shield, obscuring her eyes and mouth, making her expression harder to read. Granted, there's also a third effect of the close–ups, which is to underline the widow's determination and her frightening force of will. When her features fill the

60.

← Opposite
The indistinct, opaque nature of the truth, and how it oozes and spreads away from us in a way that is both random and relentless, is symbolized in recurring shots of liquids and puddles.

frame, she seems titanic, especially in more emotionally raw or frantic moments. When the camera pulls out, revealing her entire body, it becomes impossible not to see just how small she actually is. In the scene after she burns down the junk collector's house, as she naps under a tree, she seems tiny and almost frail. The contrast serves as a reminder that, as in the films preceding this one, all of Bong's characters, no matter how monstrous they may seem and no matter the awful things they may do, are only human. ****

61.

→ **Right**
In *Mother*, as in *Memories of Murder*, the face is presented to the viewer as an emotional map to be read on numerous occasions. Kim Hye-ja, firing on all cylinders, is heartbreakingly expressive—in close-ups, she appears to be an unstoppable force of nature, but wider shots reveal just how small she is. Bong offers a subtle variation on this motif by also focusing on the protagonist's hands which—knowing what we know by the end of the story—have their own tumultuous tale to tell.

2009
Mother
2h 8m

Director	Bong Joon Ho
Writers	Bong Joon Ho Park Eun-kyo
Key Cast	Kim Hye-ja Won Bin
Budget	$5 million *Estimated*
Producers	Choi Jae-won Seo Woo-sik
Music	Lee Byung-woo
Cinematography	Hong Kyung Pyo
Film Editing	Moon Sae-kyung
Production Design	Ryu Seong-hie
Art Direction	Ryu Seong-hie

어머니의 정의

MOTHERS FOR JUSTICE

INFLUENCES
PSYCHO (1960)

Of all of the filmmakers that Bong has professed to admire, the one at the top of the pyramid is Alfred Hitchcock, whom Bong describes as his "mentor" despite the fact that the two never met. In fact, he has even credited *Psycho* (1960), which he recalls watching at the age of nine, with being one of the reasons he decided to become a director.

At the core of *Psycho*, adapted from the 1959 novel by Robert Bloch, is the relationship between motel owner Norman Bates (Anthony Perkins) and his strangely illusive mother. The film's big twist (turn back now if you're unfamiliar) is that Norman's mother, although a central part of the story, has been dead for years. Norman had killed her and her lover out of jealousy, then mummified her corpse, behaving as though she were still alive. He even pretends to be her, wearing her clothes and a wig to execute violent murders. The conversations that other characters overhear between Norman and his mother are, in fact, conversations with himself.

That unnatural closeness—or at least the implication of it—between mother and son in *Psycho* is evident as an influence on *Mother* (2009). "When I was making *Mother*, I also rewatched *Psycho,* because I thought that maybe when Norman Bates's mother was alive, they might have had a similar relationship as the one you see in *Mother*," Bong has said. And, similarly, in *Mother*, though the focus is reversed (the mother is the main character rather than the son), Kim Hye-ja's performance seems to take the viewer through the journey Norman Bates makes off-screen, with her grief and obsession driving her to previously unthinkable extremes as she attempts to exonerate her son for crimes he may not have committed.

Psycho may be a key text, but the influence that Hitchcock's work has had on Bong doesn't stop there. *Strangers on a Train* (1951) and *North by Northwest* (1959) were cited as influences on *Snowpiercer* (2013), and *Psycho* was a point of reference for Bong in constructing *Parasite* (2019) as well. Rather than being inspired by the character relationships this time around, Bong drew from *Psycho*'s sense of space and its diptych structure. The transition from the Bates Motel to the Bates house, so to speak, unfolds like a puzzle box; then, within the Bates house, there's the staircase, the second floor, the basement—just like the wealthy Parks' house in *Parasite*. There's also a concrete sense of progressing from one space to the next as more of the story is revealed. And even the way the audience is first introduced to the Parks' house, with the camera following Ki-woo (Choi Woo Shik) as he takes it all in, is influenced by *Rear Window* (1954) and its sense of voyeurism.

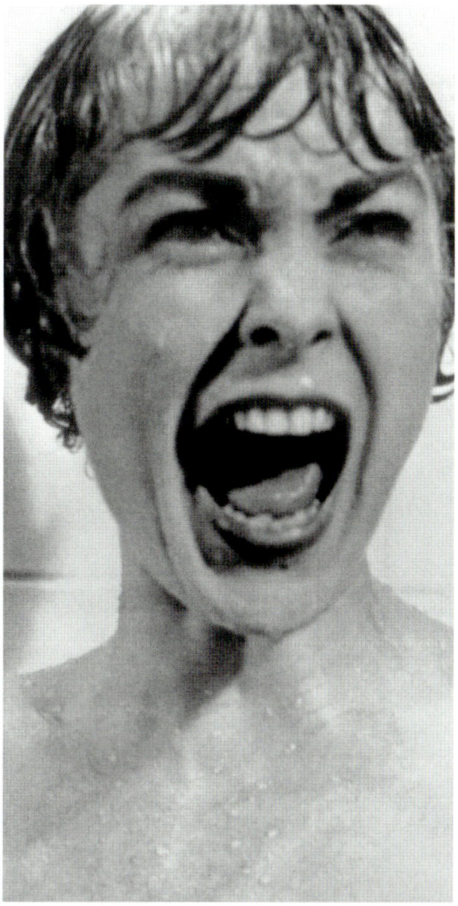

PSYCHO

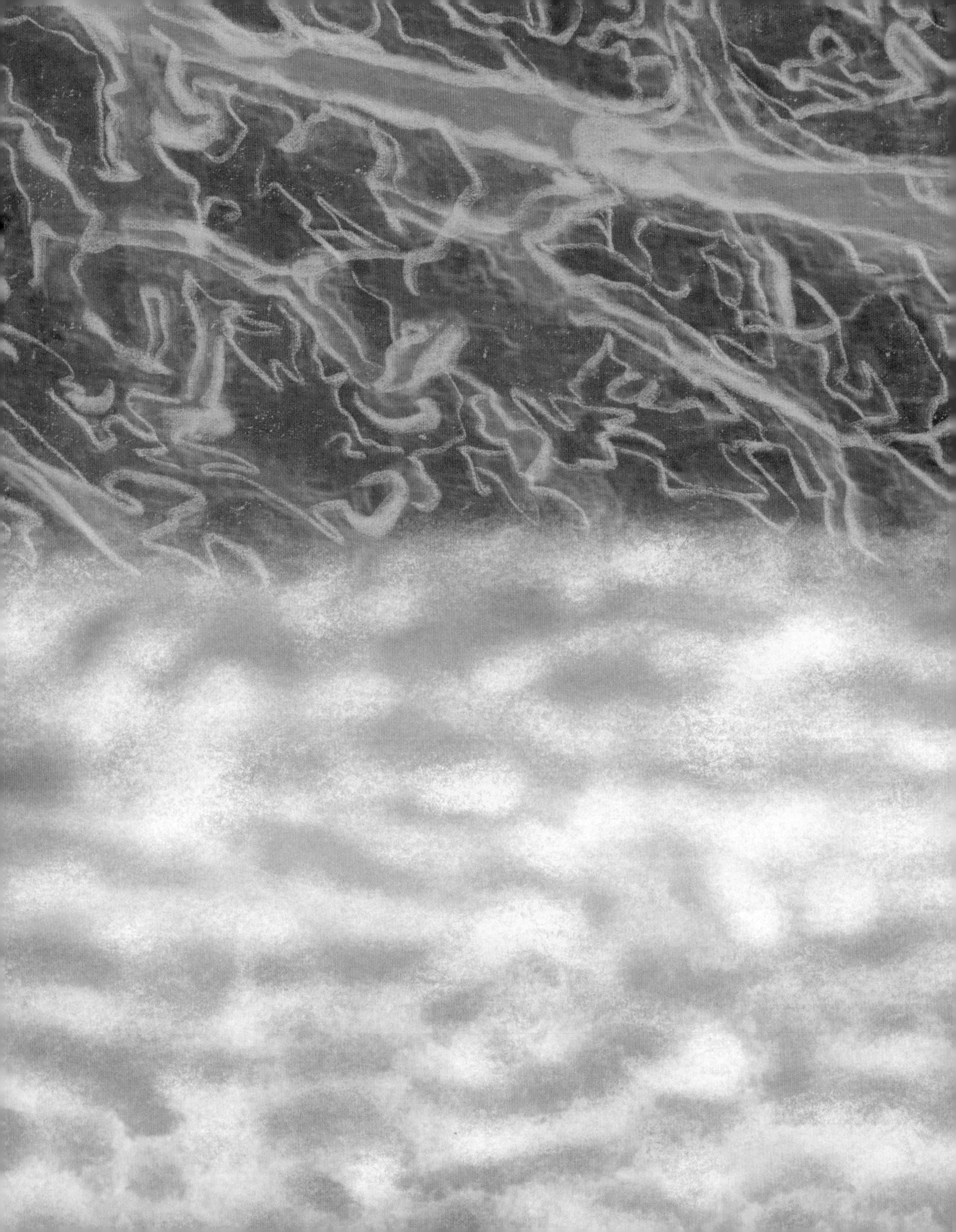

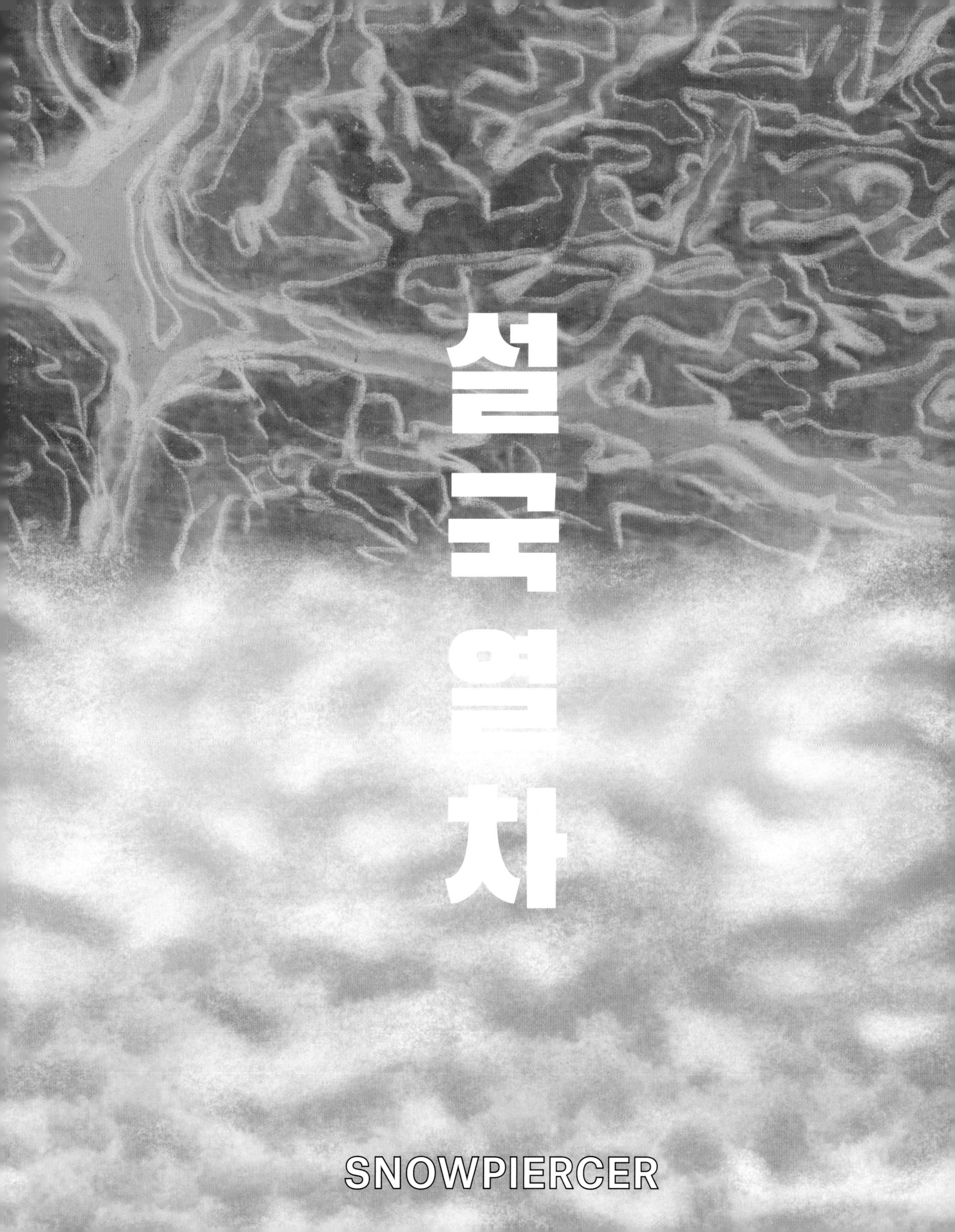
설국열차
SNOWPIERCER

62.

→ Opposite
Class oppression and exploitation are at the forefront of *Snowpiercer*, and at the beginning of the film, Bong surveys those forced to survive at the back of a train and their squalid conditions. Among the gathered crowd is Chris Evans's Curtis, soon to be the leader of a full-scale revolution.

Of Bong Joon Ho's films, *Snowpiercer* (2013) is the most cartoonish—or at least contests the title with *Okja* (2017), given that film's titular super pig—not least because it's actually based on a graphic novel (Jacques Lob and Jean-Marc Rochette's 1982 *Le Transperceneige*). It is also his most blatant in criticizing the way that money—and the varying levels of privilege that it creates—shapes the world. It doesn't feel like a coincidence that the apocalypse event that precedes the film isn't brought about by an alien invasion or a major war, but by our collective failure to stop global warming. We are, Bong says, the architects of our own destruction. Mankind's near extinction is a man-made problem, and even in such dire straits, people scrabble to maintain the class hierarchies of the pre-apocalypse world. The poor are still treated like chattel while the rich continue to enjoy unbelievable luxury. It's a grim picture of human nature and its entrenched capitalism, but no more so than in Bong's other films—the only difference is that, in *Snowpiercer*, his critique is no longer found in the subtext.

It's the year 2031, and Earth has become a frigid wasteland. An attempt to stop global warming via stratospheric aerosol injection has backfired, ushering in a new ice age. The last remnants of humanity are packed onto a train—the Snowpiercer, brainchild of a mysterious man named Wilford (Ed Harris) who now serves as its conductor—which circles the globe nonstop so it doesn't freeze to the tracks. Passengers are split into sections: the wealthy, who ride at the front, enjoy extravagances like fresh sushi and entire cars converted into classrooms and walk-through aquariums; while in the tail, people are packed elbow-to-elbow in squalid conditions and subsist on "protein bars" that look like rotten black Jell-O. Determined to flip the status quo, Curtis (Chris Evans) leads a like-minded group of fellow tail passengers in a revolt, fighting their way up the length of the train, car by car, in the hope of reaching the engine and seizing control. Along the way, they recruit Namgoong Minsoo (Song Kang-ho), the man who designed the security features on the train, and his daughter Yona (Go Ah-sung, once again playing Song's daughter), bribing them with Kronole (an addictive drug that doubles as an explosive substance) to open the locked doors they face.

Throughout the film, the open callousness of those in positions of power is striking; the idea of those at the top of the ladder exploiting those at the bottom is much more explicit here than in *The Host* (2006) or even *Parasite* (2019), which deal with similar themes but don't traffic in the same kind of clear-cut villainy. But rather than coming across as too on-the-nose or groan-inducingly obvious, the eccentric aspects of *Snowpiercer*'s setting and premise serve to accommodate its much more black-and-white sense of morality—the film isn't particularly subtle, but in Bong's hands that bluntness feels like the strike of a hammer.

To wit, the single scene that best and most succinctly sums up the film is that of the literal hammer strike.

As a contingent from the front of the train engage in what is essentially a routine abduction of children from the tail, a commotion breaks out. Andrew (Ewen Bremner), the father of one of the boys who has just been taken, throws a shoe at the head of the woman in charge. Retribution for his insubordination is immediate. For seven minutes, his arm is forced through a sort of porthole, leaving him to endure the hideously cold temperatures outside the train. During that time, the train's second in command, the ghoulishly styled Minister Mason (Tilda Swinton), lectures all of the tail passengers, emphasizing the necessity of order: "I am a hat. You are a shoe. I belong on the head. You belong on the foot." It's a cruel, cold speech, and one that instantly makes it clear the degree to which Mason and her cohorts believe themselves to be better or more worthy than the members of their audience. When the seven minutes are up, Andrew's arm, now frozen solid, is brought back inside the train. Following a brief inspection, in which a man delicately

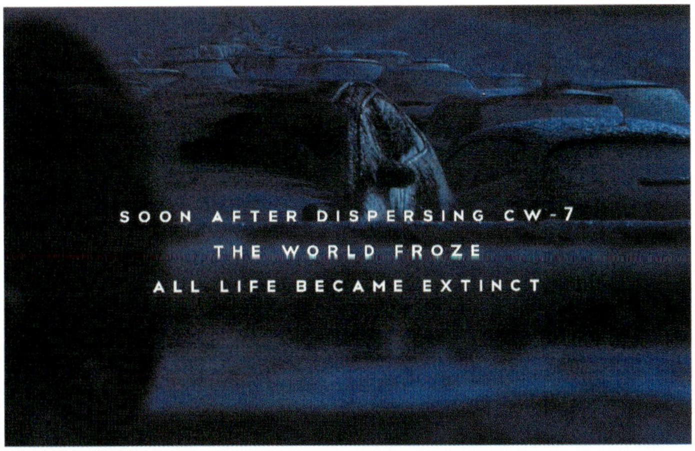
SOON AFTER DISPERSING CW-7
THE WORLD FROZE
ALL LIFE BECAME EXTINCT

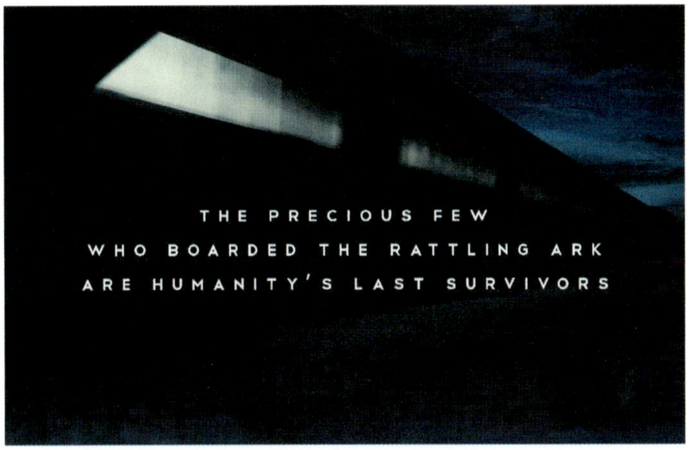
THE PRECIOUS FEW
WHO BOARDED THE RATTLING ARK
ARE HUMANITY'S LAST SURVIVORS

63.

↑ **Above**
The villains in *Snowpiercer*—which include Tilda Swinton as the buck-toothed, northern-English harridan Minister Mason—are of the comic-book variety when it comes to the intensity and ingenuity of their punishment methods. In this case, Ewen Bremner's Andrew has his arm frozen and then smashed for insubordination.

taps on the frozen flesh to check its tenor, in a sickening contrast to what follows, his arm is smashed to bits with a sledgehammer.

It's an awful punishment for a relatively minor offense (smaller still in relation to why Andrew throws the shoe to begin with), and more overtly barbaric than anything that happens in, say, *Mother* (2009) or *Memories of Murder* (2003). Even *The Host*, despite featuring a giant monster and a bevy of self-absorbed government officials, never treads into such outlandishly evil territory. But the scene firmly establishes the divide between the front and the back of the train, and the lengths to which the characters will go in order to maintain the status quo.

None of Bong's films lack for style: the subtle shifts of the autumnal color palette in *Memories of Murder*; the expressive use of focus and slow motion in *The Host*. Yet *Snowpiercer* is the most immediately arresting of Bong's works when it comes to utilizing color, light, motion, and total absurdity. In other words—as perhaps may be obvious, given the film's graphic novel origins—it's a comic book movie. Even the character designs indicate the shift in aesthetic and adherence to reality. Mason is the obvious bellwether, with her Coke-bottle glasses, giant fur coat, rows of fake medals, and pronounced false teeth; she's a caricature. So is Claude (Emma Levie), Wilford's assistant, whose defining characteristics are her bright yellow coat and robotic detachment—upon being hit with a shoe, her only reaction is to taste the blood that it draws. Even the legions of goons sent to stop the tail's rebellion fit into a cartoonish mold, as most of the soldiers have their faces covered, which achieves the dual effect of making them feel like anonymous peons (presumably how the front passengers they're protecting actually see them) and also less human, and thus more frightening. The biggest fight in the film, which occurs shortly after the loss of Andrew's arm as the tail passengers decide to force their way through the train and take over the engine, heightens that sense of being unknowable. As the train passes through a tunnel, its passengers are plunged into complete darkness, rendering the rebels helpless as the soldiers, equipped

64.

↓ **Below**
Bong employs a sophisticated color palette in *Snowpiercer*, but never as a shorthand for the tone of the drama. The muted grays and greens of the train's tail give way to bursts of color as the rebel passengers make their way to the front, yet the emotional arc of our hero, Curtis, does not run on similar rails.

with night vision goggles, carry out a massacre. The scene begins in green and black, from the perspective of the soldiers, then shifts into darkness that's broken only intermittently by flashes of light through the train's windows. Flailing limbs are visible for split seconds; a sliver of light passes over a slack-jawed, bloody face, then over Curtis's frozen, agonized features as he takes in what's happening.

But it's not just lighting that does the heavy lifting here—the color palette of the film also shifts drastically, with the muted browns and icy blues of the tail section exploding into a rainbow of colors once Curtis and his band progress farther through the train. This *Wizard of Oz*–esque transition is even more jarring because the brightness coincides with the discovery of just how well-off the front passengers are, with each successive car more lavish than the last. But as the rebellion creeps farther and farther up the train, the colors shift back, the hues darker and more muted once again. When Curtis finally reaches Wilford's engine, the predominant shade is gray, and the preceding room is a grim red, filled with smoke, as if to suggest that, despite how far the tail passengers have come, they've ended up back where they began. The colors of this climactic scene—so pale that Curtis appears as white as a sheet—just drive the sense of hopelessness home.

And though the film's final survivors, Yona and Timmy (one of the abducted children, played by Marcanthonee Reis), represent humanity's best hope for the future, *Snowpiercer* is still mostly Curtis's story. Everything is seen from his perspective—we never get to see things from the perspective of Mason and her acolytes, nor do we jump backward to check on anyone who isn't in the group of passengers trying to make their way forward on the train. Even the cinematography and editing follow that sense of constant forward motion—as in *Mother*, handheld shots are used to create anxiety and uncertainty, and an early shot that surveys an entire car of the train by turning it on its side is designed not just to impress on a technical level but to cement a sense of left-to-right progression and motion. After all, put

65.

→ Opposite
With his first predominantly English production, Bong takes the opportunity to play with language: Song Kang-ho's security expert Namgoong, who only speaks Korean, has to communicate through a portable machine. The slowness of communication is often used to ratchet up tension as guards attack the revolutionary forces from both sides.

as simply as possible, *Snowpiercer* is about a group of people getting from point A to point B, clearing the obstacles in between by whatever means necessary.

Snowpiercer stands out in Bong Joon Ho's oeuvre for several reasons besides being his most brashly comic work. For one, it's the only one of his films that can easily be traced back to someone else's story. *Memories of Murder* is also technically an adaptation (though of a stage play rather than a graphic novel), but the events it depicts are a well-known part of Korean history, and the debt that the film owes to the play are in the details rather than in the overall premise. That said, *Snowpiercer* also plays relatively fast and loose with its source material—the graphic novel introduces the idea of a train circling Earth, but there's no revolution, no tail rebellion. The main character, Proloff, just wants to make a better life for himself. Even the reason for Earth's freezing over has changed: In the graphic novel, it's a war that causes the new ice age, not a bungled attempt at solving climate change.

In another big leap, *Snowpiercer* marks Bong's first English-language film, though the nature of the story means that a good chunk of the film's dialogue is still in a foreign language. As such, it's in *Snowpiercer* that Bong's fascination with language first becomes apparent. It's a more prominent theme in *Okja*, as a deliberate mistranslation causes a significant shift in the story, but its importance in *Snowpiercer* is more straightforward—translation devices are needed for Namgoong and Curtis to communicate with each other. That relatively slight plot function, however, leaves space for a scene in which Namgoong chews Curtis out for mispronouncing his name. It's a passing moment, but surely relatable for anyone who has dealt with the fickle nature of romanization. (Even Bong's name is often mispronounced in a similar way.) There are other small things that get lost in translation throughout the film, too, like the way the devices only sometimes choose to translate cursing, or the way Yona slips back into Korean in moments of desperation. Language, in that instance, is a shorthand for expressing the bond between father and daughter.

But it's not just a language barrier that divides Curtis and Namgoong—the two characters are also kept apart by what they ultimately want from their lives. Curtis believes that he can change the system and make things fairer for the tail passengers by seizing control of the train. Namgoong, in contrast, wants to break out. The difference in their modes of thinking turns out to be the key to the film's ending.

Throughout the film, class solidarity comes across as an almost cultish obsession. In some cases, it's beautiful—the scene in which Curtis calls for light, prompting a relay race to bring him a torch from the tail to the middle of the train (shot, notably, with real fire), is a prime example of the principle, as in *The Host*, of the weak helping the weak. But that solidarity exists on the other side of the spectrum, too, as those enjoying lives of privilege on the train are hardly willing to give that up. In some cases, it seems like a form of brainwashing has occurred: Alison Pill's performance as a chipper, almost delirious schoolteacher for the front section's children feels as though it's been ported directly in from propaganda cartoons—her eyes roll back in bliss as she sings Wilford's praises, and the picnic basket she carries turns out to hide a machine pistol. It's also

66.

← Left
A frame from *Le Transperceneige* by Jacques Lob and Jean-Marc Rochette, the first of a post-apocalyptic graphic novel series that began in 1982, about a train circling Earth after the world freezes over and its thousand and one cars.

Lock the gate!

67.

↑↓ **Above and below**
As a film inspired by a graphic novel, *Snowpiercer* takes things to the next level when it comes to striking images, from that of a torch being borne through the length of the train to the cartoonish trappings of a school car and its teacher (Alison Pill).

68.

↓ **Below**
Of Bong's cast of characters, some of the most affecting are those who have succumbed to the system they live in. Both Paul (Paul Lazar) and the violinist Gerald (Robert Russell) are fully aware of how inequitable and brutal the train's current caste system is, but, given the chance to move incrementally forward, do so instead of attempting to enact change.

shocking to see the soldiers (who are the closest thing this movie has to a middle class), in the midst of a brutal attack against the tail, all pause to count down to and cheer in the new year. Everybody with something to lose wants to maintain the status quo, and clings to useless traditions as a way to enforce it. One of the film's late reveals—that the tail rebellions have actually been arranged by Wilford, with help from Gilliam (John Hurt), the man who served as a de facto leader and mentor for the back end, to prevent overpopulation on the train—underlines the point.

The inability to or fear of going against the system—or even being unwilling to give up what little privilege one is given—also manifests in less obvious ways, such as when Paul (Paul Lazar, in his second Bong film following *The Host*, and in a part that was written for him), who has been moved to the middle of the train to look after the manufacture of the protein blocks, doesn't protest his task despite now being aware that the blocks are made of cockroaches. To him—and to many others—saying no seems impossible. And the violinist (Robert Russell) seen at the beginning of the film, despite initially refusing to leave the tail without his wife and witnessing guards beating her in retaliation, seems content enough to play solo for the schoolchildren at the front of the train.

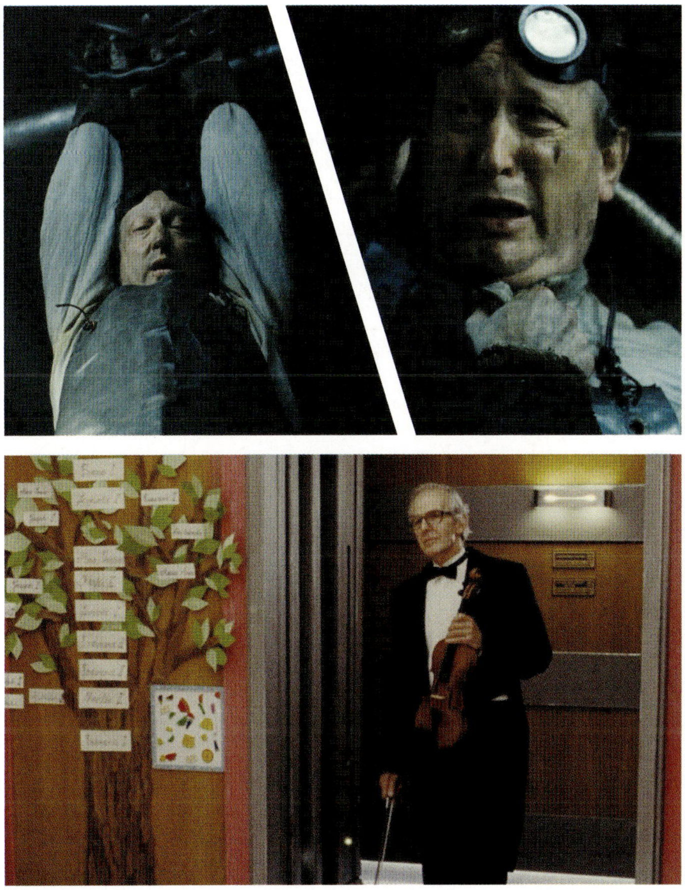

That said, what makes *Snowpiercer*—and Bong's work in general—so remarkable is the willingness to sympathize with the characters' poor choices. "I think that's the reality we live in," Bong has said. "Breaking or escaping from the system isn't an easy task. It's easy to go with the status quo." Ultimately, the fact that Curtis almost gives in to Wilford is unsurprising. As the tail passengers progress up the train, it becomes clearer and clearer that the systems keeping them in their place are more complicated than they realize; for example, the engine isn't, as they initially believe, in the middle of the train, but at the front, and the person sending secretive notes back to the tail, warning them as to what will happen next, isn't actually a spy or someone with the tail's best interests in mind. It's Wilford, engaging in population control.

69.

↖ **Opposite and above** The brutality the ominous upper classes employs to quash Curtis's rebellion is on full display in a bloody axe fight in a single carriage. In the space of a single skirmish, Bong mischievously alters the environment, first shrouding the battle in pitch darkness, and then in glowing torchlight.

70.

→ **Opposite**
The entwined fates of Curtis and Edgar (Jamie Bell) come to full fruition late in the film, after the latter has fallen in battle. By delving into the history of their relationship, Bong offers a fascinating, credible, and controversial underpinning to Curtis's motivations for wanting change.

71.

↓ **Next Page**
Bong conveys the claustrophobia of being trapped on a train by seldom allowing the camera outside (we do get a few peeks through windows), making the few exceptions—such as this stunning, digitally-rendered aerial shot of the engine darting across a snowbound landscape—all the more striking.

On top of it all, actually breaking out of the Snowpiercer still feels like a tall order. Namgoong tells Curtis that he thinks survival outside is possible, but the movie begins, after all, with a scene of a man's arm being frozen solid after just seven minutes outside of the train, and the frozen bodies visible outside—remnants of the last rebellion—are hardly encouraging for insurgents. But even Wilford's attempts to win Curtis over make it clear that the system is irreparably broken. Though Wilford says that Gilliam was his friend, he also explicitly states that Gilliam's death was punishment for the rebellion taking too many lives from the front of the train—there's no question that he doesn't truly see the tail passengers as human.

It's perhaps unsurprising, as such, to discover that Bong's grim, layered portrayal of human nature met with requests for less dialogue and more action from the American studio system. Initially acquired by the Weinstein Company in 2012, *Snowpiercer* was meant to enjoy a wide release, but disagreement over the final cut led to a now infamously fraught rollout. Harvey Weinstein, nicknamed "Harvey Scissorhands," wanted to cut a full twenty-five minutes from the film, and, as Bong recalls, wanted more action, a voice-over to explain the end of the film, and "more Chris Evans." For months, they failed to come to an agreement of which cut of the film would be released. Even worse, when Weinstein's preferred cut of the film received poor marks with a test audience, the former producer felt the solution was to cut even more, rather than deferring to Bong's vision. Eventually, after Bong's cut tested better, and press leaks about the protracted edit put pressure on the Weinstein Company, a compromise was reached: Bong's version of the film would be released, but via a much smaller limited release through Radius, the distribution company's independent arm. (Had Weinstein's cut been released, Bong has said, he would have taken his name off of the movie.) After initially opening in just eight theaters—essentially being buried—positive reviews (from the *New York Times*, *Entertainment Weekly*, *Hollywood Reporter*, and *The New Yorker*, among others) ultimately pushed *Snowpiercer* to a wider US release.

The actor Chris Evans may seem like an oddity in Bong's cast list, but a single look at the character he plays makes the choice much clearer. From the beginning, Curtis is positioned as someone the other passengers—particularly Edgar (Jamie Bell)—idolize, seeing him as a natural (if reluctant) leader. He looks after the kids in the tail section, and when the time comes, he puts himself directly in harm's way in order to determine whether or not the soldiers corralling the tail actually have bullets in their guns. In other words, he's supposed to be a hero. But the way that Curtis is lit and shot as the tail passengers make their way up the length of the train is almost always in a foreboding, villainous way: The knit of his brow casts shadows over his eyes as if to subsume them in darkness, and the grime and blood in which he's covered only make him seem more sinister and inscrutable.

These visual hints pay off fairly early—less than an hour into the film, Curtis is forced to choose between capturing Mason and saving Edgar's life. The stereotypical hero would choose Edgar. But Curtis, following only a moment's pause, goes after Mason instead, leaving Edgar to die. The decision comes as a shock, but is crucial both in establishing what kind of man Curtis is—that is, not your typical good guy—and what kind of world the characters are living in. Edgar's death directly follows a similar choice made by Mason—when Grey (Luke Pasqualino), a particularly skilled tail fighter, threatens to kill her assistant Fuyu (Steve Park) unless the soldiers relent, she lets him die rather than cede any ground. Curtis's choice is arguably made with less ease, but whatever affection Curtis bears for Edgar is vastly overshadowed by how much Edgar obviously loves him. During the very same fight in which he dies, Edgar throws himself onto a man who is about to attack Curtis, making it clear that he'd happily put his life on the line for the sake of Curtis's safety. What he doesn't yet realize is that Curtis wouldn't do the same for him.

Granted, Edgar and Curtis's relationship is more complicated than it initially seems, as revealed in

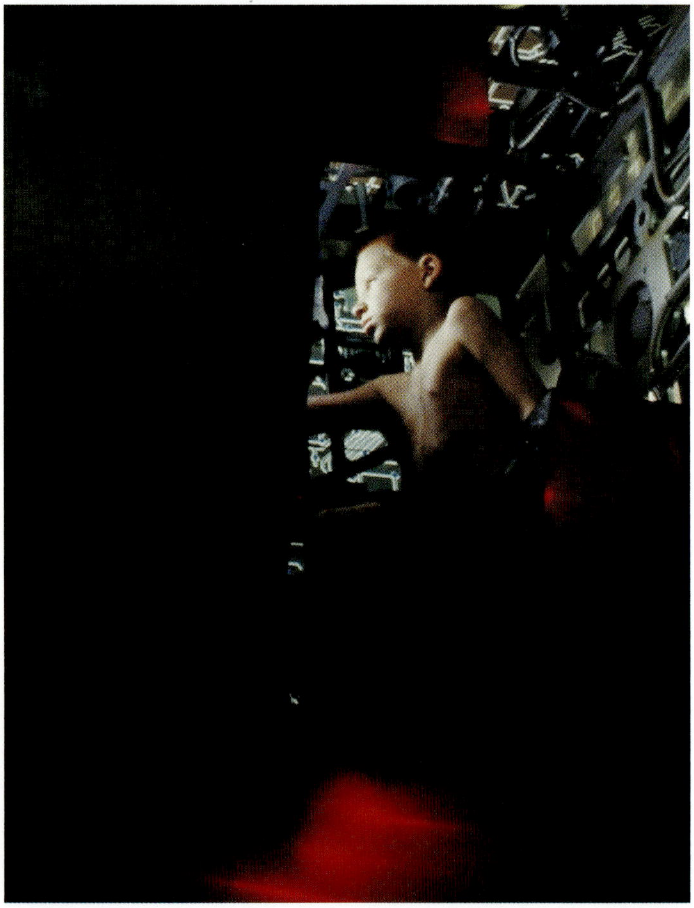

Snowpiercer's most disquieting scene. Right before arriving at the engine room, Curtis tells Namgoong about what early life on the train was like. After being starved for a month after the train embarked, he says, the tail passengers turned to cannibalism. A group of men approached a woman and her baby, killing her with the intention of eating the child. Another man stood up to them, cutting off his own arm in return for sparing the baby's life. That man was Gilliam, the baby was Edgar, and the murderous man was none other than Curtis. "You know what I hate about myself?" Curtis says, barely holding back tears. "I know what people taste like. I know that babies taste best."

It'd be a shocking, grim admission from anyone, but is even more disturbing coming from the film's main character. That he feels conflicted about it doesn't dispel the fact that we now know that he has killed and eaten human babies, and even his eventual redemption, refusing Wilford's proposal to take his place, is complicated by the fact that he almost accepts it. (Bong has said that he views Curtis as having succumbed "almost 99 percent" to Wilford's seductive line of reasoning.) It's only Yona's last-second discovery that Wilford has been stealing children from the tail to replace the engine's broken parts, condemning them to live and die inside the machine, that finally convinces him not to switch sides. That said, the revelation does finally instill some selflessness in Curtis—earlier, he confesses to Namgoong that he tried to follow Gilliam's example and cut off an arm, but couldn't go through with it. Upon finding the children in the train's engine, he does his utmost to get them out, and succeeds in rescuing Timmy—but at the cost of his arm. And, finally, he sacrifices his life in order to shield Timmy and Yona from the Kronole blast that finally derails the train.

All of the other casting choices are similarly a little twisted—Song Kang-ho and Go Ah-sung are once again playing father and daughter, but instead of being separated as they are in *The Host*, they're practically glued together, here. Though there's a slow-motion shot that feels like a conscious nod to the sequence in *The Host* in which Go's character is abducted, Namgoong and Yona

72.

← Opposite
Wilford's utopian vision and dedication to the smooth and constant running of the engine—and thus the perpetuation of the human race—is tinged with horror as it relies on grim child exploitation. The climactic images of children trapped in mechanical prisons are emblematic of Bong's yen for plumbing dark extremes to bolster his thesis.

73.

↑ Above
The seemingly benevolent Wilford lays out the crooked logic of the capitalist framework he lives to preserve. In Curtis, we see how easy it is to be lured in by the material and intellectual promises of class hierarchy.

are otherwise an inverse of Gang–du and Hyun–seo, not in terms of devotion but in terms of character arc. Namgoong ultimately sacrifices his life for his daughter's in a way that Gang–du could not, and Namgoong's louche, disagreeable attitude feels fundamentally at odds with Gang–du's sweet, earnest nature.

For the most part, *Snowpiercer* fully embraces the bleakness of its imagined future, from the reason the train exists to begin with to the social hierarchy upon it to the implication that the only real way to fix the system is to break free from it entirely. But unlike *Mother*, *Snowpiercer* is filled with little glimpses of hope. It's not entirely certain whether or not Yona and Timmy will be able to survive outside the train, but Namgoong's observation that the climate seems to be getting warmer and the fact that they no longer have to adhere to a caste system that's based, in the end, on nothing, at least gives them a chance at a better life.

Even before the finale, Bong's depiction of this dystopian existence is filled with small moments of warmth that suggest that, even in such harsh conditions, and among the worst of people, slivers of humanity can be found. Most notably, Mason's two henchmen, Franco the Elder (Vlad Ivanov) and Franco the Younger (Adnan Haskovic), share a bond that's touching despite the brutal nature of the characters. It's the death of Franco the Younger that drives Franco the Elder through most of the film—it's clear that he'd do anything to avenge the other Franco's death, even putting the train's ecosystem at risk and killing the soldiers he's supposed to be aiding. The relationship between the two Francos isn't made explicit (though an interview with costume designer Catherine George reveals that they are supposed to be brothers), but the gestures they share at least establish their bond. From the first moment they're on screen, they are leaning on each other, and obviously affectionate in a way that directly contrasts with their jobs on the train. And in the very same scene, as Mason proselytizes to the gathered crowd, we see Fuyu taking notes, presumably in the hopes of one day either rising to her station or at least becoming a little more important in Wilford's eyes. It's a small character detail, but one that immediately tells us more about Fuyu, and gives more weight to his eventual death.

Edgar and Curtis's relationship is fraught from beginning to end. Yet Edgar's boyish idolization of Curtis is a recognizable impulse in a world that can sometimes feel foreign in how exaggerated it is, and Curtis, despite throwing Edgar to the wolves and arguably being more motivated by Gilliam's perceived selflessness, has at least tried to turn over a new leaf and work for the betterment of the tail passengers. There's a warmth to Gilliam, too, in how much he clearly cares about everyone in the tail—even if, eventually, he's revealed to be working against them—and in his strangely sweet bond with Grey, as they dote on each other in the few scenes we see of them together. And, of course, the desperation of all of the parents—Namgoong, Andrew, and Tanya (Octavia Spencer)—to keep their children safe is among the most potent emotional hooks the film has to offer. Even if the world of *Snowpiercer* is far removed from our own (though not as far removed, Bong argues, as we would like to think), the parental instinct to protect is palpable.

And, even aside from hope, *Snowpiercer* maintains a strange sense of humor—a Bong trademark. A tense battle begins with the gutting of a fish as a warning as to what the soldiers intend to do to the would–be rebels. Halfway through the fight, Curtis slips on the fish's entrails. In another scene, a passenger clad in angel wings attempts to attack Namgoong, and ends up getting crushed to death in the train's gears. These little details, because of their silliness, end up helping the whole endeavor feel more grounded.

The layers to *Snowpiercer* all lie fairly close to the surface. The oppressive nature of class division is obvious, and is inherently baked into why Curtis is

74.

↖ **Left and above**
Bong leaves a bread-crumb trail of empathy and humanity through the dismal confines of the train as both mad-eyed henchman (Vlad Ivanov's Franco the Elder) and mystic sage (John Hurt's Gilliam) have the capacity for love.

leading a rebellion, in contrast with the way *Memories of Murder* and *The Host*'s social commentary requires more careful viewing to parse out. The film marks a new level of boldness in Bong's work when it comes to anti–capitalist themes—*Okja* clearly pits its characters against a major corporation despite being a girl–and–her–pig story, and *Parasite* is an upstairs/downstairs story no matter how you slice it.

Snowpiercer is, by contrast, a little clunky—though that sense is more about execution than the fact that the film wears its heart on its sleeve—but it represents a turn for Bong. Post–*Parasite*, asking what his defining characteristics are as a filmmaker will usually prompt answers describing his deftness with tone and material, and a preoccupation with the trap that is capitalism. But for all that *Parasite* makes that anti–capitalist bent unmissable, it's always been a facet of all of Bong's films—the difference is only, again, in how obvious it is. Up to this point, other details have always come first—with *The Host*, for instance, most of the buzz was about the film's perceived anti–American undertones. But in *Snowpiercer*, describing the plot in anything but the simplest terms (a group of people attempt to get to the front of a train) must include the fact that the train is divided by wealth, or at least the shadow of it.

The film uses its cartoonish qualities—its colorful characters, its varied and dramatic palette—as sheep's clothing to slip the wolf, its ultimate messaging, into mainstream pop culture. The hero's path that Curtis appears to be following is totally debunked by the film's end, both when it comes to how the train actually works and the futility of any rebellion. It's telling, too, that the film's final shot is not of Curtis or some kind of heroic triumph. Rather, as Yona and Timmy stumble, dazed, out into the snow following the train's derailment, they spot a polar bear. The bear, a concrete sign of life in the supposedly desolate outside world, is the last image that Bong leaves us with. In other words, the survival of the human race is bigger than just one or two people. **▮▮**

75.

↓ Below
The final shot of the film, in which a polar bear is spotted wandering the barren wastelands, is classic Bong: a hint at the potential for happiness rather than a more overtly sentimental and obvious kiss–off.

2013
Snowpiercer
2h 6m

Director	Bong Joon Ho
Writers	Bong Joon Ho Kelly Masterson
Key Cast	Chris Evans Jamie Bell Tilda Swinton Song Kang-ho Go Ah-sung
Budget	$40 million *Estimated*
Producers	Jeong Tae-sung Steven Nam Park Chan-wook Lee Tae-hun
Music	Marco Beltrami
Cinematography	Hong Kyung Pyo
Film Editing	Steve M. Choe Kim Chang-ju
Production Design	Ondrej Nekvasil
Art Direction	Stefan Kovacik

EAT THE RICH

RENTAL
ARRI
27

INFLUENCES
NAOKI URASAWA

On more than one occasion, Bong has said that, in another life, he might have become a comic artist. It doesn't actually seem like too much of a leap in imagination—Bong drew comics for his college newspaper, and his storyboards are so meticulous and well-drawn that several have been published in book form. He has also spoken at length about manga artists he admires (Minoru Furuya, Taiyō Matsumoto, Yoshiie Goda, to name a few), but the name that crops up most often is Naoki Urasawa, best known for the series *Monster* (1994–2001), *20th Century Boys* (1999–2006), and *Pluto* (2003–2009).

Bong has referred to Urasawa as "this era's best storyteller," and in a 2006 conversation between the two talents, he recalled that he'd been reading *Happy!* (1993–1999) while writing *Barking Dogs Never Bite* (2000), *Monster* while writing *Memories of Murder* (2003), and *20th Century Boys* while writing *The Host* (2006). In that same conversation, Urasawa and Bong compared their sensibilities, noting a shared tendency to include scenes of characters eating, make sad scenes funny (and vice versa), and blur the line between good and evil.

Urasawa's work, like Bong's, often focuses on normal people dealing with situations as extreme as the end of the world, or the mundane aspects of genres we often only see as fantastical. *Pluto*, a reimagining of Osamu Tezuka's iconic *Astro Boy* (1952–1968), takes what is generally conceived of as a kids' comic about robots, and transforms it into a murder mystery that reckons with the ideas of sentience and rights for artificial intelligence. Rather than following Astro Boy himself, Urasawa's main character is a Europol robot detective, though Astro Boy remains in the primary cast. It's a complicated, heartbreaking work, and almost inconceivable in a world where remakes and reboots feel so beholden to the idea of fan service that originality is either rare or nonexistent.

Urasawa's work doesn't shy away from darker themes: *Monster* focuses on a surgeon who must come to grips with the fact that, in an attempt to introduce positive change to the hospital system, he has saved a ruthless killer; his latest work, *Asadora!*, addresses the effect of World War II on Japan. Yet, throughout, he maintains a thread of hope that keeps his work from descending into total cynicism. Bong takes a similar tack as a storyteller—though he explores some of the darkest places that humanity can go, he still retains some sense of humor or earnestness that allows for at least a bittersweet ending, if not a completely happy one.

As with Bong's admiration for Quentin Tarantino, his admiration of Urasawa is also mutual, to the point that Urasawa has posted a couple of illustrations referencing Bong and his work: once to praise *Parasite*; and again to congratulate him on his Oscar wins.

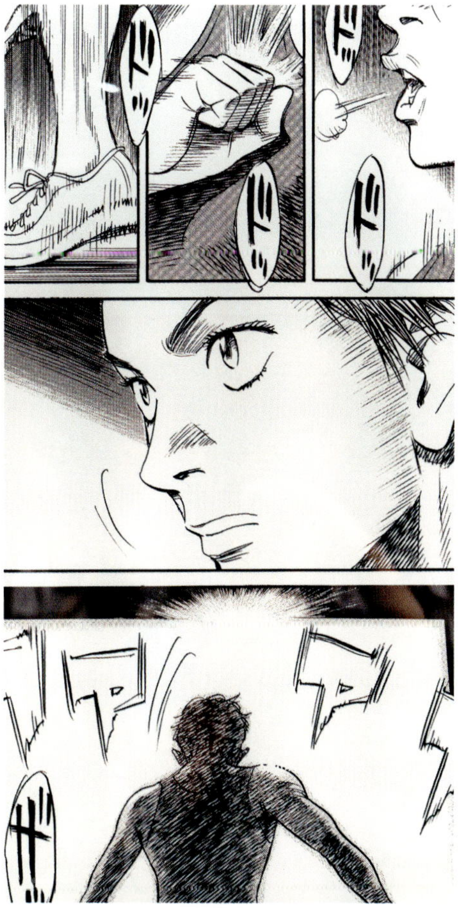
ドッ
ドッ
ドッ
ドッ
ザッ

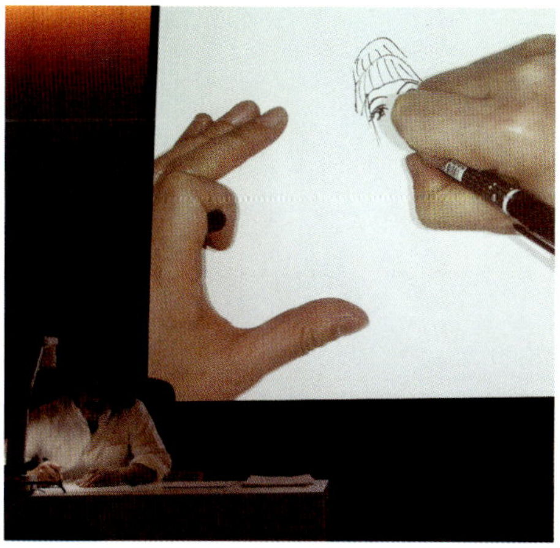

옥자

OKJA

76.

→ Opposite
Bong introduces the unbreakable bond between Mija (Ahn Seo-hyun) and her beloved super pig Okja in a way which both pays homage to classic human-animal buddy movies but also slyly satirizes their reliance on sentiment and anthropomorphism.

The introduction of *Okja*'s (2017) title character almost invites the audience to be afraid: A young woman stands in the foreground, facing the camera, as a larger force materializes in slow motion from behind her. This choreography and execution mirror a shot that's been seen in Bong's work a few times previously. In *The Host* (2006), it's the moment of Hyun-seo's abduction by the river monster. In *Snowpiercer* (2013), it's as Yona warns her friends, milliseconds too late, about the axe gang lurking behind the door they're about to open. In both prior cases, the framing is used to depict a moment of extreme peril and helplessness, and for a second, viewers would be forgiven for thinking the same thing about the character of Okja. Okja is huge, comparable in size to that of the creature in *The Host*, and an imposing presence—but Mija (Ahn Seo-hyun), isn't even startled when this marauding super pig makes her presence known, and the vibrant colors and placid tone make it all the clearer that there's no present danger.

The subtle subversion of visual language is just one of many things that sets *Okja* apart from Bong Joon Ho's previous work. If *Snowpiercer* is Bong's comic book movie, then *Okja* is his fairy tale (to wit, two of the big influences that Bong cites are Merian C. Cooper and Ernest B. Schoedsack's *King Kong* [1933] and George Miller's *Babe: Pig in the City* [1998]): A young heroine is suddenly thrust into a totally unfamiliar world in order to save her porcine friend, as the adults around her hinder rather than help her, no matter how good or bad their intentions. But even in *Okja*, the closest thing Bong has to a family fable, the director shies away from absolutes, as well as avoiding bringing events to too neat of a conclusion.

A twist on the classic formula of "a boy and his dog," except, in this case, "a girl and her super pig," *Okja* focuses on farm girl Mija and her quest to rescue her best friend, a giant, genetically modified pig named Okja, from the clutches of the Mirando Corporation. Mirando, attempting to rehabilitate their toxic public image, has launched a "super pig" program in which twenty-six special piglets (which they claim were found in Chile rather than having been genetically modified) are sent to farmers around the globe to be raised as the farmers see fit. Okja, given her massive size and sterling condition, is determined to be the best of the litter, pulling the pig and her bosom buddy into a whirlwind adventure.

On a certain level, the movie could be interpreted as a screed against the meat industry—or the food industry at large—particularly given slaughterhouse sequences so brutal that they caused more than a few audience members (including singer-songwriter Kate Nash) to become vegan or vegetarian after watching it. (Bong, too, confessed that, while researching the film and visiting real slaughterhouses, he temporarily went vegan.) But the film's small details—at the end of the movie, Mija still eats chicken, and she and Okja both eat fish—make it clear that the message Bong is trying to convey isn't that we ought to cease eating meat entirely, but to be mindful of where it comes from and how it's farmed. It's yet another example of his rejection of didacticism, where puritan morality is always tainted and people have to accept an imperfect world. The world of *Okja*, despite its cartoonish bent, is also not so black and white. Then again, of course it's not—this is a Bong film. There's nothing about *Okja* that's simple, apart from the tender bond between Mija and Okja.

Okja is an anomaly in Bong's oeuvre; his focus on more grounded stories means that a CG-powered animal sidekick isn't exactly par for the course. Yet more crucially, Mija too is an anomaly. She's one of only two female leads in Bong's works. (Characters such as Nam-joo and Hyun-seo in *The Host* and Yona in *Snowpiercer* are important, but they're not leads—more a vital part of larger ensembles.) She's also something of a paragon in the same way that most of Bong's female characters are: None of them are perfect, of course, but they tend to outmatch their male counterparts, who more often are the kind of bumbling lead that Bong favors

10 Years Later
Far from New York

(Gang-du, Doo-man, Ki-taek, et al.). Mija is smart, brave, and as earnest as can be—and too young to be as cynical or as desperate as, say, Nam-joo or the widow in *Mother* (2009).

On top of that, Mija is Bong's only child lead. Kids are a relatively rare presence in his films—they're not totally out of the equation, as *Memories of Murder* (2003) opens and closes with Song Kang-ho's character dealing with some local scoundrels, and the young Hyun-seo and Se-joo are a major part of *The Host*, but they are most often seen at the peripheries. Even if they end up caught in the crossfire of the adult drama around them, moments of violence or emotional/physical duress involving children (the final murder in *Memories of Murder*, for instance) are usually brief, or take place off-screen, as if to spare them from the same kind of torment inflicted upon their adult counterparts. There's almost an idea of purity or innocence at play—the danger they encounter is never danger that they go out of their way to seek out, and they possess an idealism that's at odds with the cynicism of the themes that Bong's work can convey.

Mija is similarly innocent: At the beginning of the film, her concerns are mainly ensuring that her beloved Okja won't be taken away, wheedling her grandfather into buying them a new TV, and getting a closer look at the Retina display on the laptop of the Mirando liaison (Yoon Je-moon) who's been charged with keeping tabs on the super pig. That is to say, the pull of money still exists in Mija's world, but she is otherwise "pure" as a character. The adventure she goes on, and the twists contained therein, are all a result of the adults around her choosing to lie to and manipulate her. Even her grandfather Hee-bong (Byun Hee-bong) is complicit—he tells the lie that lights the touchpaper on the entire story, reassuring her that Okja is theirs forever when, in fact, she will be taken away to be crowned "best pig" in New York, and likely turned into bacon.

When Okja is pig-napped, Mija makes the decision to leave the countryside to go get her back. During her ad-hoc rescue attempt, she encounters the Animal Liberation Front (notably a real organization, though

77.

↑ Above
The character of Okja represents a nexus of contradictory demands from various parties: Mija's grandfather Hee-bong (Byun Hee-bong) is emotionally detached from her future as a foodstuff; whereas the members of the Animal Liberation Front want to co-opt her as a symbol of their struggle.

the characters purporting to follow their ideals are all fictional), which is trying to get to Okja for a different reason. Mija wants to take Okja home, the Mirando Corporation wants to turn Okja into meat, and the ALF wants to use her as a mole, planting a secret camera under her ear to capture Mirando's mistreatment of the animals it's supposedly breeding ethically. Jay (Paul Dano), the ALF's leader, recognizing the bond between Mija and Okja, gives Mija the choice as to whether or not their operation will proceed—if she wants to go back to the mountains with her pig, then that'll be that. However, K (Steven Yeun), the ALF member who has been serving as translator between Jay and Mija, deliberately lies to Jay about Mija's wish to take Okja home, instead telling Jay that she's willing to go ahead with the plan.

Another big lie, this time one that triggers the most traumatic passage of the film, involves Johnny Wilcox (Jake Gyllenhaal), a slimy, manic TV personality and celebrity zoologist, whose position as Mirando's mascot is threatened by Mija's appearance. The young girl's very public attempt to save Okja makes such a big splash that the head of the Mirando Corporation, Lucy Mirando (Tilda Swinton), arranges a public reunion between the pair in an attempt to mitigate the PR damage. Johnny, meanwhile, in an act of abhorrent revenge, arranges to have Okja raped by a male super pig being kept in captivity in a Mirando laboratory, and takes samples of her meat for product testing. Distraught by what he's seeing through Okja's camera, K finally confesses to what he's done, and Jay punishes him by beating him and throwing him out of the ALF, though he keeps K's equipment to help finish the mission. Jay remains sympathetic to Mija throughout the film—he seems to be the only adult who truly understands how special Mija and Okja's bond is, as evidenced by the look of wonder on his face when he sees how seamlessly the two of them communicate—but his treatment of K makes it abundantly clear that there aren't any completely "good" adults. He even proves willing to hurt Okja, as he attempts to strike her in order to save Mija from her bite.

78.

↓ Below
As in *Snowpiercer*, brightness, ebullience, and seeming benevolence act as a shroud for something darker, represented here by Jake Gyllenhaal's celebrity zoologist Johnny Wilcox. But appearances aren't everything—even those who appear to be good or well-intentioned, such as Paul Dano's hard-nosed freedom fighter Jay, carry darkness within them.

79.

← Left
Mija's wonderment at the laptop Mundo (Yoon Je-moon) brings to check on Okja is a shorthand for just how sheltered she is, and how removed she is from the ruthless world she's about to be dropped into.

80.

→ Opposite
Okja deals with often-paradoxical arguments about vivisection, animal cruelty, and meat-eating, not so much offering solutions for change, but showing how these solutions are anathema to capitalism. Mija is happy with her rescued pig (below)—but at what price for the rest of Mirando's super pigs (above)?

In the end, both Mija and the ALF get their respective wishes, as the ALF uses the parade intended to showcase the heartwarming reunion between Mija and Okja as a platform to screen footage collected from Wilcox's lab, thereby tanking any public goodwill Mirando might have accrued, and Mija finally gets to go home with Okja. But Bong carefully keeps the film's finale from feeling too triumphant—or too much like an old-fashioned fairy tale. First things first, a hero's journey is not what Mija is looking for, and, for all that Lucy, Johnny, and the members of the ALF, not to mention Okja, might come across as cartoon characters, *Okja* is still set in the "real" world. The Mirando lab and the slaughterhouse from which Mija finally rescues her friend are disturbing to say the least, suddenly bloody and grimy in a film that can otherwise feel poppy, colorful, and larger than life.

Bong even avoids using the most obvious set piece for his grand finale. The parade, with its giant pig float and pig-costumed participants, is the perfect setting for a showdown, and even though it's the location of the ALF's big stand, it is not the climax of Mija's story. Instead, Mija's face-off with Nancy Mirando (also played by Swinton), Lucy's brusque sister who swoops in to take over following the parade debacle, occurs in a disgusting, dispiriting slaughterhouse. Where the rest of the film has boasted a bright, rich color palette, this climactic venue feels comparatively (and perhaps symbolically) drained of any life. Sickly blues are the order of the day, lending a particularly sticky, unpleasant sheen to the blood and guts on display, in one of the few instances in Bong's work when such explicit violence and bloodiness is held on screen rather than left to the imagination, or presented either quickly or in extreme close-up. The viewer is forced to face the callousness with which these animals—and the many real animals who are bred for meat—are treated.

The sense of grounding—of realism as opposed to fantasy—extends to the confrontation between Mija and Nancy, which is hardly a grand display of good triumphing over evil. In any other movie, Mija and Okja would rise to the occasion and become heroes. To a certain degree, they do. But it's not by choice, nor in a particularly orthodox way. Rather, Mija buys Okja from the Mirando Corporation with a gold pig figure that had been given to her as a gift by her grandfather. Money saves the day, as opposed to guts or goodwill. For the price of that pig, Nancy allows Mija to take Okja home—but that doesn't account for the countless other super pigs that Nancy is now speeding into production.

As Mija and Okja take their leave, they pass hundreds of super pigs slowly being shuttled into the slaughterhouse by men with electric rods, and manage to save just one baby super pig, who is thrust into their path by its parents. For the rest of the super pigs, there's no hope of a life that doesn't end by being turned into meat, nor any existence that's even a fraction as peaceful or pleasant as Mija and Okja's life in the mountains, where they amble through trees and rivers all day without any interruption. Mija has demonstrated extraordinary bravery, making her way through Seoul and New York City all on her own, and dealing with multiple adults who ought to know better, but she isn't a superhero—she can't save all of these pigs—nor does she necessarily want to be. In the film's final moments, there's no indication that Mija has any desire to engage with the outside world again. She has Okja back, and that's enough.

Ironically, of the film's adult characters, the only one who is straight with Mija is the fearsome Nancy Mirando. Unlike a prototypical villain, her aim isn't to destroy all of these pigs, but purely to turn a profit. She'll throw her own sister under the bus to keep the company afloat, so there's no question that she's ruthless, which makes it all the more surprising, at least initially, that she has no qualms about simply selling Okja back to Mija. That Okja is so important in the film is because it follows Mija's perspective. In actuality—in Nancy's eyes—Okja is just one more pig.

Both that finale and Mija's arc make it equally clear that Bong doesn't intend for *Okja* to serve purely as a condemnation of the meat industry. Even in the capacity to which it does discourage eating meat, it's less about ceasing eating meat altogether and more

81.

↑ **Above**
As the film's moral nucleus, Mija goes about her daunting rescue quest alone. She interacts with people and earnestly takes their offers for help at face value, but the way Bong places her in the frame constantly emphasizes her lonely toil.

about ceasing mindless consumption and, as many of his films are, about practicing kindness and healthy curiosity, whether it be toward humans or animals. Mija herself hammers the point home as, in the film's final scene, we see that she's made peace with her grandfather and now lives with him, Okja, and the baby super pig back at home. She's grown up a little, as illustrated by the change in her clothing—instead of her signature colorful jacket and track pants (which make her look like a typical middle-aged Korean hiker rather than a child), she's upgraded to a more adult (and marginally more feminine) white button-down shirt and skirt—but she hasn't changed in any major way otherwise. Her heroism was innate from the beginning of the movie—though she may be older and wiser now, she's still the same Mija underneath the superficial change in clothing.

Of all of Bong's characters, Mija is arguably the most removed from the rest of the world. In part, it's because she's still a child; she isn't yet as jaded as many of Bong's other protagonists. Her detachment, for lack of a better word, is also a result of the fact that she and her grandfather live in the mountains, relatively far from any other signs of human life. Upon arriving at Mija's home to inspect Okja, Wilcox and his team are all visibly exhausted, and complain about how arduous the trip was to get there.

That tension between city and country life is one of Bong's abiding interests—in *Memories of Murder*, the two lead characters initially butt heads because of their respective social backgrounds. This tension has never been expressed so explicitly as it is in *Okja*. The film's introduction, in which Lucy Mirando unveils her super pig plan to a group of journalists, is filmed in a way that echoes the glossy, hip, and smooth vibe of the presentation playing behind her. As the camera glides around the space, pastel colors and cute graphics fill the screen, though Bong firmly establishes the film's sharp edge as Lucy tells the gathered press that the super pigs "need to taste fucking good." We then hard cut to Mija frolicking in the sun-dappled countryside. The shift of focus is jarring not just because of the big change in scenery, and how relatively unkempt Mija is in comparison to the ultra-polished Lucy (Mija's hair is comparable to that of Prince Valiant's, a classic kids' bowl cut, and she hardly fears getting her hands dirty), but because Bong completely alters the sense of motion. We instantly see these two discordant worlds in tandem, which in turn drives the conflict at the center of the story.

Wide shots dominate the scenes that take place in the countryside, capturing, as much as is possible, the vastness and comparative serenity of nature. The ample frames leave more than enough room for the giant Okja to wander around, and images are composed like paintings—the first time Hee-bong appears on screen, he is seen through the open doors of the house, the framing essentially turning the image of him into a square, with the light silhouetting him against the verdant backdrop of the mountains. When the camerawork becomes more frantic—an early moment of peril incorporates handheld shots to emphasize both motion and danger—the shift demands focus and attention. There's no room for complacency anymore.

The film's color palette undergoes a similar change. Mija's taste in luridly colored clothing makes her stand out against the appealingly saturated countryside backdrop, but everything else around her is otherwise perfectly natural. When she leaves for the city, she still stands out—her red jacket draws the eye in a crowd of drably dressed commuters. Yet it's less that she stands out and more that everything around her seems dulled—that is, apart from the world of Lucy Mirando, which is bathed in a million shades of pink. The key, though, is that the Mirando "version" of the world is almost too colorful and, to that end, comes across as sterile and suspicious. The darkness and griminess of the slaughterhouse and laboratory scenes are distinctly manufactured to provide a stark contrast. The blue wash over everything makes the blood all over the floor look black and sticky, and there's no greenery or nature anywhere to be seen—

82.

← Opposite
Tilda Swinton's bouncy corporate CEO Lucy Mirando is cut from a similar cloth to her Minister Mason in *Snowpiercer*—a pantomime villain who proves to be massively out of her depth. Bong's collaborations with Swinton have yielded some of the actor's most memorable performances.

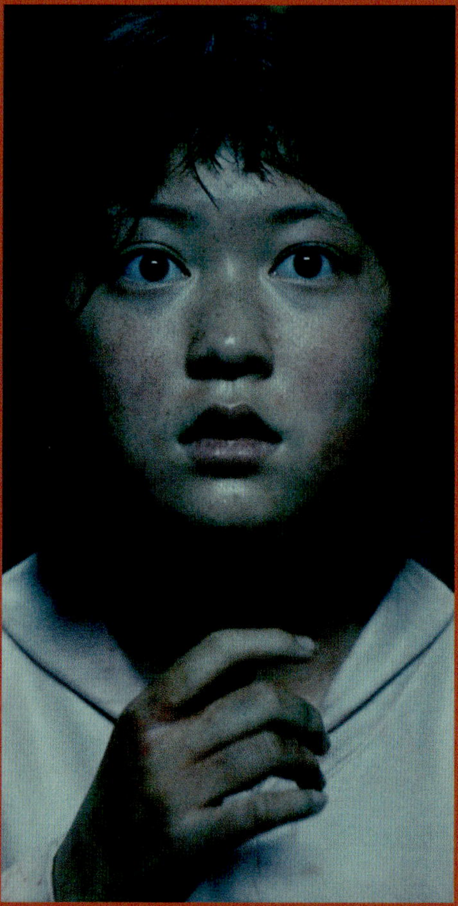

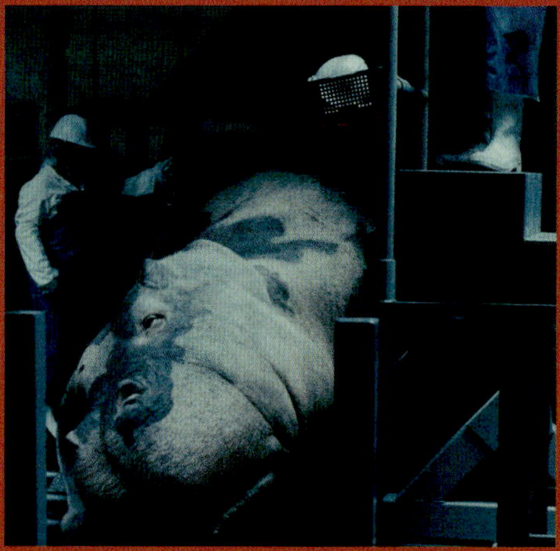

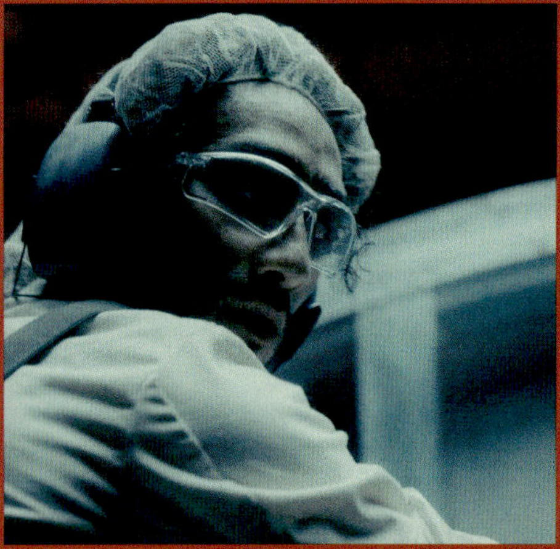

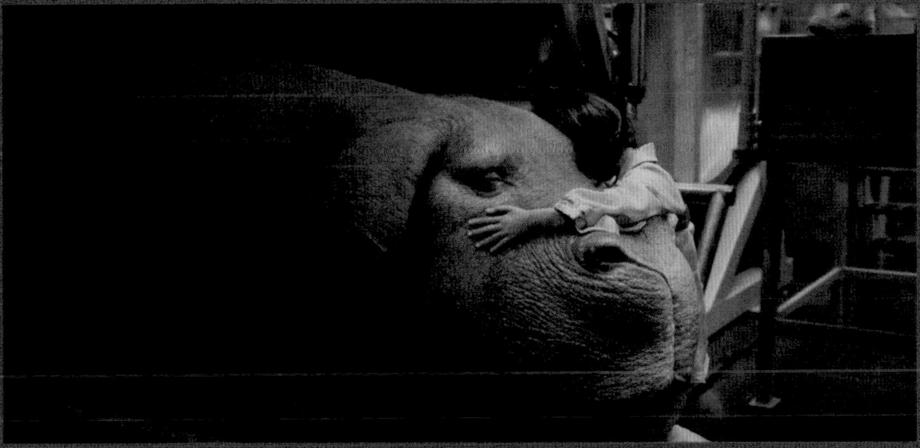

83.

↖ **Opposite and above**
At the film's climax, the simple transaction of a golden pig for a live one (Okja) is what helps Mija to achieve her goal. Ethics and sentiment are swept aside and cold, hard economics win the day.

84.

↓ Below
Despite the film's satirical bent, Bong uses *Okja* as a way to present the brutal realities of a mechanized food industry, almost leaning on the gory iconography of the splatter horror genre—a procession of packaged animals parts, rivers of blood, terrifying implements of death—to get his point across the line.

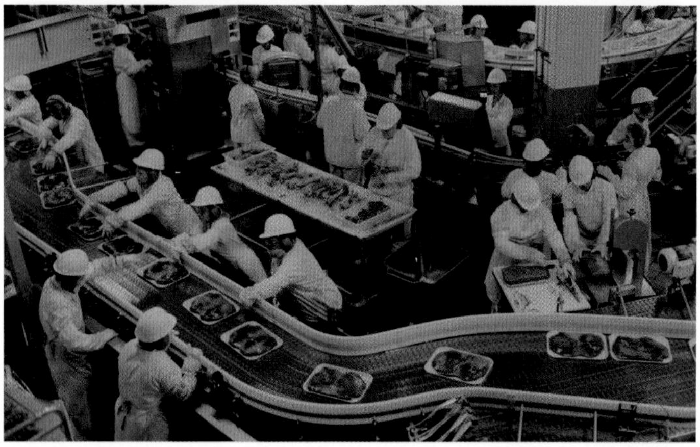

there aren't even windows. Granted, the inside of the slaughterhouse isn't *meant* to be seen—it's the ugly side of the company that Lucy has been trying to cover up this entire time. (It's an echo, in intention, of the engine reveal in *Snowpiercer* or the basement space in *Barking Dogs Never Bite* [2000], as all three hidden spaces are for the sake of the rich covering up the degree to which they'll exploit the less fortunate. In that way, it's also a precursor to the bunker in *Parasite* [2019]).

Language also serves as something of a divide in the movie, not just when it comes to Okja's inability to verbally communicate with humans, but in several other ways as well. There's K's betrayal of Mija, as he deliberately mistranslates her wish to go home. This actually prompts Mija to start learning English, enough so that, by the film's end, she bargains with Nancy without any translation necessary. Another, subtler language detail occurs around the same time—the few lines of dialogue spoken by slaughterhouse workers are all in Spanish, drawing a line between those who run Mirando (middle-aged white executives, with the exception of Giancarlo Esposito's Frank) and those who are forced to carry out the dirty work that Mirando is dragged across the coals for. And finally, there's the strange, slightly meta note of what K says to Mija right after mistranslating her response to Jay. The English subtitle reads, "Try learning English. It opens new doors!" However, the actual Korean dialogue actually goes, "My name is Goo Soon-bum!" The joke, that Soon-bum is an old-fashioned, corny kind of name, won't translate for most non-Korean viewers, hence the decision, made by Bong and cowriter Jon Ronson, to go with a different gag. Right after the line is spoken, K literally jumps out of the door of the truck they're in. "I mean, that's not that funny, either," Bong said, speaking of the scene. "I thought there was no other way except to make [the line and its translation] totally different."

The action scenes, too, illustrate this omnipresent concept of division, particularly how removed Mija's existence is from the rest of the world. The big problem she encounters at the very beginning of the film occurs when she is walking Okja through the mountains, loses

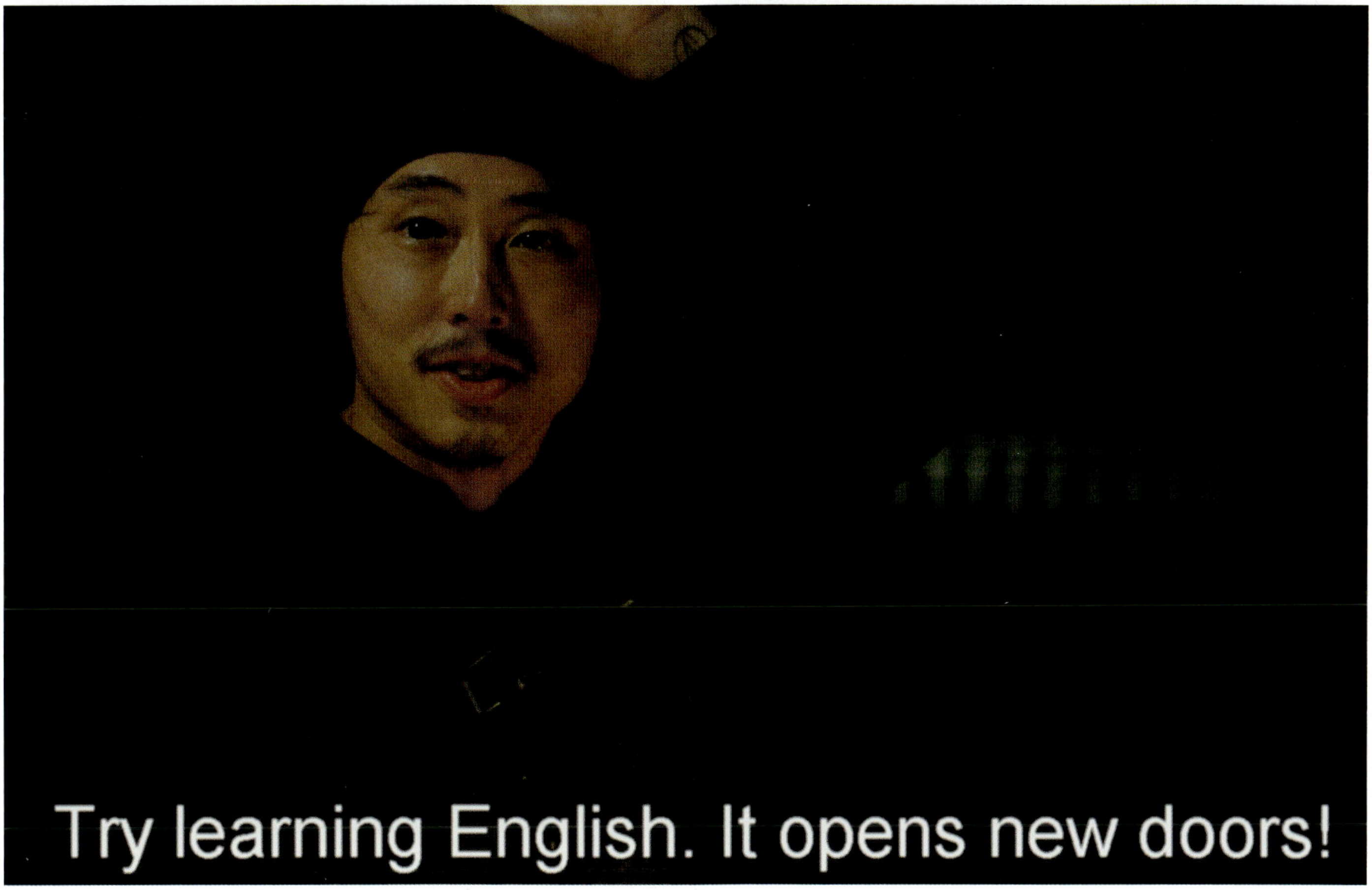

85.

↑ **Above**
Bong's persistent interest in the language barrier as a cause of duplicity and human alienation is visible in a sequence in which K (played by Steven Yeun), the only member of the Animal Liberation Front who speaks both Korean and English, tricks Mija into going along with their plan.

86.

↓ **Next page**
The big Mirando parade—itself held in one of the busiest venues possible, through New York City's financial district—would be the perfect set-piece for a grand finale, yet Bong defies expectations by setting the movie's true climax just moments later in a creepy, dingy warehouse, emphasizing the importance of story over spectacle.

87.

← **Opposite**
More than just a magical realist family caper, *Okja* digs into the idea of the genetic and emotional relationship between humans and animals, presented in the way that Okja seems to reciprocate the love that Mija extends to her.

her footing, and slips from a precipice. The rope with which she leads Okja serves as the only thing keeping her from plummeting to her death. Mija's only recourse to survival becomes Okja, and it's Okja's quick thinking that saves the day. She uses a jutting tree trunk as a sort of pulley and throws herself off of the cliff, thereby catapulting Mija back up onto solid ground. Luckily, both survive. By contrast, the big problem that Mija has to solve at the end of the film is not so much figured out with wits and bravery, but simply by complying with the tenet presented to her. Offering Nancy the golden pig figure is an ingenious solution on Mija's part, but the moment isn't there to prove just how smart she is: It's to illustrate the extent to which the ways of the world they're living in are dictated by money. Mija doesn't fight the system—and arguably doesn't even try to, beyond refusing to easily kowtow to Mirando's initial demands of her as a new mascot. Rather, she accepts it without much hesitation. Her aim is to save Okja, and if playing by capitalism's rules is what's necessary, then so be it.

From the very first moment they're seen together, there's no question that Mija and Okja are two peas in a pod, made for each other. Despite being different species, there's no pig–human language barrier between them, and they're so in tune that they seem like a single entity. While Mija naps on Okja's side, the giant super pig rolls over. Instead of falling off, Mija rolls, too, as if in a choreographed dance, ending up squarely on Okja's belly. Even their names, which, as per Korean tradition for children of the same generation within a family, share a syllable—Mi-*ja* and Ok-*ja*—indicate their closeness.

Okja also borrows, in a fashion, from Sofia Coppola's 2003 film *Lost in Translation*. The biggest way in which Bong emphasizes the bond between Mija and Okja is through brief scenes in which they "speak." Twice throughout the film, Mija whispers something into Okja's ear that the audience can't hear (nor lip-read, as she cups a hand around her mouth as she speaks). It happens once when they're alone in the forest toward the beginning of the film—that is, in a moment where a dramatic declaration is hardly necessary—and once when a traumatized Okja bites Mija, unable to recognize her through a haze of fear. With one arm still trapped in Okja's teeth, Mija lifts her ear and whispers something inside. Slowly, Okja, who until this point has acted in a frantic, disoriented manner, calms down. If anything, the dire circumstances make it seem all the more crucial for the audience to know what Mija says to Okja to calm her down, but the fact that it's kept quiet is all part of the spell that Bong casts. The story may be a work of fiction, but the privacy that Bong offers Mija and Okja makes them feel real. What they have to say to each other isn't meant for us—it's their secret to keep.

This little motif also lends more impact to the film's final moments. Back home, Mija gets ready for a meal with her grandfather. Before she fully enters the house, Okja pulls her aside. Here, as in the first scene in which we see them together, it's neatly illustrated that even just a glance between them can communicate multitudes. After contemplating Okja for a moment, Mija turns so that her ear is to Okja's snout. Unlike Mija's whispers to Okja, we can hear Okja's plaintive vocalizations, but we can't understand them, nor does Bong subtitle what's being said. Finally, Mija simply smiles at her best friend, then sits down to dinner.

The way that they're shot and framed only emphasizes their bond. Though close-ups aren't saved exclusively

88.

← **Left**
The balance between shyness and enthusiasm in Hiromasa Taguchi's (seen second from right) performance in the 1996 Japanese romantic comedy *Shall We Dance?* informed the way Bong and his team animated and characterized Okja.

89.

↓ **Below**
The film's central action set-piece is one of Bong's most raucous and dynamic—a road chase sequence that transfers to the cramped byways of an underground shopping mall, with guns blazing, retail outlets exploding, and a neat trick involving rainbow parasols to aid a quick, stylish, and colorful getaway.

for Mija and Okja, they are employed for the two girls most often, and, as in *Memories of Murder*, Bong pays special attention to their eyes. They can speak to each other just fine, but part of what makes their bond so special is the fact that they seem to possess a sort of sixth sense, and the knowing looks they share are the primary visual way of conveying that. For Okja, this is especially important, as whatever power of speech she's capable of is understood only by Mija. The tone of her grunts and squeaks (provided, in part, by *Mother* and *Parasite*'s Lee Jung-eun) goes a long way toward expressing her mood for others, including the audience, but beyond that and becoming more or less physically aggressive, her eyes have to do a lot of talking for her. (Unlike most "cute animal" characters in contemporary cinema, Okja's eyes are proportionate to her head—no super pigs exist in real life, but she doesn't require much suspension of disbelief to take seriously.) From the scene on the cliff to the chaos of the parade, a focus on Okja's eyes is necessary to make her just as expressive as the humans around her. We're meant to sympathize with her, and a relatively high degree of anthropomorphism—as opposed to *The Host*'s creature, which was more animalistic—makes it an easy task. And just as the inspiration for *The Host*'s monster, Steve Buscemi in *Fargo* (1996), informs how it's portrayed on screen, so does Okja's inspiration, actor Hiromasa Taguchi in the 1996 Japanese romantic comedy *Shall We Dance?* Buscemi's performance in *Fargo*, rather than being monstrous, is nervy, and the monster is accordingly not malicious so much as it is frantic. Okja's touchstone comes through more easily: Taguchi's character, a large man taking up dancing as a way to lose weight, dances with great enthusiasm, but immediately flinches and shrinks upon any reproach or negative energy. Similarly, Okja is surprisingly shy and fragile given her size; the immediate instinct upon seeing her is to try to protect her.

90.

✓ **Left and below**
In a delicious send-up of Pete Souza's famous *Situation Room* shot, taken in 2011 as President Barack Obama and his national security team viewed live video relay of the raid on Osama bin Laden's compound, Bong reconstructs the photograph with members of a corporate conglomerate and a super pig.

Bong's films are always doing something interesting with music: *Barking Dogs Never Bite*'s jazzy score invokes film noir, while *Memories of Murder*'s more classically orchestral, slightly synth-y score encapsulates contemporary thriller to a tee. *The Host* takes a few more musical risks, with goofy, circus-esque cues and science-fiction thrums occasionally punctuating the otherwise straightforwardly orchestral accompaniment. But *Mother* serves as a turning point when it comes to Bong's use of music, one that's crystallized in *Okja*. Unlike the films that precede it, *Mother* almost has a theme song; the same piece of music both begins and ends the film, and it is so crucial in tone to those scenes that hearing that song again will likely immediately remind any listeners of the film it's from. It's the first piece of music in one of Bong's films to really stand out.

Okja doesn't take quite as big a swing, but still devotes a big moment to a single song. It's not the first time that Bong has used preexisting music in one of his films, as the song "Woman in the Rain" plays a key part in *Memories of Murder*. But when he deploys John Denver's "Annie's Song" in *Okja*, it's not as a diegetic device (i.e., a piece of music being heard within the context of the movie); rather, it plays ironically over a scene of chaos. Its sweet strains somehow feel perfectly suited to the moment, as does Bong's constant melding of genres and tones. Okja and Mija's first escape attempt sees them hurtle through an underground mall, pursued by both Mirando employees and ALF activists. When the chase finally comes to an end after Okja, who swerves to avoid hitting a bystander, crashes into a stall and falls to the floor, the action shifts into slow-motion, and the score stops. Then, "Annie's Song" kicks in. It's an incongruous choice—John Denver's sweet voice flows over the image of Mirando employees leveling tranquilizer guns at the ALF, who respond in turn by opening umbrellas to deflect the darts being shot at them. Up to this point, Okja has been presented as something of a wrecking ball, barreling through the landscape, but the pause and shift in tone that "Annie's Song" creates begs viewers to reassess. "[Okja's] intention is not to attack these people," Bong said of the scene. "What you see is the character who is most scared and the most fearful is Okja. It's an unintentional chaotic mess caused by a shy, introverted character who doesn't want this to happen." The song apparently came to Bong in the editing room, carried on a wave of nostalgia from his childhood, when his older brother played it so much that it got on the young Bong's nerves.

As opposed to the work of, say, Quentin Tarantino or Edgar Wright, directors who are known for their clever needle drops, the use of "Annie's Song" in *Okja* is such a novelty in Bong's work that it stands out. It's also telling of Bong's evolution when it comes to how he matches music to his images. The further one progresses in his filmography, the larger a part the music plays, enriching the story being told and creating moments that are so magical that they stick indelibly in the mind of the viewer.

Okja is also in the running to be Bong's cheekiest film, as its digs at American politics, while subtler than those in *The Host*, are more outrageous. The way that Lucy Mirando looks, for instance, was at least partially modeled after Ivanka Trump, while Nancy was styled as "a female version of Trump." Then there's the conference room scene, as a group

of Mirando executives watch footage of Mija and Okja's initial escape attempt in Seoul. The placement of the characters is a direct homage to *Situation Room*, the photo taken by Pete Souza of President Barack Obama and his national security team as they monitored the raid on Osama bin Laden's compound. Lucy sits in the place of Hillary Clinton, with Frank in Obama's seat. Given the Trump iconography that inspired the Mirando sisters' aesthetic, it's an ironic callback, and perhaps one that best illustrates another core thread to the film, of positive intentions not necessarily yielding positive results, as well as a refusal to damn (or bless) either of the political extremes he's pulling from.

Lucy's primary mission in taking over as Mirando's new CEO is to rebrand it, to move it away from the tyrannical, ruthless image her father cultivated, and to create a more approachable, more ethical (or at least ethical-seeming) company. In her attempt to do so, however, she has lied to everyone, and is ultimately exposed as a fraud. The ALF members similarly can't quite be totally good in their quest to prevent animal cruelty—they still exhibit cruelty toward Mija, Okja, and one another. Though Hee-bong cares deeply for his granddaughter, simply going ahead and doing what he thinks is best for her isn't helpful, either. And even Mija and Okja, in their struggle to return home, end up causing quite a commotion, even if the damage they incur is, in the scheme of things, negligible in comparison to the extent of harm done by the people around them. Again, nothing in *Okja* is truly black and white—that is, except the bond of love that keeps Mija and Okja together. It's the one respect in which *Okja* embraces its fairy-tale trappings: Love conquers all. **II**

91.

↓ Below
That *Okja* is so affecting has everything to do with the relationship at its center, which Bong showcases without ever tipping his hand. Throughout the film, Mija whispers messages to Okja that the audience can't hear, and at its conclusion, Okja whispers back. These secrets, kept between the two bosom buddies, have the effect of making this fairy-tale friendship feel real.

2017
Okja
2h

철창을 전부
비울때까지

Director	Bong Joon Ho
Writers	Bong Joon Ho Jon Ronson
Key Cast	Ahn Seo-hyun Tilda Swinton Paul Dano Byun Hee-bong Jake Gyllenhaal
Budget	$50 million *Estimated*
Producers	Dede Gardner Jeremy Kleiner Lewis Taewan Kim Dooho Choi Seo Woo-sik Bong Joon Ho Ted Sarandos
Music	Jung Jaeil
Cinematography	Darius Khondji
Film Editing	Yang Jinmo
Production Design	Lee Ha-jun Kevin Thompson
Art Direction	Jung Yoon-bae Deborah Jensen Gwendolyn Margetson

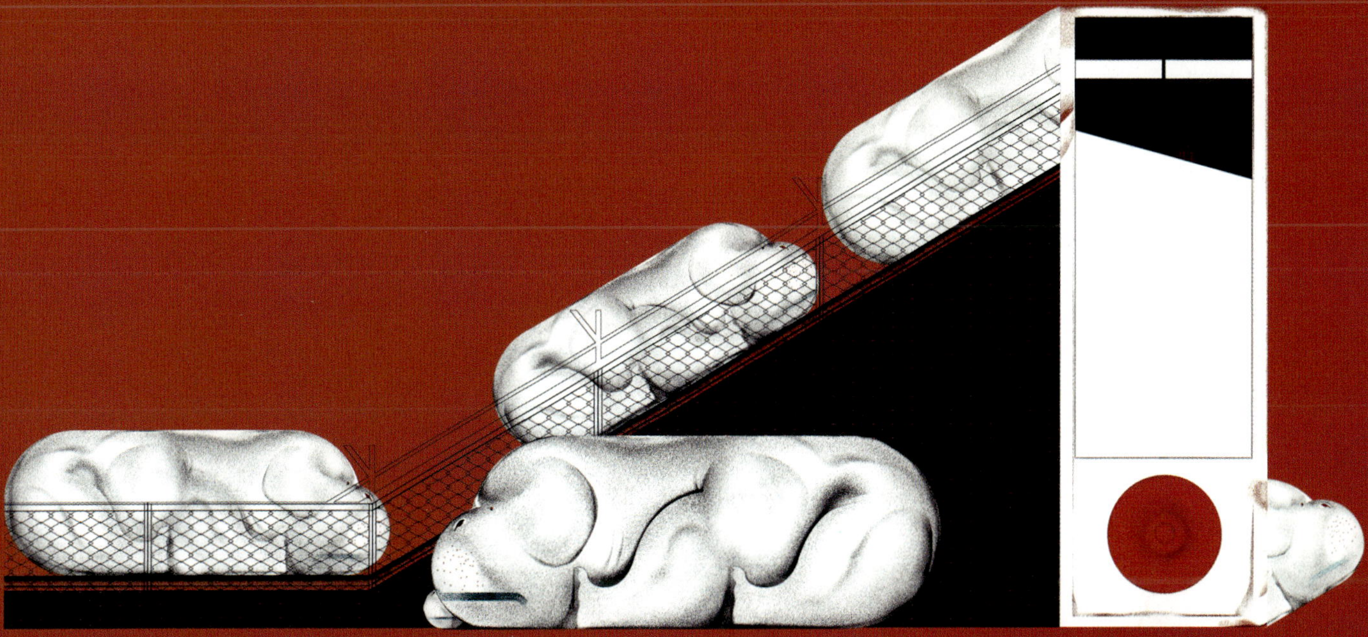

UNTIL EVERY CAGE IS EMPTY

Case Study:
Giving Birth to Okja

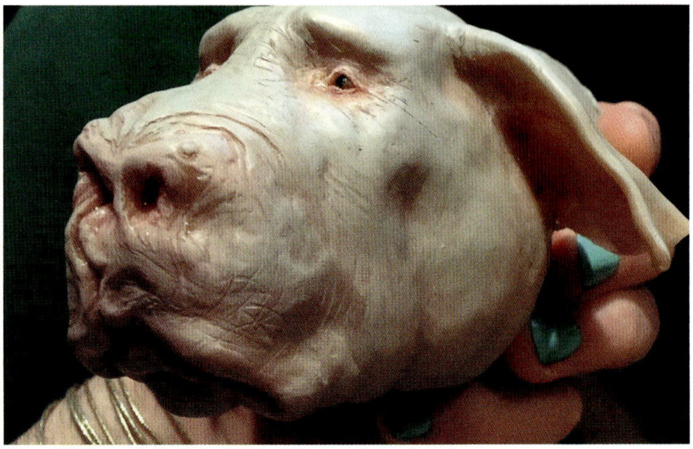

1.

2.

1. Prototype model of Okja.
2. Excerpt from illustrated storyboard, which shows blocking, transitions, and movement.
3. Creating a tactile sense of Mija and Okja's relationship.
4. Detail from the storyboard from the film's central chase sequence.
5. Sketch of Okja and Mija to give a sense of contrast in their stature.
6. Painted alt design for Okja and Mija.
7. Sketch of a tender moment.
8. Digital map for Okja's sprint through an underground shopping mall.

3.

4.

5.

6.

7.

8.

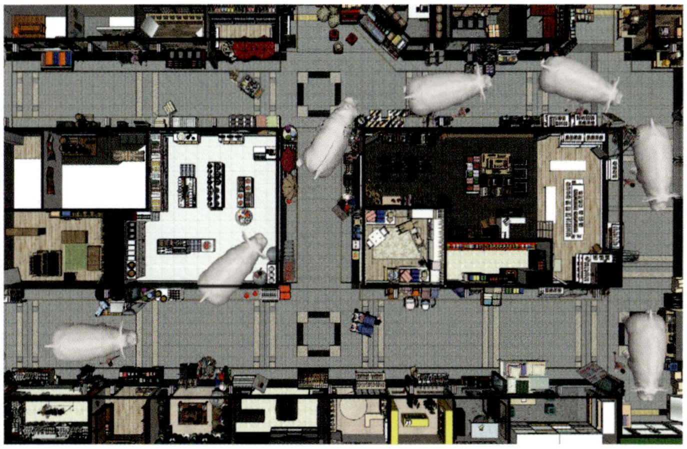

INFLUENCES
THE WAGES OF FEAR (1953)

A humorously common through line in the works that Bong cites as influential upon him is that he saw many of them at far too early an age. Among the choice handful is Henri-Georges Clouzot's 1953 thriller *The Wages of Fear*, which stars Yves Montand as Mario, one of a group of desperate men stranded in the isolated town of Las Piedras. When an oil well—owned by an American company that, not coincidentally, shares its initials with Standard Oil—catches fire, Mario and three others are hired to drive two trucks, both loaded with highly explosive nitroglycerine, necessary to put the fire out, through treacherous terrain.

In an interview during *Parasite*'s (2019) press tour, Bong had this to say about the film: "I think the experience I had that was almost close to traumatic was with this French movie, Henri-Georges Clouzot's *The Wages of Fear*. [. . .] It's the kind of film that will put you in a cold sweat. You can only feel anxious while you're watching it. I was in elementary school when I saw it on TV, and I was so overwhelmed that it kept appearing in my dreams. I couldn't escape it for about a week. It was the first time I was so taken by a movie."

His reaction is understandable. The suspense sequences in the film are almost painful to watch, and beyond the action, the events of the film are nigh impossible not to find wrenching. The men are clearly being exploited—they are chosen for the mission specifically because they're not part of a union and don't have any relatives who would come asking for them if they went missing, and are sent on what is effectively a suicide mission for just $2,000. It's not just that the mission itself is terrifying to watch; it's that the system they're caught in is corrupt and amoral, making for a conceptual rather than literal link to Bong's work.

There's also no sense of a safety net in *The Wages of Fear*—no character is truly safe, and there's no guarantee that the film will end happily. "Modern Hollywood thrillers cannot end in tragedy for its heroes, because the studios won't allow it," Roger Ebert wrote in his review of the film. "The last scene, where a homebound truck is intercut with a celebration while a Strauss waltz plays on the radio, is a reminder of how much Hollywood has traded away by insisting on the childishness of the obligatory happy ending."

These aspects of Clouzot's work—the masterful ability to ramp up tension, the inclusion of larger social commentary, the refusal to pander to the audience—are crucial parts of Bong's oeuvre as well, and though unintentional, there's yet another parallel between Clouzot's work and Bong's. Upon the American release of *The Wages of Fear* in 1955, it was significantly trimmed (around 35 minutes of footage were cut), partially because it was deemed too long, and partially because it was deemed too political (specifically too anti-American), complaints that are reminiscent of those leveled against Bong's early works and, in particular, the near-butchering of *Snowpiercer* (2013).

EXPLOSIVES

"LAST WORD IN MOVIE SUSPENSE"
LIFE MAGAZINE
You sit there waiting for the theatre to explode!
H. G. CLOUZOT'S
"WAGES OF FEAR"
EXPLOSIVES
YVES MONTAND
CHARLES VANEL
PETER VAN EYCK
VERA CLOUZOT
FOLCO LULLI
WILLIAM TUBBS
A Filmsonor Production
dca
"One of the great shockers of all time" – TIME MAG.

기생충

PARASITE

92.

→ Opposite
Introducing the Kims. Bong presents the semibasement domicile inhabited by a family of lovable hustlers at the top of *Parasite*, drawing on its awkward architecture, lack of privacy, and poor Wi-Fi connection (leeched from the cafe upstairs). Without ever resorting to stereotypes of poverty, we can instantly see who the Kims are.

Bong Joon Ho's films are full of surprises, but arguably none more so than *Parasite* (2019). At first glance, the story is relatively straightforward: The Kim family are barely making ends meet, living in a sub-basement apartment and folding pizza boxes to earn money. Opportunity comes knocking in the form of the wealthy Park family, who first hire Ki-woo (Choi Woo Shik), the Kim family's son, as an English tutor, and then, upon his recommendation, hire the rest of the Kims without realizing that they're all related to each other. The plot could easily conclude there, with the Kims pulling one over on the obliviously rich Parks, but as with all of the stories that Bong tells, it's not nearly so simple. There's no clear division between good and evil, hero and villain—the only real line is between rich and poor, two states of being that aren't moral arbiters in and of themselves.

As in *The Host* (2006) and *Mother* (2009), the film's true conflict arises from the all-encompassing trap that is capitalist society: In order for one person to advance, another must fall behind. *Mother* deals with the idea more explicitly than *The Host*, which overall is one of Bong's more hopeful pictures, while *Parasite* wrestles with this notion head-on. Unbeknownst to both the Parks and the Kims, the Park family home sits atop a bunker. Inside that bunker, the husband of the former housekeeper, who has been ousted in order to provide the Kim matriarch with a position within the house, has been hiding from debt collectors for the last few years. The discovery sets off a harrowing chain of events that ends in tragedy—and ultimately frames every character as a victim to some degree.

It is almost an understatement to describe *Parasite* as a masterwork, even if its accolades indisputably declare it as such: It won the Palme d'Or at the 2019 Cannes Film Festival, and then there's its history-making Best Picture Oscar win. It's a refinement of ideas that Bong has been exploring throughout his career—the influence of money, how misunderstandings can spiral out of control, how evil is less about monsters and villains and more about the corners that people are backed into—and, like Bong's other works, *Parasite* becomes all the richer the more time one takes to inspect it.

The best example of how masterfully *Parasite* is constructed is "The Belt of Faith," a seven-minute tour de force sequence that serves as a sort of conclusion to the first half of the film—and is so much of a key to the movie that it even gets a brief (and brutal) reprise.

One by one, the Kims have infiltrated the Park house; first, Ki-woo is hired as an English tutor for the Parks' daughter, Da-hye (Jung Ji-so), after being recommended to the family by his friend Min-hyuk (Park Seo-joon). When the Park matriarch, Yeon-gyo (Cho Yeo-jeong), mentions that her young son Da-song (Jung Hyeon-jun) needs an art tutor, Ki-woo brings his sister Ki-jung (Park So-dam) into the fold, introducing her as "Jessica," a friend of his cousin's. While being driven home by Yoon (Park Keun-rok), the Parks' chauffeur, Ki-jung takes matters further into her own hands, surreptitiously leaving her underwear in the car. Yeon-gyo and Dong-ik (Lee Sun-kyun), the Park patriarch, all too ready to jump to the conclusion that their driver is engaged in illicit activities, promptly fire him upon discovering the offending piece of clothing, and Ki-jung happily takes the opportunity to recommend her father Ki-taek (Song Kang-ho), posing as her uncle "Mr. Kim," to take the driver's place. As Ki-jung makes her sales pitch to Yeon-gyo, the one remaining member of the Park family's original staff, the housekeeper Moon-gwang (Lee Jung-eun), slowly approaches in the background, returning from walking the family's three small dogs. Her simple presence reminds the audience that there's still one person left for the Kims to get rid of if they all want a new job. Oblivious to what's been happening in her own house, Yeon-gyo agrees to meet Ki-taek. "This chain of recommendations is the best," she says. "How should I describe it? A belt of trust?" As soon as she utters the words, composer Jung Jaeil's accompanying cue kicks in.

PIZZA GENERATION · FRESH & PURE PIZZA · SINCE 2010
PIZZA
ITALY

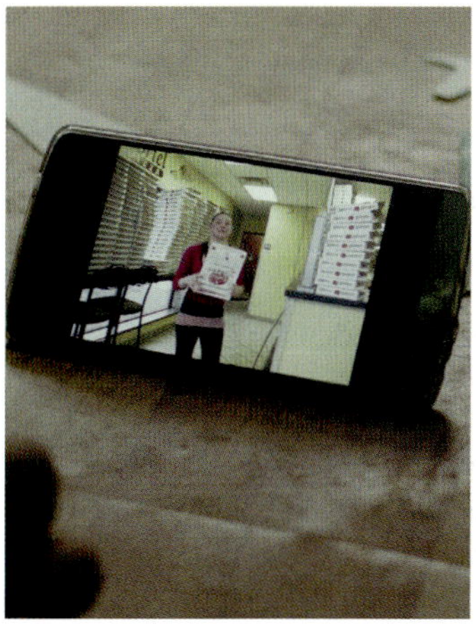

With each new film, Bong's use of music and sound becomes more virtuosic. Like most contemporary filmmakers, he uses music to help inform the tone of what's playing out on screen rather than using it as a form of narration (i.e., faithfully following what's unfolding on screen as was often the case in silent films), and though *Parasite* is no exception, "The Belt of Faith" comes closest to breaking the rule. Jung's score shifts in tempo and tone to match the changing scenes, starting as something relatively sedate as we first see Ki-taek and Ki-woo at a Mercedes dealership, reacquainting Ki-taek, whose former jobs included being a driver and a valet, with the features of the luxury car. It's just one part of the con, and the way Bong lets us in on it makes it feel like we're watching a heist. Because we've spent the most time with them, and because they're positioned as underdogs, we naturally sympathize with the Kims and root for them to succeed. However, "The Belt of Faith" is essentially *Parasite* in miniature—a perfect encapsulation of the dynamics at play within the larger movie. To get his job, Ki-woo lies about being a college student. For Ki-jung to become "Jessica," even more lies are told. And for Ki-taek and his wife, Chung-sook (Jang Hye-jin), to take positions within the Park household—in addition to furthering the lies the Kims are telling—two people must first lose their jobs. (In a much smaller but equally telling detail, early in the film, Ki-taek flicks away a stinkbug at the same time that he chows down on a moldy piece of bread. Though he treats it with disdain, they're not actually so different: They're both struggling to survive.)

When Ki-jung gets the driver fired, there's arguably some sense that she's acting in retaliation, as Yoon is a little forward with her, insisting on driving her all the way home until Ki-jung lies and tells him she already has a boyfriend. But there's no real justification for getting him fired from his job. The Kims know this, as illustrated by the fact that, as soon as Ki-taek becomes the Parks' new chauffeur, their scheming to get Moon-gwang out involves pointing out her perceived character flaws. In other words, they're trying to justify what they're doing in order to ignore the fact that their success comes at the cost of harming others—as in *Mother* and *Snowpiercer* (2013), the "weak" are fighting among themselves rather than collectively searching for a way forward.

Even in the sequence's small details, it's clear that the Kims' attitudes have changed now that they've experienced some good fortune. Besides being willing to frame two people in order to get them fired, they go further with the lies they tell—in a very Bong-esque aside, we get to see Ki-taek rehearsing a lie about Moon-gwang contracting tuberculosis from a script that Ki-woo has written for him, taking notes as to how emotional he should become as Chung-sook and Ki-jung also mouth along the dialogue behind him. On top of that, we see the family discussing their plans at the very pizza place for which they were folding boxes at the beginning of the film—their waitress, who'd scolded them earlier in the movie, practically throws their food on their table, as Ki-jung shoots her a pointed gaze. It's a brief moment, but a significant one that serves as an indication that the Kims have risen in station, or at least think that they have.

With Bong's predilection for unflinchingly depicting stark human brutality, the manner in which the Kims get rid of Moon-gwang feels very apropos. As with Yoon, they come up with a reason for her to be dismissed that's sensitive enough that the Parks won't explicitly state it, leaving the victim no chance to defend themself. Upon learning that Moon-gwang is severely allergic to peaches, they exploit that knowledge to have her sent to the hospital, where they surreptitiously photograph her before using the picture to convince Yeon-gyo that her housekeeper has contracted tuberculosis. As the cherry on top of the sundae, they induce yet another allergic reaction for Yeon-gyo to witness, staining a used napkin with sauce—fake blood—to really seal the deal. It's all staged and shot so slickly that it feels fun—again, it displays all the skillful mechanics of a movie heist. The score helps to get the adrenaline pumping, as the flurry of notes constantly suggests motion and constantly changing direction. But the piece, which is

93.

↖ Top left
The house on the hill, a miracle of pristine modernist architecture and elegance, lived in by the super-rich Park family, and diametrically opposite to the Kim home. The design of the house's interior is also key to how the narrative plays out and how the drama is choreographed.

94.

↙ **Left and below**
Tutor; art therapist; chauffeur; housekeeper. The Kims cleverly exploit the weaknesses of the Parks to insidiously become a part of their household. They are a literal manifestation of the film's title, but the true meaning of the film is far more complex and intangible.

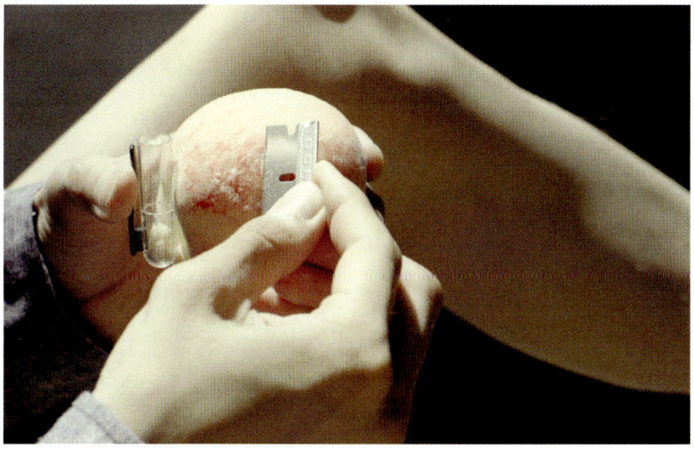

95.

← Left
The peach has become perhaps the iconic image of *Parasite*, and it's a simple chemical reaction—namely the violent allergic reaction suffered by officious housekeeper Moon-gwang (Lee Jung-eun) when peach fuzz is sprinkled in her vicinity—which helps to set the narrative freight train in motion.

96.

← Opposite
Each of the three married couples in *Parasite*—the Kims, the Parks, and the ill-fated Moon-gwang and Geun-sae (Park Myung-hoon)—has a different relationship to love, as exemplified by how they interact with each other in moments of (relative) privacy.

traditionally classical in sound, retains an edge thanks to its minor key. The music's kinetic, lush nature helps disguise the reality that it's accompanying a tragedy, in much the same way our empathy for the Kims helps blind us to the harm that they're causing. The retching coughs that Moon-gwang suffers after being exposed to peach fuzz are awful, as is the knowledge that the Kims could, in toying with another person's medical affliction, potentially kill them. And of course, that's exactly what happens later on. When the particular melodic line used in "The Belt of Faith" returns, it's as the Kims, caught between a rock and a hard place, remove Moon-gwang from the equation for good.

What is key to *Parasite* as a whole is the fact that none of the characters are villains—or, depending on how you spin things, all of the characters are. The Kims are the film's central focus, and their designation as de facto protagonists is what makes it all the more crushing when we witness what they, too, are capable of doing for the sake of a little money and proximity to status. The Parks, who do all that they can to appear cultured and sophisticated, aren't as subtle about their distaste for working-class people as they think they are—a major point in the film is that the Parks are repulsed by the odor of people not from the same socioeconomic class. "You know when you boil a rag?" Dong-ik says. "It smells like that." But even so, they're out of touch more than they are evil or blatantly cruel. They live in their safe, moneyed world, and have no interest in anything outside of it.

Moon-gwang and her husband Geun-sae (Park Myung-hoon), despite being the ones to bring the Kims' scheme tumbling down, are hardly villainous characters and are victims themselves. They're also tender toward each other in a way that feels absent from Dong-ik and Yeon-gyo's relationship, and more fraught in Ki-taek and Chung-sook's. The brief flashback in which they recall happier days spent in the house is the most romantic scene in the film (though it ends, in the present, in violence). That the moment—in the Parks' sunny living room, Moon-gwang and Geun-sae dance to the crooning of Italian pop singer Gianni Morandi—is the film's sweetest seems strange given that *Parasite* is the most overtly sexual of Bong's films. It's not that his other films don't contain sex, but, as in *Memories of Murder* (2003), it's perfunctory, not sensual or meant to stimulate in any way, or, as in *Mother*, it's a source of anxiety rather than titillation. And romantic love hasn't, until this point, really entered into the equation. Granted, it's not totally uncomplicated in *Parasite*, either. The one couple we actually see getting intimate is the Parks, who take their speculation about their driver's supposed illicit activities and turn them into a sexual fantasy conducted where their son might see them—as well as, unknowingly, in front of the Kims. But physical intimacy doesn't translate to emotional intimacy, as Ki-taek's conversations with Dong-ik about love reveal. ("We'll call it love," Dong-ik says, when Ki-taek asks if he loves his wife.) The Park marriage isn't a warm one, a facet stressed in how differently the bonds between the other characters are realized. Money, as it turns out, can't buy everything.

One of the most striking scenes in the film is a glimpse into Ki-taek and Chung-sook's relationship. As the family members sit in the Park house, Chung-sook jokes that Ki-taek would scurry away like a cockroach in the event that the Parks came home. Annoyed, Ki-taek grabs the collar of Chung-sook's shirt, as if to strike her. The mood suddenly changes. For a long moment, Ki-taek and Chung-sook just stare at each other. Then, slowly, they break into laughter. "I fooled you, didn't I?" Ki-taek asks his kids, while Chung-sook, easily twisting his arms, says, "If it was for real, I'd fucking kill you." It's good-natured ribbing, but at the same time, the look on Chung-sook's face in that moment of tension speaks volumes. We already have a sense of just how many jobs Ki-taek has held and lost (driver, valet, cake shop owner, etc.), as well as just how precarious the Kims' financial position has been. Ki-taek and Chung-sook have been through hell

97.

→ Opposite
Parasite not only comprises a shifting power structure between numerous family units, but it also accounts for the power structures within the units themselves. Chung-sook appears to wield the lion's share of power and influence within the Kim clan, while the bullish Moon-gwang is dominant as an adjunct of the Park family, but more submissive within her own strange marriage.

together—and, at least on Chung-sook's part, have had to give up a lot. Though it's never explicitly discussed, Chung-sook's past includes a stint as a champion shot put player. There's a framed silver medal in their apartment, as well as a photograph of her in action. That it's silver is telling—always the bridesmaid, never the bride. Nevertheless, Chung-sook is now a far cry from where she once was. (In a heartbreaking note, when their apartment is flooded during a near-biblical downpour, that medal is one of the few things Ki-taek manages to grab. As close as they were to having nothing, the loss of their home is devastating, and Ki-taek's choice to grab the medal speaks to just how much he cares for his wife. The medal is irreplaceable.)

The other relationships in the film are also considered in how they're presented—Ki-woo and Ki-jung, for instance, are opposites. Ki-woo is the optimist, striving to become more like the smooth, sophisticated Min-hyuk and sincerely believing that he will be able to improve his station in life. His obsession with the scholar's rock that Min-hyuk gifts their family serves as a physical representation of that belief, though Ki-woo's repeated insistence that it's "so metaphorical" helps lend it more of a sense of mystery (can an object within a movie really be so symbolic if the characters themselves comment on it?). His striving, though, isn't always a good thing—Min-hyuk makes it clear that a big reason he's recommending Ki-woo as Da-hye's new tutor is that he doesn't think Ki-woo will try to make a move on her. Unfortunately, in his preoccupation with Min-hyuk's seemingly perfect life (in a later moment of trouble, Ki-woo wonders what Min-hyuk would do in his shoes, while Ki-jung points out that he would never be in such a situation), Ki-woo sets the romantic wheels in motion almost immediately. Ki-jung, on the other hand, is the family cynic. When the rest of the family worry about the fate of the driver, trying to reassure themselves that he's landed on his feet after being fired due to their deception, Ki-jung is the one to put a stop to the conversation, telling the family that they ought to worry about themselves, not about others. Granted, her cool self-centeredness is mostly a front—after the Kims trap Moon-gwang and Geun-sae in the basement, Ki-jung is the first person to wonder if they ought to go downstairs and try to make peace.

And though they're not bonded in the way that the rest of the characters are in the film, there's an invisible thread tying Chung-sook and Moon-gwang together. Both parts—the mother, the housekeeper—are typically secondary roles, meant to quietly support (or, in some cases, nag) their male counterparts. In *Parasite*, however, those roles are reversed—there's no question that, despite the fact that Ki-taek and Geun-sae may get more to do, they're passive in comparison to their partners. Chung-sook and Moon-gwang are assertive in ways that their husbands are not—it's because of Moon-gwang's death (and preceding plea for her husband to remember Chung-sook's real name) that Geun-sae, who initially comes across as a bit of a wet blanket, makes a hundred and eighty-degree turn into murderous maniac. And it's Chung-sook who is the most fiercely protective of her family, as she ultimately proves willing to kill in order to defend them. Subtle details throughout the movie—still drinking cheap beer after the family all get jobs in the Park household, even though Ki-taek, Ki-woo, and Ki-jung indulge in more expensive alcohol, and noting, at the beginning of the film, that food would have made a better gift than the scholar's rock—also place her as the most grounded. These women are their respective families' anchors, and easily the fiercest—and strongest—characters in the movie. By contrast, Yeon-gyo, who Min-hyuk describes as "young and simple," lives up to her reputation. It's her naïveté that allows for the Kims to infiltrate the house, but that doesn't mean that she isn't clever. "She's smart . . . It's just that she trusts people too easily because she's never experienced anything bad," Bong has said of the character. "I think you need to have something bad happen to you to start doubting people. She just never had that kind of thing happen to her." As for the Kims, Moon-gwang, and Geun-sae, the degree to which life can be a struggle is foremost in their minds.

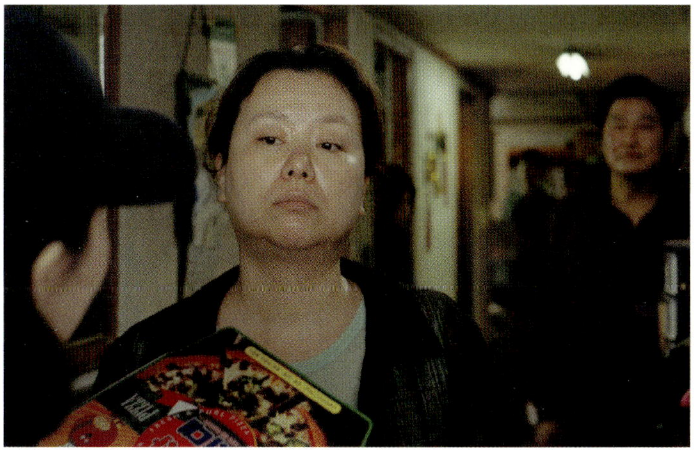

It is a testament to Bong's storytelling skill that he drops *Parasite*'s big twist exactly halfway through the film rather than at the end.

With the Parks out of the house, on a camping trip for Da-song's birthday, the Kims indulge in a staycation. As they enjoy having run of the house, the doorbell rings. It's Moon-gwang, but a drastically different Moon-gwang from the one we've seen before. Rather than her usual prim, clean-cut self, Moon-gwang looks as though she's been put through the wringer—she's soaked in rain, there are bruises on her face, and, for all that she attempts to act as though everything is normal, she is clearly desperate. She forgot something in the basement when she was dismissed, she tells Chung-sook, who, as the new housekeeper, is the only person who's actually supposed to be in the residence.

It's here that *Parasite* takes a thrilling, shocking, unpredictable turn. Just as the film reaches the halfway mark, Moon-gwang opens a secret door that leads to a bunker underneath the house. Up to this point, the film feels fairly cut and dried. It's an upstairs/downstairs story, with the main question hanging in the air being: Will the Kims ever be found out? The moment Moon-gwang shows up, there is an instant tension, not just because the Kims are in danger of being exposed, but because the presence of a third party—besides the Parks and the Kims—turns the expected equation on its head. This isn't a story of one versus the other. In this story, nobody wins.

The introduction of the bunker also nudges the film into horror territory, in equal parts thanks to the sense of disorientation that the introduction of a totally new part of the house creates, the uneasy waves of emotion that spring forth from Moon-gwang's overly obsequious manner, and the reveal of exactly what's lurking down there. As it turns out, Moon-gwang's husband, Geun-sae, has been living in the bunker for more than four years, hiding from debt collectors after his Taiwanese cake shop—incidentally a business venture that Ki-taek also tried and failed, reflecting a real fad (and resulting bubble) in Korea—

98.

↓ Below
Just as he doesn't wholly glorify the working class pluck of the Kims, Bong extends empathy to the detached and haughty Park family. Yet the character who oscillates most wildly when it comes to audience affinity is the scatterbrained, gullible, and entitled (though ultimately well-meaning) matriarch, Yeon-gyo (Cho Yeo-jeong).

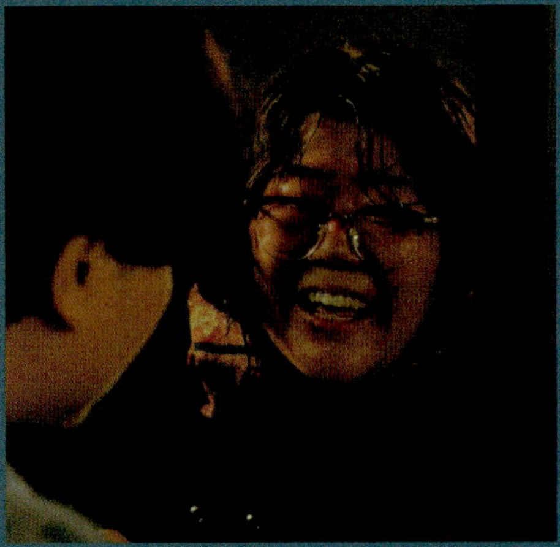

99.

↖ **Opposite and above** Bong and the film's publicity team made public pleas for audiences to refrain from mentioning anything that occurred in the film's second half: a sudden and unexpected trip into the Park family basement where the recently fired Moon-gwang has been hiding her husband, who is wanted by local loan sharks. The cool, seemingly effortless manner in which Bong orchestrates this rug-pull makes it a plot twist for the ages.

100.

← **Opposite**
Ki-woo's attempts at reconciliation see him descending into a cool green light—and the wrath of the recently widowed Geun-sae. Bong employs the claustrophobic architecture of the bunker to create tension and play with space: Chung-sook's body is framed in a square, and Geun-sae's initial attempt on Ki-woo's life becomes a halo-like circle.

101.

↓ **Next Page**
In the films of Bong Joon Ho, people always contain hidden depths and secrets. In *Parasite*, so does the central location, whose doorway is hidden in plain sight (and presents one of the most memorable images in the film) and wreathed by the Park's extensive collection of ornamental ceramics and glassware.

went bust. The scene that follows is wrenching; Moon-gwang, on her knees, begs Chung-sook not to inform the police, calling Chung-sook "big sister" and using formal speech in a show of deference. "As fellow members of the needy, please don't," she says, to which Chung-sook responds, "I'm not needy." It's a shocking answer given that Chung-sook has essentially stolen Moon-gwang's job. Even though she was in a similar position until very recently, she doesn't show any pity, and it's clear that, in the moment, she looks down on Moon-gwang. (Interestingly, one of the things that Ki-jung says when they're hatching the scheme to get Moon-gwang out of the house is that she acts like she owns the place, which is exactly how the Kims are acting, now, too.)

It's this tension—the unfortunate tearing each other down in the hopes of advancing their own positions by ultimately miniscule increments—that carries the rest of the film. Immediately after telling Moon-gwang off, the Kims' ruse is exposed, as the rest of the family, who had been hiding around a corner, tumble into view, and Moon-gwang quickly puts the puzzle pieces together. As soon as the tables are turned, Moon-gwang becomes hostile, dropping formal speech as Chung-sook—suddenly vulnerable—picks it up. But it's of no use. Whether it's a combination of the fact that Chung-sook showed no pity and the knowledge that the Kims are responsible for their current misfortune, or that she, like Chung-sook, sees ruthlessness in this situation as practicality, Moon-gwang takes a video of the hapless Kim family and threatens to tell the Parks.

For a brief moment, Moon-gwang and Geun-sae—the least fortunate people in the film—hold the upper hand, and they lord it over the Kims in a humiliating way: They make them endure the same punishment typically doled out to misbehaving children and students in Korea, forcing them to kneel and keep their hands held up in the air. It's only a physical altercation between the two parties that turns the tables once again, though at an awful cost: Having received word that the Parks are coming home early thanks to inclement weather, the Kims rush to get rid of any trace that they—and their unexpected guests—were ever there. Over it all plays "Zappaguri," the semi-reprise of "The Belt of Faith," which ensures that the audience never forgets that this is a hell of the Kims' own making. As with "The Belt of Faith," the score here is as much about communicating a mood as accompanying what's happening on screen, and the end of the sequence is, in true Bong fashion, both hilarious and horrifying. As Ki-taek attempts to stow Geun-sae and Moon-gwang away in the bunker, Moon-gwang, hearing the sounds of the returning Park family, makes a break for it. As she runs up the stairs, yelling for help, Chung-sook, who is in the kitchen cooking in anticipation of the Parks' return, subtly maneuvers to the basement entrance and, as Yeon-gyo enters the kitchen, doesn't even turn around to look at Moon-gwang as she kicks her back down the stairs. The moment is so deftly executed that it's hard not to laugh—but the true end of the sequence is just an instant later, as Moon-gwang tumbles down the stairs and hits her head *hard* against the concrete floor. The music cuts out abruptly, leaving just the sickening *crack* of the impact behind.

What sets *Parasite* above the competition in its depiction of have-nots fighting with other have-nots is in the road that leads to the ultimate outcome. In *Mother*, there's no real space for compromise. When the widow kills the junk collector, it's in a fit of desperation in which she doesn't seem to have control over her own actions, and later, when she confronts the boy who has taken the fall for her son's crime, she clearly feels remorse, but doesn't do anything to help him. In *Parasite*, even as the Kims attempt to conceal what's happening from the Parks, they worry to themselves as to how Moon-gwang and Geun-sae are doing, wondering if they ought to bring food down to the bunker and try to broker some peace. The tragedy is not that they don't act on those feelings, but that they aren't given a chance to. Because of Da-song's birthday celebration (which, in large part, comes off as a party meant more for the adults than the children), they don't get the chance to defuse the metaphorical bomb

102.

→ Opposite
There's a running gag about precocious Park progeny Da-song's (Jung Hyeon-jun) wish to play "cowboys and Indians," and his desire is catered to in the film's bloody final showdown. As a rampaging Geun-sae joins the fray with a giant knife, grim reality takes over from the fun and games—just as it has from the Kims' initial ruse.

before it explodes. By the time Ki-woo goes down to the bunker, Moon-gwang has already died, and Geun-sae has nothing on his mind but revenge. In the film's most terrifying scene, lit in sickly greens rather than the film's otherwise neutral tones, Geun-sae ambushes Ki-woo. For Ki-woo, coming down the stairs, there's nothing visible beyond the tiny rectangle of the landing. The moments that follow—a halo of wire rising above Ki-woo's head as Geun-sae sneaks up behind him, the abrupt zoom out as the wire closes around his neck, Ki-woo's frantic but futile escape from the bunker, and the awful moment when Geun-sae brings the scholar's rock (the very thing that Ki-woo thought would bring their family prosperity) down on Ki-woo's head—feel as though they've been pulled directly out of a horror film. These characters are reaching their breaking points. The monster has been released.

Carnage ensues, with each element serving as a last, defining cry for each character. Geun-sae is, on a surface level, the scariest of the cast. Unlike the other adults who've gathered at the Park house, he's dressed entirely in black as opposed to the largely pale shades that are used to symbolize wealth. (Even his hair, thinning at the top, widens the divide between him and the Parks' polished friends.) After grabbing a knife from the kitchen, he strides directly into the party and stabs Ki-jung in the chest, derailing the original (and now bitterly ironic) plan for Dong-ik and Ki-taek, wearing war bonnets, to "attack" Ki-jung, then allowing Da-song, described as an "Indian otaku" by his mother (a kind of appropriation that only underlines the Parks' obliviousness to anyone not in their sphere), to save the day. Ki-jung, for her part, doesn't express any horror or surprise, instead uttering an annoyed, "Ah, shit," as she falls to the ground. Ki-woo, out cold, is carried out of the party by Da-hye. Da-song, upon seeing the "ghost" who's been haunting him for the past few years, promptly faints. For a moment, basic instinct wins out—Ki-taek, Chung-sook, Dong-ik, and Yeon-gyo instantly focus on their respective children. Ki-taek runs to Ki-jung's side while Chung-sook flies at Geun-sae with an axe. Dong-ik and Yeon-gyo, having grabbed Da-song, flit around the periphery, with Dong-ik screaming at Ki-taek first to drive the unconscious Da-song to the hospital, then to throw him the car keys. Unfortunately, the keys land under Geun-sae, who has just been stabbed through the torso with a skewer by Chung-sook—a final humiliation as he literally becomes just another chunk of meat. The reactions the two men extend to each other are polar opposites. Geun-sae is obsessed with Dong-ik—he sings a special song every time Dong-ik comes home, using switches in the bunker to manually turn on the entrance lights, and screaming, "Respect!," at the ceiling to thank Dong-ik for giving him (albeit unknowingly) a place to live. When he sees Dong-ik, he still shouts out, "Respect!," even though he's dying. Dong-ik, by contrast, makes a noise of revulsion as he catches Geun-sae's scent, going so far as to hold his nose while retrieving the keys. For Ki-taek, this is the final straw. Grabbing Geun-sae's knife, he stabs Dong-ik in the chest, killing him.

In a sequence that's shocking for how violent it is (particularly in comparison to the film's first half), Ki-taek killing Dong-ik makes for the biggest twist. Geun-sae's rampage is one we can see coming because the inciting incident is so fresh in our minds, but for Ki-taek, it's a slow burn. What is key to note is that the Kims aren't struggling for work because they aren't looking for it or are otherwise unqualified for it—what separates them from the Parks isn't brains or drive, it's circumstance. But, while the characters recognize that about their immediate family, they fail to offer the same consideration to anyone else.

As one of Bong's most frequent collaborators, Song has been called upon multiple times to hold the entire screen with just his gaze. *Memories of Murder* ends with a close-up on Song, and asks him to take on the seemingly impossible task of conveying the grief experienced by a generation of Koreans in a single look. *Parasite* asks him for a similar miracle—his character, Ki-taek, comes across as fairly easygoing, and becomes animated when having fun with his family. Yet the more that Ki-taek interacts with the Parks, the more the film

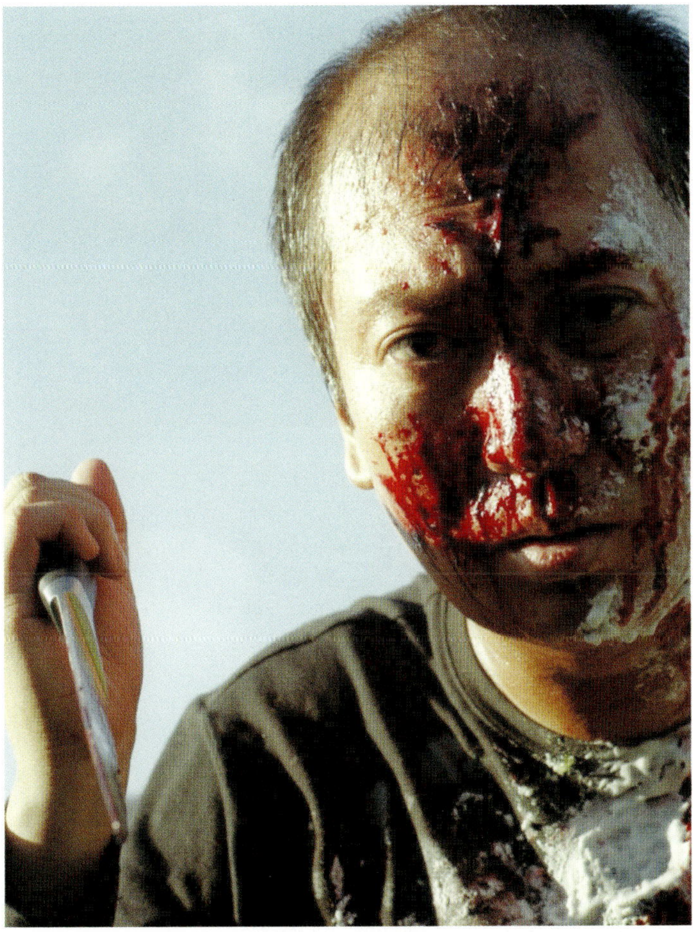

103.

→ Right
The two very different houses in the film—the Parks' mansion and the Kims' semi-basement apartment—nevertheless contain superficial similarities that serve to connect the two families. Levels are everything: The Kims' home literally shows how low on the status ladder they are, while the Parks' house is divided into levels that subtly separate them from their staff.

104.

← Left
Shots that adopt a bird's-eye view are a rarity in *Parasite* but serve the distinct purpose of suggesting distance. During the flooding sequence, it captures all of the water that has flooded down to the lower levels from the palatial estates above. In the film's finale, it follows and isolates Ki-taek (Song Kang-ho) as he is effectively forced to leave his family, after the bulk of the film has had the Kim family occupying the same shot.

hints at just how much Ki-taek has gone through to get to this point. There's the now-infamous shot of Yeon-gyo in the back of the family car, chatting away as Ki-taek, in the driver's seat, wears a stony, almost resentful expression. A similar look crosses his face in the film's finale—the panic and anguish on his features as he tries to keep track of his family disappears while he sees the way Dong-ik reacts to Geun-sae. Just as the widow in *Mother* loses control of herself when confronted with the reality of what her son has done, Ki-taek seems to become an entirely different person when he stabs Dong-ik, no longer able to simply grin and bear the lack of respect that the rich hold for the people who work for them. It's not a premeditated act of malice—it's not that Dong-ik has really done anything worth getting killed over. It's just that, in that moment, it's all too much for Ki-taek to bear.

The visual language in *Parasite* makes it impossible to forget the way that money has literally and metaphorically stacked these people on top of each other: Bong utilizes bird's-eye view as well as straight-on shots to make it feel as if the characters are trapped inside an ant farm. Granted, it's an apt feeling—they *are* trapped. Even the very beginning of the film, when the camera tracks down from the street-level shot of the semibasement window to Ki-woo sitting underneath, evokes a sense of limbo. The Kims' apartment literally exists half above ground and half below. If their economic status descends even a little bit more, they'll be swallowed up completely. The Parks' bunker serves a similar purpose; not only is it below the basement, it's actually completely unknown to the Parks (who barely even go into the basement to begin with, leaving it to their house staff). Geun-sae's circumstances are completely inconceivable to them—they think of him as a ghost, a monster, rather than a real person. But the idea of having nothing isn't so far removed from the Kims.

Similarly to the way wide shots were used in *Okja* (2017) to emphasize a sense of scale, Bong deploys them in *Parasite* to shrink the Kims down. The first time Ki-woo goes to the Park house, a two-story beauty (notably a set constructed for the film rather than an existing building) with a yard that's so big and so full of greenery that it seems like it's in a totally different world, he's shown going up the street in a wide shot in which he appears miniscule. Then, when the Kims flee the Park house after discovering Geun-sae in the bunker, they're shot straight-on, but from such a distance that they might as well be insects, scurrying down zigzagging flights of stairs. The vertical distance separating the Parks from the Kims seems incalculable, as the Kims continue to descend, descend, descend. When they arrive home, it's to discover that their neighborhood has flooded, whereas the Park home is pristine, untouched by the unfolding natural disaster. On the street, the sewage water comes up to their knees; in their semibasement apartment, it's up to their waists and, eventually, to their necks.

Bird's-eye view shots occur twice in the film, and underline the top-down structure in which the characters are ensnared. The first time it's used, it's to watch the flooding of the Kims' neighborhood. People do whatever they can to stay above water, turning doors into makeshift boats and swimming through the sewage. The second time, it's as Ki-taek flees Da-song's birthday party. Again, as in the wide shots and the previous overhead shot, he becomes like a rat in a maze, scampering to figure out how to escape. In the few other times that the film utilizes closer overhead shots, it's for a similar effect—to emphasize the powerlessness of the person being looked down upon (Ki-woo being dragged across the floor, the dying Geun-sae looking up at Dong-ik).

The difference in status between the Parks and the Kims plays out in smaller ways as well, from the Kims being forced to hide under furniture and crawl on the floor in order to escape the house when the Parks return home early, to the way where they sit in the car divides them into passenger and hired chauffeur. Even language puts up barriers—Yeon-gyo continually uses snippets of English to make it clear that she's educated and sophisticated, and Moon-gwang, while trying to appeal to Chung-sook, does the same in an implicit attempt to pull herself up into a perceived higher, more equal social rung.

And even more so than Bong's other films, *Parasite* is a movie that's loaded from top to bottom with crucial details. There's the fact that, when Moon-gwang returns to the house, she cuts the CCTV wires so that she won't be seen, later making it possible for Ki-taek's escape from the party to go unnoticed. Then there's the flickering of the entryway lights, which we know, once we meet Geun-sae, are actually messages from the bunker and not just the foibles of automatic lights. It's also, despite the arc of the story, incredibly funny in classically Bong ways—for instance, we see one of the Park family dogs eating the meat from the skewer that's been thrust into Geun-sae's body. And for all that *Parasite* was acclaimed as a "universal" film at the time of its release—and, certainly, it's a film in which any viewer should find a minefield of riches—it is, like *Memories of Murder* and *The Host*, also a deeply Korean film. Catching references like scholar's rocks, ipTIME, KakaoTalk, and the entire concept of *jjapaguri* (the latter two translated, respectively, as WhatsApp and ram-don in the English subtitles) as well as castella cake shops aren't crucial to enjoying or understanding the movie, but ground the movie in a reality that, for some viewers, won't really feel that far away.

The beginning and end of *Parasite* are mirror images. A hanging laundry rack full of socks dangles in front of a narrow semibasement window. Slowly, the camera tracks down, revealing Ki-woo looking inquisitively at something he's holding. In the film's opening, the window reveals a sunny day, and Ki-woo's object of attention is his phone as he tries to figure out whether or not they can still leech off of their neighbor's Wi-Fi. In the film's finale, it's a snowy winter night, and the thing Ki-woo is holding is a letter to his father, which he has no way of sending.

In the end, Ki-taek, who asks Geun-sae, "How can you live in a place like this?" when he first sees the bunker, ends up hiding there, tapping a Morse code message to his son through the lights in the hopes that, someday, somehow, he might see it. The unstated fear of sinking completely below the ground has come true. As Ki-woo writes his letter back, instead of simply getting up from his seat as he does at the film's start, he looks up, directly into the camera, leaving the audience to decide what they think will happen next. Will the cycle repeat again, or will there actually be a change?

The echo—reminiscent of *Mother* opening and closing with Kim Hye-ja's dancing—suggests a circular story, one that has ended in the same place that it began, and reads as cynical in that respect. No one has emerged from the movie's events without suffering some major loss—four characters have been killed—and Ki-woo's plan to save up enough money to buy the house is, realistically, a pipe dream. However, the credits, or rather, the song that plays over them, provide a glimmer of hope. "Soju One Glass," composed by Jung, written by Bong, and sung by Choi, sounds cheerful and upbeat, in defiance of lyrics that describe nothing but hard, strenuous labor and inclement weather. It's as if to say that, at the risk of sounding trite, life is what you make of it. As in *Okja*, which acknowledges and engages with the fact that stopping all people from eating meat is an impossibility (and that the meat industry is not an inherent evil) and, rather, that being more conscious is the key, *Parasite*'s ending seems to beg for more compassion for one another. Though *Snowpiercer*'s finale suggests that Bong thinks the only way to fix capitalism is to escape from it completely, that conclusion is feasible only because *Snowpiercer* is a work of science fiction set in a post-apocalyptic future. *Parasite* isn't nearly as removed from contemporary reality, and adjusts its expectations accordingly. Looking back through Bong's oeuvre, it's eminently clear just from where a work like *Parasite* would come, making it all the more impressive (and important) that the film is still so vital, so compelling, and so unpredictable.

105.

← Left
The film ends enigmatically with Ki-woo (Choi Woo Shik), recovering from massive head trauma, looking directly at the camera with an inscrutable expression after fantasizing about being reunited with his father. As usual, Bong refuses to explicitly spell out what any of it means, leaving it to the viewer to decide the Kim family's fate.

2019
Parasite
2h 12m

Director	Bong Joon Ho
Writers	Bong Joon Ho Han Jin-won
Key Cast	Song Kang-ho Lee Sun-kyun Cho Yeo-jeong Choi Woo Shik Park So-dam Lee Jung-eun Jang Hye-jin
Budget	$15.5 million *Estimated*
Producers	Kwak Sin-ae Moon Yang-kwon Bong Joon Ho Jang Young-hwan
Music	Jung Jaeil
Cinematography	Hong Kyung Pyo
Film Editing	Yang Jinmo
Production Design	Lee Ha-jun
Art Direction	Se Jin-lim Mo So-ra

PROPERTY IS THEFT

맘스크린 지퍼백
카놀라유

INFLUENCES
THE HOUSEMAID (1960)

Kim Ki-young's *The Housemaid* (1960), a thriller about a family that falls into disarray following the arrival of a new maid, has the distinction of being considered one of the best Korean films of all time. Produced between two fraught periods of Korean history—after the resignation of Syngman Rhee, South Korea's first president, in 1960, and before the ascension of military strongman Park Chung-hee in 1962—*The Housemaid* is practically scandalous in relation to the control the government would later exert over the film industry, especially as Myung-sook (Lee Eun-shim), the eponymous housemaid, is so overt about her sexual desire.

The object of her want is her employer, Dong-sik (Kim Jin-kyu), a composer who gets by teaching piano lessons while his wife (Ju Jeung-ryu) labors at a sewing machine to help support them and their two children. Though Myung-sook is originally hired to help ease Dong-sik's wife's burden, she seduces and becomes pregnant by him, setting off a chain of events that tear the family apart—until it's revealed that Dong-sik has just been reading about these events in the newspaper.

Bong Joon Ho has cited Kim Ki-young as one of his major influences, as well as citing *The Housemaid* as a key reference for *Parasite* (2019). It's easy to see the similarities between the two films—*The Housemaid* takes place in a two-story house, symbolizing the family's wealth (as does the piano they own), and very much functions as a satire of contemporary society, of expectations for and the pains of striving toward respectability. Even Bong's visual language in *Parasite* feels inspired by *The Housemaid*'s careful cinematography and editing, with shots that carefully segment the house and the characters within.

Bong also seems to have taken a leaf out of Kim's book in terms of characterization: In a Criterion Collection interview done as part of Martin Scorsese's World Cinema Project (Scorsese is also a fan of the film), Bong notes that the women in Kim's films are driven by desire—sexual and otherwise—while Kim's male leads tend to be idiots: "They look really stupid and indecisive." A similar dynamic applies to Bong's films, as his female characters often possess a degree of common sense and level-headedness that his male characters lack.

But what is arguably key to connecting the two films is their attitude toward moral binaries: Myung-sook's arrival heralds the splintering of Dong-sik's family, and the film frames her as something of a monster, but at the same time, it isn't as if Dong-sik doesn't have a choice in his seduction, and he remains in a position of power over her as her employer. Similarly, in *Parasite*, neither the rich Parks nor the striving Kims are totally good nor evil—they are simply doing what they believe they must in order to survive.

단편영화 및 뮤직비디오

SHORT FILMS AND MUSIC VIDEOS

106.

↓ Below
Kim Roi-ha stars as *White Man*'s (1994) nameless protagonist. A theater actor up until that point (*White Man* would be his first film credit), Kim was introduced to Bong by a mutual friend, and, as Bong had run out of money by the end of the short's production, accepted a voucher for a button-up shirt (which Bong had received from his father) as payment for his work.

WHITE MAN (1994)

Made six years before Bong's feature debut, *Barking Dogs Never Bite* (2000), the short film *White Man* (1994) is instantly recognizable as a stylistic and thematic bellwether for much of the rest of his work. Even in just its eighteen-minute run time, the film tackles class division, the ways in which those with means will take advantage of those without, and the systems meant to keep these artificial divisions in place.

The film's title alludes to the rise of the white-collar, middle-class professional, a.k.a. the "yuppie" class, and lends an extra dimension to a film that could, on a surface reading, simply be taken as the story of one man's strange day. An unnamed protagonist, played by Kim Roi-ha (who would later also star in *Barking Dogs Never Bite*, *Memories of Murder* [2003], and *The Host* [2006]), discovers, in a moment reminiscent of the opening of David Lynch's *Blue Velvet* (1986), a severed finger in the parking lot outside his apartment, and brings it around with him for the rest of the day.

Eventually, it's revealed in a news report that the finger belonged to a factory worker who, after losing it in an industrial accident, brought it with him to assault his company's CEO. The same report also notes that government negligence has led to the pollution of a dam with clumps of oil and dead fish—caused by improper disposal of waste from nearby construction sites—making the water unsafe. While the broadcast is the only explicitly stated hint at conflict between economic classes, *White Man* is loaded with details that bolster its central theme, from the immediate disparity between the well-to-do apartment complex in which the main character lives (the same complex, as it happens, that the unfortunate CEO lives in), and the ramshackle houses that are just one neighborhood over. As in *Parasite* (2019), stairs and a literal upstairs/downstairs contrast are used to emphasize the divide—after Kim's character's car breaks down, he's forced to walk home, and a seemingly endless stairway serves as both a literal and metaphorical chasm between the poor and the newly developed apartments above.

107.

↓ **Below**
The distinguishing feature of *Memories in My Frame* (1994) is its use of space and framing. When the young boy (Choi Sung-woo) is shown in the city, he's always boxed in; when he dreams of the countryside, it's colorful and expansive, a far cry from the confines of his new home.

Class themes aside, *White Man* also hints at Bong's sharp, unique sense of humor. The man's reaction upon finding the finger is not to report it to the police, or even just to leave it alone, but to keep and wash it. He uses it to dial a phone, to type, to strum a guitar—it's gross, yes, but hilarious at the same time. Ultimately, he gives it to a dog (who shows no interest in it), but the brief friendship between man and digit, as it were, is perfectly oddball while it lasts, as is the film's suggestion of just how separated this white-collar man is from the kind of circumstances that would result in such an injury. Even the film's opening, in which he removes a goldfish from its bowl and forces it to inhale cigarette smoke, makes it clear that this man stands at a significant remove from those less fortunate than he is.

Though its choppy tempo and formal rough edges give it away as an early work, *White Man* still impresses with its boldness, from its morbid sense of humor to its visual language to the choice to keep its primary theme largely in the background. That is to say: it's prototypical Bong.

MEMORIES IN MY FRAME (1994)

Of Bong's shorts, *Memories in My Frame* (1994) is the simplest and shortest. A young boy (Choi Sung-woo) comes home from school to discover that his dog is nowhere to be found. Later, he hears barking. Is it just his imagination, or has his dog really come home?

There's not much more meat on the bone than that, but if the short film doesn't offer much by way of story or depth, it makes up for it in composition and emotion. In a 2021 interview with director Rian Johnson, Bong recalled that, when he was nine years old, his family relocated from Daegu to Seoul, and had been forced to leave their dog behind. Bong cited the experience as a core inspiration behind the story for *Okja* (2017) ("At that time, the dog was kind of like my soul mate") as well as that film's city/countryside divide, but the event's fingerprints are clearly visible on *Memories in My Frame* as well.

After the dog's disappearance, the boy dreams of an endless field. As he walks through brilliant green grass, we hear the sound of a dog barking. The boy wakes and goes to his window. There's nothing outside. Still, the boy goes out onto the street to take a look around. The next morning, he closes the front gate of the house as he leaves for school. A few moments later, he returns, reopening the door, presumably just in case his canine friend should wander back home.

Where *White Man* is an early indicator of Bong's preoccupation with class systems and structures, *Memories in My Frame* is a clear statement of his interest in the differences between urban and rural landscapes (between nature and the varying degrees of influence mankind exerts upon it). As in *Memories of Murder* and *Okja*, the divide between country and city isn't analagous to that between good and evil. Rather, it brings up the question of how coexistence is possible. *Memories in My Frame* may not dig into the dilemma to such an explicit degree as Bong's feature works, but it's present in obvious and subtle ways. The story behind why the dog is missing isn't directly synchronous with Bong's personal experience, as this pooch seems to have run away rather than being given away, but there's an undeniable difference between the life the boy lives now and his life prior to moving—the way his home is shot, focusing on the house gate and, inside, the boy's window, creates a sense of being boxed in that is diametrically opposite from the openness of the countryside dream sequence.

Even though the short is a simple one—even in comparison to *White Man*—Bong demonstrates his skill in using visuals to tell a story rather than spelling every beat out through dialogue and exposition. In fact, there's barely any dialogue at all—the only spoken words in the short are in its introduction, as the boy searches for his dog. Granted, there's not too much to really have to explain, but the way Bong chooses to show us each beat lends depth to the proceedings. Having the boy turn in his dream and in his bed, and cutting them together to seem like the same motion, holding on the boy's window as he peeks out and then runs outside, rather than following him through the house and then onto the street—these shots are not just aesthetically appealing, but emphasize the contrast between dreams and reality, interior and exterior space. And the film's open ending, which leaves it to the viewer to guess whether or not the dog will come home, also feels of a piece with Bong's feature work. Rather than providing a clear-cut, "happy" answer, he leaves us on a note of ambiguity.

INCOHERENCE (1994)

Produced as a part of Bong's training as a student at the Korean Academy of Film Arts, *Incoherence* (1994) is much more blatant than *White Man* (which was produced while Bong was still attending Yonsei University) in its social critique. Divided into four parts—three chapters and an epilogue—the short, which Bong says was inspired at least in part by the unconventional structure of Quentin Tarantino's *Pulp Fiction* (1994), follows three different men as they land in hot water.

The first chapter, "Cockroach," focuses on a professor (Yoo Yeon-soo) whose sexual daydreams threaten to derail his class. Bong introduces us to him as he fantasizes about one of his female students while walking through campus, imagining pulling her loose sweater back over her bare shoulder. In his office, he browses a copy of *Penthouse* before heading to class. During his lesson, he realizes that he's left the handouts meant for his students on his office desk, and the female student volunteers to retrieve them. When he realizes that the issue of *Penthouse* is still on his desk, and that she'll see it if she isn't somehow intercepted, he rushes up the stairs in an attempt to get to his office first. Despite his best efforts, she beats him there by a hair, and it's only his Hail Mary—chucking a book across the room and landing it perfectly on top of the magazine (much to his student's surprise), claiming that he saw a cockroach—that allows him to escape the encounter unscathed.

"Up the Alleys," the second chapter, presents a game of cat and mouse. A jogger (Yun Il-ju) sits on a stoop to rest, drinking from one of the milk bottles left by the door. When a paperboy (Shin Dong-hwan) stops by, the

man offers him the other bottle for his trouble before continuing on his run. However, as soon as the jogger is gone, the home's actual owner (Kim Seon–hwa) appears, saddling him with the blame for her missing milk deliveries as well as, in retribution for his perceived thievery, canceling her newspaper subscription. As the hapless paperboy continues on his route and the jogger finishes his run in the same neighborhood, they keep glimpsing (and pursuing and fleeing from) each other.

The final chapter, "The Night of Pain," much like its precursors, mixes suspense with slapstick, as a drunk man (Kim Roi–ha) tries to find a place to relieve himself. After failing to get off of a bus at the correct stop due to his intoxication, he squats on the lawn of an apartment complex, dreaming that he's in a restroom, until he's told off by the building's security guard (Park Gwang–jin). Though the guard is understandably brusque, he gives the drunkard a relatively generous offer: to go into the apartment basement, do his business on a newspaper, and then throw it away. Resentful of being scolded, the man first rants at the guard (from behind a door, through which the guard can't hear him), then, it's heavily implied, leaves his poop in the guard's rice cooker.

Each chapter of the short is darkly funny, but it's the epilogue's reveal that is the true punchline. In the short's conclusion, we see that all three men—the professor, the jogger, and the businessman—have been invited onto a news show to address "the moral crisis in our society."

The professor teaches social psychology, the jogger is in fact the editor–in–chief of the newspaper the paperboy was delivering, and the drunk is a public prosecutor. As they denounce the very behaviors that we've seen them indulging in (the professor, for instance, says it was a good thing that the Korean edition of *Penthouse* was suppressed), we also see the other people they interacted with—the student, the paperboy (whose briefly–seen brother is played by none other than Bong), the guard—going about their lives. Though they've been fooled by these hypocrites, and hold less "respectable" jobs, they're portrayed as more honest. The so–called experts, in reality, have no leg to stand on—they proclaim

108.

↖ **Top left**
Given the relatively brief space that a short film provides, Bong gets immediately to the point in introducing the three main characters of *Incoherence* (1994). Within the first few seconds of each chapter, we instantly get a sense of who these men are at their basest level—which makes the eventual reveal that they are all hypocrites especially funny, and especially biting.

their shock that the ringleader of a recent spate of murders was considered trustworthy by those who knew him without batting an eye at their own uncouth comportment.

The film's Korean title is 지리멸렬, which Bong, speaking to critic Darcy Paquet for a segment on the Criterion Collection release for *Memories of Murder*, affirms is less a one–to–one translation of "incoherence" and more an amalgam of "ludicrous, pathetic, cheap, foolish, and messy," making it clear just how Bong feels about his three leads and their ilk. Though villains and antagonists in the mold of these men exist throughout Bong's feature work, those longer runtimes also allow for added dimensions—there's not really room for sympathy for the main characters in *Incoherence* whereas, in movies like *Parasite* and *Mother* (2009), Bong stays away from such clear distinction between sympathetic and derision–worthy. He makes even his ostensible protagonists casually capable of both cruelty and hypocrisy.

"BUT" (2000), "LONELY STREET LAMP" (2003)

The two music videos Bong directed stand out from the rest of his oeuvre, as the "stories" being told are informed by the songs they accompany. Both songs—"But" (by Kim Don–kyu) and "Lonely Street Lamp" (by Han Young–ae) released in 2000 and 2003, respectively—tread an overtly romantic territory that's rare for Bong, though less so in his short works (see: 2008's *Shaking Tokyo*).

"But" stars Park Hae–il and Bae Doona (who would later play siblings for Bong in *The Host*) as a former couple. While riding the subway, a man (Park) is shocked to see his ex–girlfriend on the other side of the car. As he chases her through an increasingly dreamy set of subway cars, it becomes clear that she's a figment of his imagination. However, there's still hope for him—a different woman on the train picks up an old photograph he drops in a clear moment of connection.

"Lonely Street Lamp," meanwhile, is a little more straightforward. Various couples, young and old (and even

109.

↓ Below
The two music videos that Bong has directed are a showcase for his sense of humor and whimsy, as both are much more blatantly silly (and romantic) than Bong's feature work. "But" (2000) turns a subway into a fantasy–like landscape, while "Lonely Street Lamp" (2003) sees a revolving door of lovey–dovey couples, emphasizing the loneliness of its lead character.

a man and his dog), canoodle and caress one another under a street lamp. The only loner is a forlorn young woman (Kang Hye-jung, who shot to stardom the same year for her role in Park Chan-wook's *Oldboy*) who loiters around the steps the lamp illuminates, as if hoping its romantic energy might rub off on her. Miraculously, it does—an equally awkward man (Ryu Seung-beom) is seen standing around on his own, and eventually, the two loners meet, falling into an endearing courtship (reminiscent of the whimsical flights of fancy practiced by French filmmaker Michel Gondry), remaining still while the world wobbles around them.

Arguably, the biggest thing to take from these two works is their playfulness, not just in terms of tone but in style as well. Bong doesn't shy away from moments of fantasy or magical realism in his feature films, but he certainly doesn't go as far as "But" does (the characters' chase sequence—with plenty of slow-motion running and longing glances—takes them through a car that's lit entirely in blue). And "Lonely Street Lamp," though more grounded than its counterpart, is charmingly twee in how it brings its central couple together. If *White Man* and *Incoherence* serve as foundational texts for the thematic drive of Bong's work to come, "But" and "Lonely Street Lamp" hint at how deft he is as a storyteller. The story in both videos is fairly rote—it's the execution that makes them fun and notable.

SINK & RISE (TWENTIDENTITY, 2003)

Sink & Rise (2003) acts as something of a precursor to *The Host*, which premiered three years later, not just in terms of its setting (the action centers around a snack stand on the bank of the Han River) but in tone. Sandwiched between two of Bong's bleaker features, *Memories of Murder* and *Mother*, *The Host* lands on the more optimistic side of the scale, ending on a hopeful note rather than a cynical one. *Sink & Rise*, part of an omnibus of films in celebration of the twentieth anniversary of the Korean Academy of Film Arts, is similarly a little brighter, as well as suggestive of the subtle magical realism that is now common in Bong's films.

110.

↓ Below
Though ultimately more of an experiment than anything else, *Sink & Rise* (2003) is a prime example of Bong's ability to show, not tell. The characters, who do not have any explicit backstories spelled out for them, still feel relatively fleshed out thanks to the quirks of their outward appearances and how they interact with each other.

A father and daughter (Yoon Je-moon and Jung In-sun, notably also seen as the little girl at the end of *Memories of Murder*) come across a snack stand run by an old man (Byun Hee-bong). As the dad reminisces about eating boiled eggs as a child (in an attempt to keep his daughter from choosing a more expensive snack), he claims that they float in water. When the shopkeeper argues that they don't, the two men make a bet. The dad will throw a boiled egg into the Han River. If it floats, he and his daughter will take all of the snacks they can carry. If it sinks, he will give the shopkeeper his child. Egg after egg sinks until suddenly a giant egg appears, bobbing on the surface of the water. Though all three observers are shocked, the father and daughter quickly regain their senses, rushing back to the snack stand to claim their prize. The very last image of the short—of the father and daughter running away with their arms full of snacks, gleefully laughing—feels like a joyous burst of adrenaline.

Shot in one take, *Sink & Rise* packs everything into its details, from the bruise on the father's face to the grubbiness of both his and his daughter's appearances and his use of English in an attempt to prove his intellectual superiority. Though it seems fairly slight—its arc is lighter than that of Bong's previous shorts given its relative lack of concern for any broader context—it still packs a punch as a technical experiment, not to mention just how unforseeable the ending is. There's no explanation for the giant egg, and the father and daughter express no real curiosity about it, as the food that they've won takes precedence. Even as an audience member, though the natural impulse is to want to know more, the main story, as it were, still lies with that little family unit. As they run away—to the tune of "Aquarius/Let the Sunshine In"—it's impossible not to share in their joy, even if larger mysteries remain unsolved.

INFLUENZA (DIGITAL SHORT FILMS BY THREE DIRECTORS, 2004)

Like *Sink & Rise*, *Influenza* (2004) boasts an experimental edge, as it's entirely made up of footage from "observation cameras and CCTV security systems" in Seoul, per an intertitle. The effect that this stylistic choice has is immediate: the fixed and detached nature of the footage (that is, the idea that there's no one "directing" what's going on) sets the viewer at a disorienting remove from the action. Even in the film's very first scene—an extended shot of traffic over a bridge—it's hard to know where to look until a little circle pops up, indicating Cho Hyuk-rae (Yoon Je-moon, once again), the short film's main character and at this point barely a speck on the screen, gazing over the edge. The sense of distance between the viewer and the unfolding events also ups the tension ante, as even the suggestion that this is found footage rather than a staged film creates an overarching sense of danger and helplessness. To add to that unease, Bong often allows the cameras (so to speak) to keep rolling even after the action has ceased.

The story itself, though aligned with Bong's usual interests, is unusually dark. Cho—who, again, we are introduced to while seemingly pondering suicide—is doing his best as a salesman hawking ineffective instant glue. When he loses his stock after nearly being arrested, he's driven first to picking through garbage to find food, then to committing petty crimes that grow increasingly violent in order to get by. What begins with stealing credit cards escalates to carjacking, attempted bank robbery, and murder. In the film's conclusion, he and his partner (Go Soo-hee, previously seen in both *Barking Dogs Never Bite* and the "Lonely Street Lamp" music video) are finally apprehended. When they try to rob an old man at an ATM, the ensuing commotion draws too much attention and the police are called. Cho, in a rage, murders the old man, and his accomplice holds the door to the bank shut as a crowd gathers outside.

Remarkably, the short isn't totally devoid of humor: During their attempted bank robbery, Cho draws a customer ticket, and is rewarded with a prize for being the twentieth customer on the twentieth anniversary of the branch's opening, and a scene in a parking garage is only intermittently seen as the preprogrammed security camera rotates back and forth. But those moments aside, *Influenza* largely feels hopeless, and doesn't pull any punches in its depiction of brutality. Cho isn't portrayed as

inherently cruel—rather, he is pushed to such extremes by his circumstances, from which it seems there's no escape. The film's most striking scene, in retrospect, actually comes early on, as, while picking through garbage, he comes across a piece of salvageable food. Right before biting into it, he clocks the security camera watching him and holds its gaze for a long moment. He doesn't want to be seen eating from the trash, but can't afford not to. He puts the item aside. Almost immediately afterward, a man walks by and drops a knife. Cho picks it up, but its owner backtracks to retrieve it. The moment is the most explicit in the film in terms of messaging (Bong otherwise allows events to play out without any obvious construction or a heavy directorial hand): Cho has hit rock bottom, and when the idea of turning to violence is presented to him, it seems like his only option. This idea—of the shame and hopelessness that can be felt by those who have been beaten down to such an extent—recurs throughout Bong's feature work, whether in *Snowpiercer* (2013), as Curtis admits to cannibalism, or in *Parasite*, as Moon-gwang grovels for mercy.

Cho's descent is awful to watch, and is made worse by how it plays in tandem with the indifference of the people around him. Nobody thinks to offer him aid—more often, passersby ignore him. When he's picking through the trash, the only people who interact with him are a woman seeking to offload her garbage, and the man with the knife. Granted, even Cho is guilty of turning a blind eye. While eating at a convenience store, he witnesses a man assaulting a woman, brutally beating her and then dragging her out of sight. Rather than intervene, Cho continues to eat, and isn't even shaken by what he's seen.

The short's final scene serves up a terrible irony in that respect: It's only as Cho reaches the end of the road, as it were, that people finally care enough to interact with him in any capacity. Most of the observers are horrified, but others seem gleeful—in particular, there's one man who attempts to record the murder with his phone camera and ends up in an altercation with another man as they jockey for space. Even in this instance, the way that people react, rubbernecking and

111.

↑ **Above**
Influenza (2004) achieves a chilling sense of detachment through the mode in which it's shot. The apathy projected by the CCTV and security camera footage extends to the characters' behavior toward each other—the viewer can't intervene, but the onlookers, who do have a choice, choose not to.

112.

↓ **Below**
Bong's contribution to the *Tokyo!* anthology (2008) is remarkably sweet, and perhaps the most fully realized of Bong's shorts. Lovingly designed and shot, the warmth that the production exudes sits at first at odds with the protagonist's chosen exile, then in harmony with his desire for connection.

gawking, is damning. It's not just the larger system that is responsible for Cho's dire straits, but the people within it as well. If no one cares enough to create change, then none will occur.

SHAKING TOKYO (TOKYO!, 2008)

Shaking Tokyo (2008) has the distinction of being Bong's most romantic work, as love tends to figure into his feature work mostly in the familial sense and, when not platonic, is seen either in passing or in a much more complicated context, as in *Mother*. This short (part of an anthology of three shorts filmed in Tokyo by non-Japanese directors, with Michel Gondry and Leos Carax rounding out the trio), by contrast, has a love story at its center, focusing on the importance of human connection.

The film stars Teruyuki Kagawa as a hikikomori (a term for both those suffering from and the actual condition of suffering from acute social withdrawal—essentially recluses) who hasn't left his apartment for a decade. His only interactions with others are through delivery people, most notably the staff at a local pizza place from which he orders every week, and even then, he avoids eye contact and never steps beyond his doorway. That all changes, however, when a new pizza delivery girl (Yū Aoi) enters into his life. Not only do they make eye contact when she arrives, but an earthquake that occurs at that very moment causes her to faint. For the hikikomori, this is as much a seismic event as the earthquake itself—he's being forced to interact with another human being, and what's more, he's fallen for her at first sight. Noticing a series of tattoos on her body labeled "sadness," "hysteria," "headache," and "coma," he presses "coma." The action causes both his hair to stand on end and her to jolt out of her unconscious state. Strangely enough, she doesn't seem at all put off by the obsessively neat nature of his apartment—empty pizza boxes are stacked from floor to ceiling, as are water bottles, toilet paper rolls, and cups of instant noodles. "This place is really perfect," she says, before abruptly leaving.

113.

→ Opposite
Iki (2011), Bong's most recent short film, is a study in telling a many-faceted story as simply as possible. With a single setting and just two characters (one of them not an active presence until the short's final moments), its focus is entirely on the emotions being conveyed.

Stricken by their encounter, the hikikomori calls the pizza place again the next day, hoping that she'll deliver his order again. Instead, he gets the store's manager (Naoto Takenaka), who barges in, tracking rainwater everywhere, and uses his phone without even asking for permission. (In a funny aside, he yells at the person on the other end of the line, "I'm much more introverted than you are!") When the hikikomori finally manages to ask after the young woman, the manager first jokes that she's his wife, then comes clean, explaining that she'd quit her job while saying "she'd never come out again." In other words, he'll need to overcome his fear of going outside if he ever wants to see her again.

When he does work up the courage to step foot beyond his apartment, he discovers that, during his decade as a hermit, the rest of the world has withdrawn as well. Plants have become overgrown, and the streets are empty, save for a delivery robot that has replaced human couriers. As he runs to the woman's house, he spies people through their windows, and guesses to himself just how long they've been shut-ins. When he finally reaches the delivery girl's home, he tells her through her window, "If you don't come out now, you never will." At first she resists, locking her door, but as he desperately shakes the doorknob, another earthquake occurs. The chaos sends everyone in the neighborhood out onto the street in a panic, but that collective connection doesn't last—as soon as the tremors cease, people slowly retreat back to their homes. When the hikikomori realizes that the delivery girl has come out of her house, too, they get into a scuffle as he attempts to prevent her from going back inside. Though she initially resists, she stops when he presses one of the tattooed buttons on her arm, this one reading "love." As they hold each other's gaze, the world begins to shake once again.

Even aside from its sweet central storyline, *Shaking Tokyo* is charmingly, beautifully shot. The neatness of the hikikomori's apartment immediately provides a sense of who he is, and his reintroduction to the larger world is just as disorienting for the viewer as it is for him, as bright, washed-out shots make it momentarily difficult to figure out what's going on. And as he discovers that the rest of the city—and perhaps even the rest of the world—has become hikikomori as well, the tone briefly shifts into creepy, eerie territory. (A moment in which a woman disappears behind patterned glass is nightmarish to watch.) But there's a strange kind of beauty, too, to the sequence in which the hikikomori runs through the abandoned streets, wandering through a disarmingly serene version of the iconic Shibuya Crossing. Finally, there's the short's conclusion, which captures both the nervousness and thrill of a new connection.

Though it's a relatively happy ending, the fact that everyone around the central couple has once again retreated from the world at large suggests that there's still some work to be done. "I had an image of the people of Tokyo as oddly repressed, defensively lonely," Bong said, speaking about how he came up with the short's story. "I think I had a desire to wake them up, shake up and liberate such people. That's where the title *Shaking Tokyo* came from and how the motif of the earthquake also came about." But there's still hope, as the shaking begins again—perhaps some other people will find each other, this time.

IKI (3:11 A SENSE OF HOME, 2011)

In the aftermath of the March 11, 2011, Tōhoku earthquake and tsunami, filmmaker Naomi Kawase invited a group of international directors (including Apichatpong Weerasethakul and Jia Zhang-ke) to contribute short films, each running 3 minutes and 11 seconds, in tribute to the victims for an anthology titled *3:11 A Sense of Home*. Bong's short, *Iki*, is among the twenty shorts included in the film, and it tackles the complicated nature of grief and its attendant emotions (despair, anger, denial).

A young woman (Go Ah-sung) walks down a stretch of beach. She's clearly uneasy, as her body language is erratic and she picks at a bunch of reeds she has clutched in one hand. As she continues on, it's revealed that she's

come across the prone body of a young child. At first, she doesn't seem to know what to do—she even almost laughs before approaching the girl, then proceeds to poke her cheek, press her ear to her chest to try to find a heartbeat, and then try mouth-to-mouth and CPR. When nothing seems to work, she turns first to anger—she slaps the body—and then she breaks into sobs. As she cries, the child opens its eyes.

There's no dialogue, largely because it's not necessary. The emotions that Go's character experiences can be communicated without language. The short's style, to wit, is in service of her performance—the focus is always on her reactions as she attempts to resuscitate the young girl. It's easy to imagine a more melodramatic, less subtle version of this short, and it's to Bong's credit that he doesn't take a more on-the-nose route, as the film works even outside of its intended context. What is notable is that, despite everything, the film ends on a tentatively optimistic note. Any attempt at an explicit reading will only come across as prescriptive or trite, but it doesn't feel incidental that the short ends with the little girl opening her eyes rather than remaining still.

INTERVIEWS

HONG KYUNG PYO

CHOI TAE-YOUNG

YANG JINMO

TILDA SWINTON

JUNG JAEIL

CHOI WOO SHIK

HONG KYUNG PYO

Cinematographer

Collaborations

Mother

Snowpiercer

Parasite

Hong Kyung Pyo, a veteran and pioneer in the Korean industry, has the distinction of having served as cinematographer on some of the biggest Korean films of the last few decades. After making his debut on the scene as part of the crew of *That Which Falls Has Wings* (1990), Hong would go on to work on such films as *The Foul King* (2000), one of the films credited with making Song Kang-ho a true star; Na Hong-jin's *The Wailing* (2016); Lee Chang-dong's *Burning* (2018); and, of course, three movies with Bong: *Mother* (2009), *Snowpiercer* (2013), and *Parasite* (2019). Their collaboration has been such that, in an 2020 interview, Bong said that any Korean films he'd make in the future would be with Hong.

You first worked with Bong on *Mother*. How did that collaboration come about?

I knew Bong from his days as an assistant director. I was a first camera assistant, a focuspuller, on a piece called *Motel Cactus* [*Image right*]. We got close then, and we talked. We said that we should work together if we ever got the chance. At that time, Bong Joon Ho and Jang Joon-hwan (director of *Save the Green Planet*), were both assistants and they were also classmates in the Academy, so they were close. We knew each other well before that, too, because the [film] scene in Korea is small and we worked at the same film company—*Memories of Murder* and *Save the Green Planet* were done at the same company, so we saw each other often. When Bong was in LA after *The Host*, we met there, and I think that was when he first talked to me about a project called *Mother*.

What was your initial conversation about the look of *Mother*?

I heard about *Mother* really early—a year or two years before starting actual work. I knew that he was writing a script called *Mother* with Kim Hye-ja in it and it was about a mother. We did research and exchanged lots of photos and images to narrow down what we wanted the look to be. We didn't get the specifics nailed down, but we kept up a conversation about what would work best, and all the while he worked on the script.

You used vintage anamorphic vintage lenses on *Mother*. I'm curious how you arrived at that choice.

I got the final version of the *Mother* script, and while reading it, I thought that it had a really classical feel to it, like an old film. I loved it. I genuinely felt that it was a masterpiece. Just from the script, I felt the story needed something special to convey that weighty, serious, and classic feeling. Back then, ten years ago, people weren't using anamorphic lenses that much, though they seem to be coming back now. But I wanted it to be *Mother*'s signature look. While researching lenses I heard that a small company in Germany had those lenses, so I went there and tested them, and brought them back for shooting.

The opening scene where Kim Hye-ja is walking through a field is so striking. Can you tell me about filming that

scene? There's a behind-the-scenes video where Bong and the rest of the crew are also dancing so she wasn't embarrassed to do it herself.

Yeah, we were dancing on set. As DP, that scene is a really long take—she walks from far away to all the way up to the camera, and the camera looks like it's on a high angle, but when she comes up to the camera, the camera comes down to eye level and tightens in, with her continuing to dance. The camera then follows her movements very minutely. It looks graceful, but on set Bong was dancing next to the camera, and the music on the set was different—we were playing Korean trot music. It was something a little more upbeat, to alleviate Kim Hye-ja's awkwardness, and also to encourage a degree of comfort with the emotions in the scene. And yes—we were dancing to try to make her feel more comfortable.

I also want to talk about the final scene of *Mother*, where she's dancing on the bus. I understand it was a very difficult shot to get, in part because the bus is moving, and in part because you wanted to get the light at a specific time of day.

From the first moment I received the film script, the first and last scenes of the movie seemed really important. At first, we talked about doing [the final shot] of the film with CGI, since it would be difficult to shoot it with real sunlight, but Bong and I wanted to shoot it for real, with natural light, real sunlight, so we did quite a lot of location hunting. There aren't that many places in Korea like that—low and open spaces where the sunlight can come through like that when it sets. Originally we found a space, a wide open field in the Jeollanam-do area, but there were scheduling issues. The timing had to be right with the winter sun and everything, so we went through a complicated series of adjustments and eventually shot in a space near Incheon Airport outside Seoul. [*Image left*] We did tests, too. We got together early in the morning, when the sun was coming up from the opposite side, to see the feeling of when it was coming up. We did some rehearsals with extras, and then did the actual shoot in the afternoon, when the sun was setting. I think we got the okay on the first or second take. Back then we were shooting with film, and that day we actually shot until we used up all the film. And we even shot that, the film rolling out. I was using this long zoom lens, and Bong was talking to me over the radio while we were shooting. We were lucky to get that shot.

How has your process of working with Bong as a director of photography and cinematographer changed as productions have switched from film to digital?

I shot *Mother* and *Snowpiercer* on film. *Snowpiercer* was the last Korean movie to be shot on film. When we got back after *Snowpiercer*, no one was shooting on film. Even now we have the idea of wanting to retain that film feeling, which was also true when we were doing *Parasite*. We did a lot of tests around that. Things are pretty different now. I'm from the old generation, the analog generation. I still gravitate towards that certain atmosphere—or emotion—that film has. But with digital, it's true that things are more convenient, and quicker. But emotionally, I still like the old film movies, personally.

You mentioned that you started talking to Bong about *Mother* one or two years before it actually began shooting. How early were you brought on for *Snowpiercer*? And do you remember your initial discussions about what that movie was going to be?

He first talked about *Snowpiercer* while we were shooting *Mother*. Bong always has two or three other scripts developing in his head while he's shooting a movie. I always tell him that it's nuts the way his mind works. On this side of his brain there's *Mother*, and then on this side, *Snowpiercer*, and then another movie on another side. I received the script for *Snowpiercer* about a year after *Mother* was done. With the script he had included some conceptual art—some of the core scenes, like the first scene inside the train, with the people sitting—and other images to aid understanding. It was originally an animation with a very complex line of movement. That's how the first Korean version of *Snowpiercer* came to me. I really like that version. The story is actually quite different from the English version. Have you read it? The original Korean draft?

I read it in English, not Korean.

The Korean version is somewhat different, with Bong's characteristic nuances, his humor. Those really come to life in Korean, but [they get lost when] translated into English. But it got translated into English for the final version. With Bong, I always receive these things early. With *Parasite* too, it was while he was preparing for *Okja*. Before he started *Okja*, we met at a coffee shop in Seoul, and we'd been exchanging phone calls before that. I was working on *The Wailing* and other projects, and he brought me a thirty–page synopsis of *Parasite* and told me that was what he would be shooting after *Okja*. He told me that it was a movie centering around the flooding of a semibasement home, with water everywhere, and he asked me to think about how I might reproduce that. After *Okja*, he had a completed script, which was, in many ways, different from the synopsis he'd shown me earlier. But I was very surprised, reading the script. I'd seen *Mother* and *Snowpiercer*, and I saw the script for *Okja* as well, but reading *Parasite* I thought . . . wow. The world was much smaller in scale, focusing on a family. But the story within felt somehow expanded. I got the feeling that the structure was really solid, that the composition was perfect. I always ask him how on earth he writes these stories, how he wrote *Okja* and *Snowpiercer*. I tell him he's nuts.

***Snowpiercer* presents a unique set of problems because you're shooting within a confined space—the train itself—but then also having to convey the sense of forward movement, both because the train is moving, and also because the characters are moving from the back to the front of the train. What were your thoughts in terms of how to really bring that to life on screen?**

Snowpiercer is a train movie. The train is long and narrow, and from the beginning, Bong and I decided on a directionality—always from left to right. After writing the screenplay, Bong did about eight months of preparation in the Czech Republic, and in the beginning it was me, Bong, and the producer—the three of us went early and spent maybe five months in preproduction. We decided then that, when talking about the screenplay, it was going to be important for the audience to understand in what direction the train was moving, and so we designated some rules. The composition will always be such that the train seems like it's moving from left to right, and that's how we framed it. And from inside the train as well, we only shot in three directions. The camera from the front, the camera from this one side, and from the back, and it would never cross over to the other side. So, watching the movie, you'll see that there's only ever the frontal view, the one side as the train moves to the right, and then the rear view. We only used these three views while shooting the movie.

How do you decide which aspect ratio to shoot the films in?

It has to do with the core feeling of the movie. In *Mother*, the first scene is in an open field. So the feeling of a field, and the wide open spaces of the countryside. With *Mother*, wide shots were written into the screenplay, and there are a lot of shots where the character is very small in the frame and shot from far away. Because of that wide feeling, I went with a wide anamorphic ratio. The widest, 2.39:1. With *Snowpiercer*, since it's inside the narrow train space, people are crammed together, so we used 1.85:1. While the space was, of course, important, Bong said that *Snowpiercer* is about the people, the story of the people inside the train, so we used 1.85:1 to showcase the people a little more. And then with *Parasite*, it's back to a family story, and when the four of them sit side–by–side to eat, we wanted all of them in the frame without getting cut, so we used a lens that would get them all together.

You've said that it was on purpose that the Kims are almost always in the same frame, whereas the Parks are usually separated. How early on did you make the choice to present the two families in these different ways?

For that, I worked a lot with the artistic director in preproduction and talked about what to do with those two families.

I told you that I received the screenplay for *Parasite* really early. That made it so that we were able to do lots of tests, and we went to actual semibasement spaces to do test shoots and costume tests. We didn't have an actual rich person's home to work with, but we visited the homes of wealthy people. To be honest, the fancy house presented some challenges. The semibasement wasn't hard, because we had a place we could go to for shooting, and real references. But rich

people's houses are all specially designed, so the artistic team created a 3D model, and we talked about camera work and other things using that model.

I understand that the scene in which the Kims are fleeing the Park home in the rain was one of the most difficult things to shoot.

We had to use an incredible amount of water to have it continuously raining, especially the sequence when they're first descending. We had to shoot that in an existing wealthy neighborhood. It really was only possible because it was Bong Joon Ho. I don't think they would've agreed otherwise, especially at night. We had this huge crane, and we asked all the surrounding houses for permission, and everyone was cooperative. Even in terms of the logistics, pouring that much water out from that spot will inevitably result in a huge flood down in the lower area, so it's also dangerous, because there's so much water and it's moving so rapidly. We had to stack sandbags and make sure that the water was under control.

Can you tell me about finding that location and actually getting the shots?

Director Bong always described this film as a descending movie. The camera needed to work vertically to convey this feeling of height. In the beginning, the family goes up and down stairs—Bong called it a stair movie. Inside the houses, too, characters going up and down stairs was critical. But because the semibasement house and all of the Park house was a set, and that particular stair scene was the only one to take place in an actual location, finding the right place was of paramount importance. Our location team really meticulously combed through all the possible spots in Seoul. Now, with Seoul so developed, a lot of those stairs outside semibasement spaces or in poorer neighborhoods are disappearing. We found a couple, but they were subsequently torn down and gentrified.

You've noted that you tend to watch other movies to prepare for shoots, and in the case of *Parasite* you watched Orson Welles's *The Trial*. Do you remember what you watched before *Mother* and *Snowpiercer*?

There was nothing like that for *Snowpiercer*, it was mostly just for *Parasite*. For *Mother* I looked at some Hellen van Meene photography, not really any movies. Sometimes Bong will just show me these images on his iPhone—he'll send them to me before starting on a movie. Especially with *Parasite*, he suddenly sent me these shots from an old Orson Welles movie, *The Trial* [*Image left*]. He showed me these images full of people, and was saying that maybe we could do that in *Parasite*, with Ki-woo, after the flood, when everyone is packed into the gymnasium. It was less that he asked me to watch the movie and more certain scenes from movies. Or like, some stairs in a French movie. He asked me to look at those for the feeling of those scenes; the movie itself had nothing to do with *Parasite*.

I was watching an interview with you where you were saying that the scene of the Kim family on the Parks' lawn actually wasn't originally in the script, and was something that you fought to include in the film. What made you want to shoot that to begin with, and what made you fight for that to remain in the film?

As the cinematographer, I felt that the movie needed some kind of a full shot. It was all too character-driven, and so I wanted to have something with space. I went hunting, and when we were building the set I saw the sun setting. This was before the building was constructed, and I thought that it would look really cool when the sun set there. With the emotional through line of the movie, too, I thought it would be nice to have, at that point, something beautiful but also a bit ominous. Bong said there wasn't such a shot in the original screenplay, but he thought having one outside would be nice. I was really happy about that. I took the camera outside and tried shooting when the sun was going down. And luckily, there came a day with that view—like in the movie—with the red sun setting and the storm clouds above. It serves as a kind of foreshadowing for what's to come.

I understand that you used one camera and shot everything yourself for *Parasite*, which is fairly rare. What made you want to work that way on that movie?

Bong himself generally only uses one camera. If you look closely at his storyboards, they're old style—sort of painting a picture with the camera. In a certain space, if the actor is acting, the camera is in one spot, then another, and then it pans. But once you start using two cameras, things get awkward. Even for conversation scenes, generally he'll have the one camera moving around. Of course, sometimes he'll have two, but generally it's just one—at least to start with. Bong doesn't like using two cameras. He'll use two just for special circumstances, like a car accident scene, or a conversation scene where the emotions of the speakers dictate that they don't move around. Except for those niche cases, he generally works with a single camera. So we mostly used one for *Snowpiercer*, and two in the action sequences. *Mother* was almost exclusively shot with one, with the exception being the car accident scene, where they're passing by and *bam*! There's a collision. Only that scene used two cameras. With *Parasite*, we never used two.

One of the things that's fascinating about *Parasite* is that you did a black-and-white version of it. You've said that you knew that you wanted to do a black-and-white version of the film fairly early on. At what point in the process were you discussing that with Director Bong?

We first talked about the possibility of doing a black-and-white film [*Image below left*] when we were first researching and preparing for *Mother*. But realistically, shooting in black and white was a risk at the time, and there were the producers and investors to think about. We were also not completely ready. We'd talked to the artistic team about the colors and done a lot of preparation for that, so we shot it in color and forgot about it. But then, in LA, we did the postproduction and color correction for *Snowpiercer*. During that time, I suddenly had the thought that it might be nice to do *Mother* in black and white, which was a continuation of the thought that I'd had back when I'd been looking at the photographs while originally preparing for the film. I made a real proposition to Bong while we were working on *Snowpiercer*: I told him I'd go to Korea and dig out all the *Mother* materials and create a black-and-white version, just as something commemorative.

Originally, we didn't think about releasing it at all. It was just supposed to be a commemorative thing for me and Bong, sort of like a present from me, since we never got to do a black-and-white version. So I came back to Seoul, found the negatives at the Korean Film Archive, and did a black-and-white version of *Mother*. I finished it and showed Bong, and seeing *Mother* in black and white, I felt that it was totally different. For some reason, it was really easy to concentrate on the main character. After all that time had passed, watching it again, it came to me as something very new. Other people, too—their reactions were that it felt fresh, whatever the reason for that might be. So that's how that project came to be. And surprisingly, what was originally just supposed to be a little commemorative thing got released, and shown in theaters. With *Parasite*, we talked about this while we were making the film, that we should make a black-and-white version after shooting. So we did.

Do you have a favorite shot or a sequence from the three Bong movies that you've done?

I would have to say the last scene of *Mother*. That scene, even if I wanted to shoot that scene again, it's nature. You have to be really lucky. With *Parasite*, everything was artificial, so if you didn't like something, you could just shoot it again. But with *Mother*, and that scene, no. *Snowpiercer* was shot one hundred percent on a set, and *Parasite*, too, more than ninety percent on a set. But *Mother* was shot almost ninety percent on location, and when you're shooting on location, you're somewhat reliant on nature. So that last scene of *Mother* is a scene that can only be described as heaven-blessed, which is why I really like that scene. That can only be done with luck.

CHOI TAE-YOUNG

Sound Editor

Collaborations

Barking Dogs Never Bite
Memories of Murder
The Host
Mother
Snowpiercer
Okja
Parasite

Of all of Bong's collaborators, sound editor Choi Tae-young is arguably his closest, if only by virtue of the fact that he's worked on all of Bong's films to date. (For *Parasite*, Choi and his sound team won the MPSE award for sound editing on a foreign language feature film.) He is a prolific artist—his IMDb credits number one hundred at time of writing—as well the cofounder of the audio post-house Livetone, which has become something of a powerhouse in the Korean film and TV industry since its conception in 1997. Speaking to the sound library A Sound Effect about what he was most proud of in his work on *Parasite*, Choi said, "Collaborating with the most creative director I've ever met, I'm always working on sound as a new challenge and I'm most proud to continue to expand my Bong-style sound field."

You're the only collaborator of Bong's to have worked on all his films—I'm curious how you first met, and if *Barking Dogs Never Bite* was your first collaboration, or if you had worked together before that?

Director Bong was the assistant director on *Motel Cactus* in, I think, '97. We met then. This was with Uno Films, which was the predecessor of Sidus Pictures. I heard that he was debuting with *Barking Dogs Never Bite*, and so we worked together on it. After seeing *Barking Dogs Never Bite*, I thought, "Oh, this is going to flop, this is going to be the end of his career." As I predicted, the film didn't do very well, and so he disappeared for a while. Then we met again for a movie called *Memories of Murder*. After editing and the turnover—the beginning of the postproduction for audio is something called spotting, where we look at the edited video and discuss the sound—I told the director, "Wow, this movie is going to draw an audience of five million." And it turns out I was right. After that, we worked together consistently, and I don't really know why he keeps working with me. I tell him jokingly that I'm tired of working with him, and that he should find someone else. I think our relationship lets us joke around like that.

Has your method of working together changed over the years? Since you've worked together for so long, I imagine you understand each other quite well now.

It goes without saying that Director Bong's style of audio direction changes with every film he does. It evolves. With *Barking Dogs Never Bite*, which was his first film—and back then it had been about two or three years since I started working in film sound—I think his directing, or the work process itself, was more, how to put it, saturated with elements that served his own experiments, as compared to the present day. Of course, he was also thinking about the audience, but was more focused on himself. Then, starting with *Memories of Murder*, the direction became more . . . commercial? If *Barking Dogs Never Bite* was more of an independent-style movie in terms of his direction of film sound, starting with *Memories of Murder* he began to think a lot more about sound as befitting a commercial movie. Afterward, with *The Host* and *Mother*, his methodology of sound

direction continued to change, all the way up to *Parasite*. Because I worked with him for so long, following *Memories of Murder* I started to be able to read his patterns, and I became able to discern what he was thinking. After that, Director Bong gave me more general guidance rather than specific instructions for a scene. He would relay to me the overall context of the film or the overarching emotional through line, and just ask me to take care of it. When we worked, he would really say things like, "I trust you to take care of it," which was a lot of pressure for me. I felt that it was a lot more responsibility, and that if something went wrong, I wouldn't be able to blame it on his direction, since I was the one designing things, and that I needed to take responsibility for my part of the project. In the final mixing stages, Director Bong always approached the sound from the point of view of the audience, and he gave a lot of thought as to how the sound would be delivered to the audience and what emotions it might evoke. Sometimes, Director Bong will go in a direction that I don't understand at all. So I'll ask him, "Is this really what you want?" and he says, "Yes." But then, we do something called a technical screening, after all the mixing, in the theater. And during the tech screening, I'll be like, "Oh . . . that's why he went in this direction," and understand his choices. I find myself agreeing with them.

Nowadays, when I work with him, the pressure doesn't really come from worrying about the choices he's going to make, or what he's going to think about a certain choice, but rather from the thought that the onus is on me—that when he listens to the sound, or when the audience hears the sound, Director Bong's intentions have to come through clearly. In perhaps more complicated terms, my biggest task is to make sure that his subjective intentions are delivered through me and through sound in an objective manner. When this goes wrong, when his intentions are delivered subjectively, the commercial audience may experience confusion as to how they are supposed to understand a given point. The thing about sound is that, because it is emotions being delivered through sound, sometimes the listener may receive it in a way that has nothing to do with the creator's original intentions. When this happens, the audience may not be able to hear the dialogue at certain points, or question why the movie is unfolding the way it is, or mistakenly assume that some sort of technical error has occurred. That's the hardest part.

When you worked on *Okja*, I heard that Director Bong sent you some material about the film over [South Korean mobile messaging app] KakaoTalk, even before starting preproduction. I'm curious, not just for *Okja* but for other films as well, what kind of materials he sends you in these early stages.

He started doing that even for *The Host*. He made a model of the creature, and he gave me the script with the model and urged me to start thinking about it early on. With *Okja*, even before he wrote the script, Director Bong produced a film called *Sea Fog* [*Image top left*]. On the first day of shooting for *Sea Fog*, I visited the set, since it was a film he was producing, and he called me over and started showing me strange pictures of some pig creature. At first, I thought it was some comic strip, or an animated movie, but no, he told me it was Okja. He told me that this was the next movie he was going to do, and that he wanted me to see the model and start thinking about what this creature would sound like. That was two years before shooting for *Okja* began. After producing *Sea Fog*, he wrote the *Okja* script and continued to send me creature models of Okja as they were developed. Even today, after this interview, I'm seeing Director Bong.

Does Director Bong always bring you on board very early?

For sounds that don't come from everyday life, sounds that need to be newly designed, and for films that need creature sounds, Director Bong lets me know in advance so that I can prepare. I see it as a form of being considerate. It's much better than having to do things last minute, and he knows that I'm always busy. He gives me these things to think about early on so I can consider them over a long period of time and keep them with me, as a form of homework. Films where we've done that have been *The Host*, then *Snowpiercer*. With *Snowpiercer*, I knew about it around the time we finished *The Host* and before we started working on *Mother*. He told me he was going to be doing a movie about a

train, and asked me to start thinking about it. And of course with *Okja*, and now, up through his upcoming film, we've continued this sort of exchange.

What kind of work did you do to create the sounds for *The Host*? In the case of the creature, it's not really the Godzilla kind of sound that we've heard in the past.

For the monster in *The Host*, we started by using dog sounds in our design. If a dog makes [*growling noises*], we would turn that into [*creature noises*], like so. But once we actually tried pairing those sounds with the monster, they didn't match up. Why? Because dogs are mammals, and they live exclusively on land, while the monster goes in and out of water, and is something that is not quite a reptile. So that was something of a failure. Then we turned to sea lion sounds as the base for the audio design. When you design with these animal sounds, the easy parts are the general things like the creature's breathing [*monster breathing noises*], or its attack sounds [*monster attack noises*]. For the attack sounds, because we needed higher pitches we used pig [*squealing noises*] and monkey [*screeching noises*] sounds, and then pitched them higher, creating three or four layers within the design. However, there were elements where the animal sounds weren't enough. First, when the monster is sleeping and snoring [*snoring noises*]. It's seen snoring in the movie, before Hyun-seo runs away, when she's trapped. But we can't tell a sea lion, "Hey, you, start snoring." There was no way we could convey that snoring sound with an animal. One of the most difficult tasks Director Bong gave me for *The Host* was that he wanted the monster to be saying something as it is burning to death. I asked him what he wanted the monster to say, and Bong said—he actually swore as he was telling me—"You fuckers! I'm a victim too, of your toxic waste!" And of course, we couldn't get animals to say those things.

Bong wanted this subjective emotion and intention, of feeling wronged, to be delivered through the voice of the monster as it burned to death. This was an issue that just couldn't be solved with animal sounds. Coincidentally, while I was working on *The Host*, a movie came out called *King Kong* [*Image left*], by New Zealand Director Peter Jackson. I looked up how they did the sound for that movie, and I found out that in the scenes where King Kong had to communicate with people, like his breathing or when a certain emotion needed to be conveyed, they used an actor—Andy Serkis, who was also Gollum [*Image left*] in *Lord of the Rings*—as well as dubbing techniques to design the sound. I told Director Bong that we should borrow this idea, to use a person's voice, and I asked him to find the best actor to play the monster's voice. He enlisted actor Oh Dal-soo. Mr. Oh saw the material beforehand—this is before MOVs [digital video file] existed, so we gave him the material on VHS tapes—and practiced, and came in to record. But the first day was a flop. Why? Because Mr. Oh was going [*monster screeching noises*] for thirty minutes, and his throat went hoarse. After two or three days, when Mr. Oh had recovered a bit, he came back, and you know the scene where the creature eats people and spits out the bones? This vomiting is also impossible to capture with animal sounds. So Mr. Oh would go [*vomiting noises*], and we used that to design the sound. And then Mr. Oh made snoring noises [*snoring noises*], and we pitched that down to [*low snoring noises*]. For the climax, when the monster is burning and falling over, Mr. Oh did [*high screeching noise*], and we took that, pitched it down, and morphed on animal sounds to create [*monster screeching noise*] as it died. Bong really liked that. So when the creature is expressing an emotion, you need a human voice.

And with Okja, I understand that it was the voice of actress Lee Jung-eun.

Okja was different yet again. We could've gone with another male voice, but Director Bong said, "Okja is female, a very introverted character, and shy." So I thought, "Geez, how do you express that an animal is introverted and shy?" In *Okja*, a moment toward the beginning that showcases her feminine and shy nature is when Mija is picking up the fallen persimmons, and Okja comes down the slope, and Mija washes the persimmons in the stream. Then Okja slides up asking for one, but Mija says, "You already had some," and pushes her back. So Okja makes this upset sound [*whining noise*] and turns away. This is the first moment when we needed to convey that Okja is not a strong, fierce pig, but is really a shy, feminine, and introverted creature. When we were doing the sound design for *Okja*, we collaborated with Dave Whitehead, who is based in New Zealand, and he used pig sounds from the native Kunekune pig, which only lives in New Zealand, to create Okja's sound base. Then we worked with Lee Jung-eun to dub her voice on top. So Lee Jung-eun would make sounds like [*pig noises*], and we recorded those, morphed them, and mixed them. One point where Lee's voice is prominent is that moment, when Mija says, "No, you already had some," and Okja makes the [*whining noise*] and turns away. It was all using Lee's voice.

When constructing the soundscape for a film, how much of that construction is collaborative, and how much has Bong already determined in his mind?
For every project, Director Bong talks to me about the sound design in general, which is something that's different from other directors. Most directors tend to go scene by scene, cut to cut, with specific instructions. But Director Bong doesn't really go over things meticulously like that. He only talks about the points that he absolutely wants to come out a certain way. For example, with *Parasite*, the door sounds in the Parks' house—he was telling me that because it's a very wealthy family's house, it has a lot of doors: the main door; a middle door; a door leading to the basement; and the doors to each person's living space. And so the sounds of the doors were important, as well as the iron gate, the first door to that house. There had to be a gravitas to the sound of it opening. He picks out these specific points where he has a clear vision of what he wants and relays them to me. In *Mother*, when Kim Hye-ja is chopping herbs [*slicing noises*], the feeling of that slicing, that it could serve as a foreshadowing for the climactic tragedy of the film . . . a tense or brutal slicing sound would work well. He only tells me when he has these specific sounds in mind, and the rest is just up to me, whatever I want. And then, during final mixing, he listens from the audience's perspective, and if he comes up with a new idea, he lets me know. I'm not sure about when he's shooting, but for sound, he doesn't really plan everything in advance and adhere to those ideas, but rather focuses on the basic strategy. For example, to use a soccer metaphor, he would say to me, "Okay Choi, you're the striker for this match, so you do everything you have to to score, and just make sure you're covering this point, that point, and this other point. Everything else, just have fun." So all I have to do is win. What this makes me feel is that I'm not a hired mixer or supervisor, but more that I have the ability to think about and add to many elements of this movie, just as the director does. And he is able to accept my ideas and contributions. A lot of people refer to him as "Bongtail" ("Bong" plus "detail"), but in my experience, with sound, he's really quite lax. But because he gives total responsibility to the staff member in charge, that person becomes detail-oriented in order to fulfill that responsibility. I become meticulous. So I think it might be this detail, together with Director Bong's detail, that becomes the completed Bongtail. Does that make sense?

Of Director Bong's films, *Memories of Murder* is the only period piece, and I wanted to know how you constructed the sounds of that era, and if you ran into any special difficulties in doing so.
So it was around 2001, 2002, when we did *Memories of Murder*. The backdrop for the film, though, is the '80s in Korea, and the car that Song Kang-ho drives in the movie was a Daewoo car [*Image bottom left*]—now defunct—called the Maepsy-Na. We didn't have the sounds for that car in our library, and using a 2000s car to imitate those sounds would have been faking it. So we actually rented that car. The way we did it was, there is a company that has all the actual cars you see in Korean period films, and they lend them out for shooting. We received some assistance from them, and used the same model of the car we used for filming to create the sounds—the engine, the opening and closing of doors, etc.—for that car. With *Memories of Murder*, the biggest challenges related to reconstructing the sounds of that era had to do with vehicles: the buses back then; the cars; the police cars; and those engine sounds. We recorded these, and our library also did have a significant number of old car sounds—'80s cars like Toyotas, CBs, etc. We mixed these together to create this period piece. The second era-related challenge was reproducing the ambient sounds, the sounds of the neighborhoods at that time. Back then, they had things like tofu salesmen, who went around selling

tofu with that [*ding-a-ling*] bell sound. To express those sounds, we utilized some dubbing methods. The big era-relevant issues were the ambient and vehicle sounds, but we found our way through them, and with the rest of the sound, like the dialogue and whatnot, we didn't really need to fit them to the historical setting. I think the feelings of the sounds in that era—like [*growing siren sounds*], are the most needed elements in period pieces.

On the other side of the spectrum, there's the sci-fi, dystopian film that is *Snowpiercer*. How did you construct the sound for a world that doesn't yet exist? Did you have to invent any new sounds? I'm also curious what your approach was for the fact that the characters are always inside of a train.

The biggest mission for *Snowpiercer* was to express how the sound of the train changes as the movie progresses, from the rearmost compartment all the way to the engine room [*Image above left*]. In the tail compartment, because the inhabitants are the lowest classes, it's almost like a cargo hold—very noisy. As you go further up, in the middle, the train sound becomes like the KTX, or the French TGV high-speed rails. Later, in the engine room, the noise drops down to almost nonexistent, like an aircraft. You just hear the sounds of the ventilation. So we needed a very large array of different train sounds. But to design those sounds, we needed to first record actual train sounds. I contacted Korail, which is the Korea Railroad Corporation, managing all the railroads in Korea, and sent an email to their PR team. "Hello, my name is Tae-young Choi, and I am the sound director for Director Bong Joon Ho. As Director Bong's upcoming movie is about a train, we would like to rent a train and use some train tracks for audio recording—we request your collaboration." Three months, no reply. For them, it was probably strange. How can you lend a public train to a private endeavor? So that was a dead end. But I'm also close to the head of BOOM Library in Germany, so I sent him an email. "Hey, Pierre. How have you been? I need some train sounds for an upcoming project. Could you record some train sounds in Europe and send them to me? What's the estimate?" He said forty thousand dollars, but I only had twenty thousand. So I told him, "My budget is only twenty thousand. Is there a way we can find a solution within that?" And he said, "Alright, then we'll get those sounds and sell them to you through our library. You can use them, but don't re-sell them." So basically, it was like I paid them the manufacturing expenses for material to go in their library. After that, BOOM Library made an entire train sound effect library thanks to *Snowpiercer*. They toured around Europe for close to a month collecting train sounds, starting with cargo compartments, to the high-speed TGV, all kinds. And in the Czech Republic or Romania or some other Eastern European country, they found a seventeen-kilometer-long stretch of private train tracks. So they brought a train over there and recorded all kinds of sounds, since they had a lot of freedom on those tracks.

The second thing was the engine room, and the director's request here was that the engine sound should have an emotion in it, like with *The Host*. That it's not just a mechanical sound, but that there's something in it that gives it the impression of being alive. To give this impression of life, if you look at the first scene in the movie, in the car, and it's shaking, and the train goes by [*whoosh*] and there we put in animal sounds—lion and monkey sounds. So when people hear that, there are animal sounds in it. It's one of the best tricks to make them think that there's some kind of life there. For the engine room, we mixed choir voices [*high and low singing voices*] to create the sound.

To me, out of Director Bong's films, the sound seems the most prominent in *Mother*, or at least that film seems the least reliant on the score.

Mother was a movie I worked really hard on. The sound for *Mother* was very difficult—I actually find films like *Okja* or *Snowpiercer* easier, because those mostly follow a formula. Hollywood blockbuster films move within a pretty defined formula, and they're predictable, with small modifications here and there, so those are easier. But *Mother* is totally raw. Raw sound. Raw sound means real sound. And it's so difficult to deliver an emotion to the audience with actual, real sound, because it's objective sound. In sound, we categorize sound in diegetic and nondiegetic—actual sound and commentary sound. In *Mother*, most

of the sounds are those done by Foley artists. Generally, in Hollywood or other movies, they put in sounds like *bam, fwoom, hiss, whoosh* that are called imaging sound effects. But with this movie, you can't put in any of those sounds, and the director absolutely hates those sounds. He truly abhors those artificial sounds. Because we had to design using all actual, real sounds, it was all Foley, and even with Foley, if we didn't get the sound texture we wanted in the indoor booths, we went outside and collected real footsteps and things like that. If you look at the scene in *Mother* with Kim Hye-ja and those kids in the abandoned amusement park getting beat up, to get a realistic reproduction of the Foley sounds for that scene, we actually went to a defunct amusement park in the country and collected sounds from that same kind of ride. So in *Mother*, I think the score has this function of emotional storytelling for the audience, and the rest of the sounds, like dialogue and the Foley and effects and ambience, are logical sounds. They deliver the logical storytelling through sound.

The ideal film sound would be to have a good balance of this kind of emotional and logical storytelling, and *Mother* doesn't really have that kind of a score, so the audience has to imagine the emotion through the real sound. Listening to the real sound, the audience has to feel, "Wow, this is so scary," or, "Wow, this part is tense." After Kim Hye-ja hits the old man over the head and kills him and then comes to her senses, if she were to hear those real sounds when she was cleaning up, that would signify that she was not panicking, because what happens when we're in a state of panic? Normally, we hear that high-pitched noise in our ears and all those psychological sounds just fly right out of our brains. We call that the cocktail party effect. When we go to a club, and we meet someone we like and we're talking to them, all the music and the conversations around just kind of fade away. But then, if that person swears at us, or they say something that's a turn-off, then suddenly the music and the ambient sounds rise up and we can't hear what that person is saying anymore. In the moment with Kim Hye-ja, all the sounds disappear for her because of the fear and horror she feels at what she's done.

Mother adopted—even more than *Memories of Murder*—an unfriendly, writer-centric sound design. All the footsteps, the ambient sounds, every tiny sound that I put in, there was nothing to mask those sounds. And since there was nothing to mask bad sounds, every single sound was important and had to be great quality. That was really difficult. Not much music, and within that sparse music, the sound elements had to deliver the director's intent to the audience, and all the sounds that the characters were experiencing had to be expressed with actual sounds. Those were difficult tasks—and that's also why I really like the sound in *Mother*.

You mentioned previously that sometimes you disagree with Bong's choices; do you have a particular memory of a scene where you didn't understand his intent at first, but then got it during the technical screening?

Yes. There was a scene in *Memories of Murder* over which I actually got into a fight with Bong. I was yelling at him, "I can't do it. You do it. Here's the phaser. You do it. Show me." So what it was, if you look in *Memories of Murder*, it's raining, and there's a police outpost on this isolated path in the forest, and two high school girls walk in. They're wondering how they're going to get home, and the policeman tells them to go after the rain has stopped, and he turns on some music. Shin Joong Hyun's "The Woman in the Rain" [*Image above left*] starts playing on the radio. So it starts off by coming through the radio filter sound, and one of the girls says that she's leaving. The rain is pouring, and we hear [*sings "The Woman in the Rain"*], and the sound is released from the radio filter and comes through as the score. Then we see one of the suspects looking down from a little outcrop in the middle of the mountain, watching the girl go by. It was here I was told that the music director's score [*low growling sound*] has to come through simultaneously.

Up until then I'd never done simultaneous mixing. So at first, in the premixing, I mixed it so that the licensed music played until the score music came in, and the licensed music faded away into a smooth crossover. But Director Bong came in during final mixing and told me, "Oh, this isn't right. These two have to go together, in parallel." What? Parallel? So for me, for the audience, are they supposed to follow the score music, or the licensed music? That was confusing for me. So I put the balance on the score music, and laid the licensed music under. But that wasn't what he wanted either. Then I tried the opposite, which was wrong, too. Where do I put the balance? I was thinking objectively. Then Director Bong told me to just try it the way I felt it, but I was already closed off from that kind of emotional experience because I was so pissed. He was asking me to do something I'd never done, some weird circus thing, and I lost control of my feelings and lost my temper, and started arguing with him: "I can't do it. You come here and do it." And even then, this guy never gets upset: "Come on, I know you can do it. Just give it a shot." So I came to my senses, and he told me, "Just try doing it the way you feel it." And so I opened my heart, calmed down, and gave up trying to use the physical ears attached to my head, and opened the ears in my heart. I thought about how to express this suspense and tension, how to put the emphasis on not the suspect but the high school girl. And so I tried to balance the two sounds and gave it three or four tries. And Director Bong says, "That's it!" But honestly, I was still like, "That's it?" I wasn't confident in it. Then I went to the tech screening. Watching it then, I understood what the director had been asking for. After that, I used this a lot in other movies too, and other directors would be like, "[*shocked noise*] This is incredible!" and flip out. I learned from Director Bong that you can listen to the sound of a film not only with your ears, but also with your heart.

The "Belt of Faith" sequence in *Parasite* feels almost like an eight-minute separate, independent chapter, and I'm very curious about the sound in that sequence. Which sounds you wanted to have stand out, and what you did to preserve the consistency of the sound even as the characters are moving around?

That was the hardest sequence in *Parasite*. The other sequences didn't need director confirmation. It was just, "It's good. It's good." Normally we get the final mixing done really quickly. Director Bong will come around one o'clock, and we mix reel by reel, in twenty- or thirty-minute increments. We generally get through a volume in an hour.

But the part I spent the most time mixing with Bong in *Parasite* was that "Belt of Faith" sequence. During pre-mixing, I went really safe with this part. I made it so that the audience would hear the dialogue clearly. This is the safest bet, and the easiest to mix, from my point of view. But Bong thought that, while the dialogue was important, the music was also important, so the dialogue should be delivered clearly, but the musical balance, the volume balance, should have these ups and downs, like a wave, so we also experience the damping effect of the music. Of course, these ups and downs, these waves, will have depths. I would think, "About this much depth is fine," but the director would think, "Let's go a bit farther." Regarding the exact depth, I can't know what Director Bong is thinking, since I'm not inside his head, so we went through numerous tries, and he would listen, and say, "Let's have a little more depth here or here." And then he would listen again, and say, "Let's have this much depth here." That process of fine-tuning was very difficult. I would say things like, "Director, in this scene here, if we go with your depth, the audience might have trouble hearing the dialogue, maybe we could widen this part a bit?" It was like a tuning process. I think we spent about forty minutes on this. It's unthinkable that Bong and I would spend forty minutes on one scene.

Before the release, after the tech screening, we have a press screening. On the day of this press screening, we had actually gotten back from the Cannes Film Festival the day before, and Bong was nervous about the condition of the theater. We were holding the press screening at the CGV in Yongsan, and he asked me if I could come in early in the morning. I said okay. He and I went around the whole theater, checking the sound and the conditions, but of course we can't check everything, so he designated a point to check, and that point was the "Belt of Faith" sequence. He felt that if he heard the "belt of faith" sequence, he would know the condition of the entire movie. The first reference point that he placed in regards to the condition of the theater was for *Barking Dogs Never Bite*. In that, in the beginning, there's a dog barking sound [*barking noise*]. If you listen to this on stereo, you hear it from left and right, but back then we mixed it on a 5.1 channel, and generally the condition of Korean theaters really wasn't that good, so the director asked me to play the sound from each speaker to make sure they were functioning properly. I said, "Are you serious?", and he said, "Yeah." So I made the sound go [*woof*] from the left, and [*woof woof*] from the right surround, and then again [*woof*] from this surround speaker. In *Okja* you hear bell sounds, and in *Parasite* you hear bell sounds. So these bell sounds are those references, to check that the speakers are working properly in a theater. People ask me, "What is the significance of those bell sounds?" "Oh, they're just something Director Bong asked me to put in so he could check the 5.1 channel speakers in a theater." And they don't believe me. He can be quirky like that.

YANG JINMO

Film Editor

Collaborations

Snowpiercer
Okja
Parasite

Editor Yang Jinmo first worked with Bong as the on-set editor (a practice in which an editor cuts together footage on set before the dailies are sent to the in-studio editor) for *Snowpiercer* (2013), and has since also worked on *Okja* (2017) and *Parasite* (2019), the latter of which would win him an American Cinema Editors Award for Best Edited Feature Film (making *Parasite* the first non-English-language film to win the top prize at the American Cinema Editors' Eddie Awards, in a neat dovetail with its Best Picture win) as well as garner a nomination for the Academy Award for Best Editing. His other work includes both *Train to Busan* (2016) and its sequel *Peninsula* (2020), *The Age of Shadows* (2016), and the series *Hellbound* (2021).

I read that you first met Bong at the wrap party for *The Host* and then later had dinner together. Do you remember what you talked about on either occasion?
I had just participated in my first film, called *Duelist* [*Image next page*], with Director Lee Myung-se, and there's also this Director, Yim Pil-sung, who I'm good friends with. I hung out with him a lot, and somehow found myself at the wrap party for *The Host*. We went for an after-after-party meal to sober up at a place that does soy sauce-marinated crab. Director Bong probably thought of me as a film enthusiast, just starting to work on movies. And he probably doesn't remember this, but I'm actually allergic to crab. But this place only serves soy sauce crab, so we ordered that, and the situation is I'm sitting in front of this director that I respect enormously, and you know how Korean culture is, I couldn't really say, "I'm allergic so I'll just order something else."

Right.
So I forced myself to eat it, and that's why that moment is stuck in my head. Of course, even then I remember thinking, "I really want to work on a film with a director like this." But never did I dream that that our first encounter would be so strange.

Were you okay eating the crab?
My mouth was totally swollen, and my throat.

Were you pretending that you were okay in the moment?
Yeah, like I was totally okay, when in reality, my lips were twice their usual size.

You were the on-set editor for *Snowpiercer* and *Okja*. On-set editors are not really common practice outside of Korea, and both of those films were co-productions. What was it like being on set for these films?
The situations were a little different between *Snowpiercer* and *Okja*. For *Okja*, I only did the on-set editing for the US and Canada parts, and did the main editing for the rest. *Snowpiercer* was my first time working with Director Bong, and I did the on-set editing and some VFX editing. I wasn't the main editor.

How did you come to work on *Snowpiercer*?
It was through the introduction of DP Hong Kyung Pyo, who was the DP for

Parasite as well. The reason I was picked as on-set editor was that I have a certain proficiency in English, and this was a movie with heavy VFX elements. Since college, I've been interested in VFX, and am familiar with programs for manipulating or compositing images, and with green screen removal. One of the really big perks of on-set editing is that we were all basically sharing our lives while doing *Snowpiercer*, so there were a lot of opportunities to communicate with the actors and also to observe everything that Director Bong was doing. With several months of this shared experience, we got close on a personal as well as a professional level. This continued into *Okja*, which is also very VFX–heavy. One reason Director Bong entrusted me with the editing as well is, I think, because I can mock up things like the VFX shots a bit quicker on set, so we're able to cut down on a lot of prep time once shooting is over and we start work in the studio.

Is it usually the case that the on-set editor is able to do VFX editing?
No, not really. But in my opinion, you need a weapon to stand out and I thought that VFX would be a way for me to differentiate myself from other on-set editors. So that's part of what I provide for Bong.

Bong is a very meticulous storyboarder, so he tends to know how he wants things to look. In your experience on set on *Snowpiercer* or *Okja*, were there ever moments where the onset editing ended up changing how something was shot or presented?
It's true that Director Bong is very detailed with his storyboarding, but the situation in the field is always somewhat different, and sometimes the project needs to move faster than anticipated. For example, he might have imagined four scenes, four cuts, from his storyboard, but logistical limitations only allow for two. So he would ask me, "Hey, these cuts might not be critical, can you connect these and see if we really don't need them?" Then I would do a quick edit and let him know, "Director, I don't think we absolutely need those scenes, we can just go to the next cut." These changes happen relatively often.

You mentioned that you were surprised that you got brought on in a bigger role in *Okja* after having worked on *Snowpiercer*. When did Bong first approach you about the film?
I was working on *Train to Busan* [*Image opposite page*] at the time and even then I wasn't really . . . how to put it . . . a hotshot editor or anything. I had good relationships with several great directors through working together on set, but I didn't really have the visibility for a big project like *Okja*. But I had some English skills, and I had worked on CGI–heavy films since *Snowpiercer*. I had also won a prize at the BlueDragon Awards for *Beauty Inside*, my first commercial movie where I was the main editor, and Bong was headhunting for *Okja* at the time. I was at the awards ceremony, and Bong sent me a really touching video message. And it really hit me then, for the first time, that I was going to be working with him as a main editor.

How much were you involved with the CGI for *Okja*? Because again, it's a very CGI–heavy film.
For *Okja*, my editing team did the VFX editing as well. The timeline for editing was much longer than for other movies. A lot of the acting was done by an actor wearing an Okja mask, and that had to be integrated into the editing, but it was really very difficult to know how that was going to turn out. There were a lot of moments that were fully VFX as well. So we did the dramatic editing, and then the CGI editing, but that wasn't the end, because then the CGI team would do some rough animating and send it back to us, and then we made our adjustments. And later, once we had something close to a final–quality rendering, we had to adjust again, like making cuts to the frames based on what the VFX team gives us.

So there was a lot of back–and–forth?
When we were doing the editing, the VFX producer and the post supervisor would pretty much just come to work at our studio. Then when the editing was done, they would check it, and redistribute the EDLs [edit decision lists] to the CGI teams. On some days, before starting the day's editing, we did a VFX review, where we would take a look at the stuff the vendors sent us and talk about it. All of this happened in our editing studio.

There is one scene in particular that I wanted to talk about in *Okja*, which is the big car chase when Okja's being taken away and Mija follows her from the Mirando building to street level, and then to the underground subway. Could you tell me a little bit about editing this sequence?

For the action scenes, the animatics are very precise. The action sequences are constructed really well, so the critical thing for those scenes was to tighten up the pacing in editing. We looked at the scenes frame by frame and really tried to eliminate anything unnecessary to maximize that feeling of speed.

Does that mean that it's harder to edit the quieter moments in the film?

I'm so used to editing those quiet moments that I don't really find them too difficult. But the hardest scenes, when I'm editing, are the conversations. With Director Bong, he at least introduces some variation like camera blocking, so they're interesting. But for a lot of the movies I've done, the most challenging moments are typically a scene where people are sitting around a dining room table, eating and having a conversation. As an editor, those are, in a way, the simplest scenes, but also the hardest.

When were you first approached about *Parasite*?

With *Parasite*, it was a really seamless transition, just like, yeah, we're doing the next movie. But the mindset going into it was a bit different, because with the films I'd done with Bong before, like *Snowpiercer* or *Okja*, these were global projects, with a bigger budget, and there's some pressure associated with the fact that the films are in English. But with *Parasite*, Director Bong, when he was first talking to me about it, said, "Now we can do whatever we want, and we don't have to worry about our English."

With *Okja*, Director Bong had had these worries that we wouldn't be able to do what we wanted with the editing, because there was so much CGI. So there wasn't really room for any artistry in the editing because if we tried to implement any big changes, that would affect the CGI, and then the CGI timeline collapses. *Parasite* was kind of a project for us to blow off some steam, where we could do whatever we wanted. We could try different things with the editing, take bolder chances. That's what Bong said: "Let's go Korean on this one. This is one we can have fun on." Which is why no one knew this would be such a hit with foreign audiences.

Is there any specific technique or a scene that you can call out as an example of trying something new or different?

With *Parasite*, Bong went with bold edits, and I provided a lot of technical tricks. For instance, there's the scene when Geun-sae, played by Park Myung-hoon, hooks Ki-woo with the rope and fastens the end to the metal pipes. The camera was supposed to follow the action through to the moment when the end is fastened. But in the shot, the camera didn't catch that moment. So Director Bong looked for a better take, but there wasn't one. There was a take, however, where that area was in focus, although the timing was wrong, so we just inserted that one frame, since it was such a fast cut. It wasn't a CGI thing, just an editing trick. There's also the scene when Ki-taek's family is partying and they're making a mess, and they eat dog treats, and then Moon-gwang comes back. So there's a wide shot when she rings the bell, when everybody freezes. Immediately before that is a close-up of Ki-jung, eating the dog snack. But in the wide shot, the jerky is in the wrong hand! I said that, with the doorbell ringing, everyone's going to be looking in the direction of the door. Nobody's going to know which hand Ki-jung was using. So we just kept it in, as sort of an Easter egg. Also, with the sequence in which they're making the jjapaguri, there's actually a big difference between the speed at which the scene was shot and how it's edited—you need the editing to give a feeling of speed, even though the acting wasn't that fast. So we divided the screen and had the hand come in fast, and stitched some parts together, to cut down on the time. A lot of that was done through editing, to compress the tempo a bit.

How long have you been using this technique of stitching together shots to make one shot?

For a long time! I'd heard it had been used in David Fincher's *The Social Network* [*Image next page*] and *Panic Room*. For example, after shooting an over-the-shoulder shot, if you split the screen, sometimes the timing is off with one side talking and then the next. I read that they stitched those parts together to create more of a rhythm. I was inspired by that and then I used it in our movie as if I'd invented it! For example, in the scene when Ki–woo is teaching Ki–taek to act, we would want to go with the first take for Ki–taek, and we would want the third take for Ki–woo because they each have different nuances, so we stitched them together so it looks like one continued take.

Can you talk a little bit more about the rhythm of the shots?

Generally, I think the length of Bong's shots are getting shorter and shorter. You know virtuoso directors, they have a tendency of just letting shots play out. Director Bong finds a good mix of both. With some shots, he immerses us, but with other parts he can't stand the laxness of even just a couple frames. They need to be weeded out.

I read in a previous interview with you that there's generally a little less wiggle room when it comes to working on Bong's films because he has a very clear vision. Has there ever been a moment where you have butted heads on how something should be edited?

Almost never. I see my role as someone who takes the director's vision and makes it a reality with the least amount of stress possible. Sometimes there can be friction between a producer and the director about a certain edit, but with Director Bong, since he is the producer and the director, those conflicts don't really come up. The more I work with him, the more time I invest in enhancing the sequences that he wants.

Bong is known for not shooting coverage or masters. How does that affect your editing process?

There are times when Bong will come to the editing studio and we'll be editing a scene and he'll kind of confess, "I didn't shoot this because I didn't know we would need it." He'll ask me to just make it look natural, and I look for ways to do that. But really needing a certain insert and having to use something else because we don't have it, that kind of mistake hardly ever happens. I think that's one of the advantages of the on-set editing system. If we were going to need a shot that badly, we would've known during the on-set editing.

Sometimes, I think we end up with something interesting because we don't have those. So if we were to shoot all the inserts and the coverage, like they do in the US, of course we would use them, since we probably have plenty of footage for scene changes and the like. But if we imagine that we don't have them, sometimes we actually get a really good edit by smashing together the sequence after and the sequence before. A great example is in *Parasite* when Ki–woo is introducing Ki–jung to the Parks. After that scene, there was a scene where the whole Kim family goes to the salon. Since they need to make Ki–jung-as-Jessica look presentable, there's a sequence in the salon with the family talking about how to convincingly act like Jessica. That sequence got taken out. In the context of the movie, it was quite long as well. But now, looking at the finished product, right after he says, "An English teacher I know—Jessica," Jessica is, unbelievably, already in front of the house with Ki–woo, and they press the doorbell. This end product was not the original plan, but made in the editing studio because that middle sequence was cut, and we just pasted the following scene in on the heels of the previous one. I think that actually led to a more interesting product.

Lastly, I also wanted to ask, I know that you mentioned that overall the editor's job is to assist the vision of the director, but is there a particular scene in the three movies that you've worked on with Bong that you feel the most proud of, or you feel is demonstrative of your touch?

A lot of times Director Bong leaves the montage sequences up to the rhythm of the editor. With *Parasite*, it's the most famous "Belt of Faith" sequence. I think that has to be a signature scene for me as an editor—and it was also one I had a lot of fun editing. For that, the director doesn't really talk to me about this shot or that shot, but I just fit it to the reference music that I have, and create the montage based on my instincts. Which is why, I think, it was the most satisfying, and more so after seeing the audience's reactions to it. Where was it . . . Los Angeles, I think? We did a screening of *Parasite* with music director Jung Jaeil playing the piano, and that sequence got a standing ovation.

TILDA SWINTON

Actor

Collaborations

Snowpiercer

Okja

Since first appearing in Derek Jarman's *Caravaggio* in 1986, Tilda Swinton has established herself as one of the most brilliant and chameleonic actors of our time, amassing a prolific and widely varied body of work as well as the accolades to match—an Academy Award and a BAFTA for her performance in *Michael Clayton* (2007), a 2013 tribute from the Museum of Modern Art, a spot on the *New York Times* list of the greatest actors of the twenty-first century, and the 2020 British Film Institute Fellowship. Among her most memorable roles are two collaborations (three, if you're counting characters) with Bong—the harpy-like Minister Mason in *Snowpiercer* (2014), and the diametrically opposed twins Lucy and Nancy Mirando in *Okja* (2017), all three ghoulish but still, in a testament to Swinton's skill, strangely sympathetic.

Do you recall what the first Bong movie you ever saw was?

I remember very, very well. It was *The Host*, and it was because . . . Well, I probably would have found it anyway fairly soon, but I had just flown into New York and I went to have breakfast with a friend of mine. I went to the bathroom and I was waiting in this little sort of corridor outside the bathroom in this little café in the East Village. And there was a *New Yorker* magazine lying there, and it was open on a review of *The Host* that made me want to go and see the film that afternoon, which I did. I remember this beautiful graphic—there was a beautiful illustration of the tentacles of the creature coming out. Anyway, that was my sort of conduit—the messenger that got me into the cinema—and it completely blew me away, of course. Then I just basically watched everything I could. I went full throttle and found everything fairly fast. I even managed to find *Barking Dogs Never Bite*, which Director Bong is very coy about. I don't know whether he's coy about the film, but he's very coy about anybody saying that they've seen the film. I'm a big supporter of the film. But I sort of overdosed on everything I could find. And then I met him in Cannes—I'm very, very bad at dates, so I'd have to look up when it was. I think he was there with *Mother*, or maybe on the jury? [Ed. note: In 2011, Bong was the head of the jury for the Caméra d'Or prize.] I was there for *We Need to Talk About Kevin*. He was on what I call the jury next door, and we had breakfast together.

Can I pick up on the point where you say Bong is very coy about *Barking Dogs Never Bite*? I feel like every interview he's done where he's mentioned it, he says, "Please don't go watch it, it's very stupid!" Have you talked to him about the film?

I know! Which makes us all want to see it even more! But it's true. I don't know if it's because he made it before he had his own dog, or came to know my dogs, but he's definitely very coy about it. Sheepish, even.

Do you recall what you first talked about when you got breakfast at Cannes, when you first met?

I think we certainly spent quite a long time talking about the breakfast, ordering the

food. We just immediately fell in step. We just liked each other there and then. It helped, of course, that I loved his work so much, but he was so exactly what I hoped he'd be. He was companionable and witty and curious—full of glee and mischief. We just became very close friends that very day. And he was preparing *Snowpiercer*, but quite quickly he said to me, "There's really nothing in *Snowpiercer* for you." He talked to me for about fifty minutes about whether or not I should play Claude. He asked me for a while about Claude, after we left Cannes. He kept asking me and I said, "You know what, I'm really longing to work with you, but it's not that." And then he went quiet for a few weeks. And then one day he wrote to me . . . No, I think he'd already sent me the script, just for my interest, and I'd read it and found it fascinating. And he said, "You know Minister Mason, who's described as the mild-mannered man in the suit—what d'you think about that?" And we just started to make mud pies together.

Did he ever tell you why he thought of that part for you?

No! I wish you'd ask him! No, I don't, I really don't. I've no idea.

I find it so funny that the character's original description is of a mild-mannered man in a suit, because in the film, the character is, at least aesthetically, kind of the furthest thing from that. I want to start with Mason's nose, which you've said was something you've wanted to do for a while with a character. What was the genesis of that desire?

This was the very early steps down this amazing road of working with my colleague. I think, God knows, maybe even at that first breakfast, I said I've always wanted to play a character where their nose is up like that [*pushes nose up with her thumb*]. I just personally think it's funny, and clearly you do too. And you could do it very simply and cheaply—you just need a piece of sellotape to just put your nose up like that. It does something very interesting to your mouth; it makes your eyebrows go up. The whole attitude of the character just suddenly appears. I think I already mentioned that, in theory, before the Mason idea came up—and I think he said, "Well, what would you do with that mild-mannered man in the suit?" And I said, "Well, first of all I'd do that nose!" I think, in fact I know, that the next step was, he came to Nairn, in Scotland, with [longtime producing partner] Dooho [Choi] and my great friend [costume designer] Catherine George [*Image left*]. Anyway, they came to Scotland, and I picked them up from the airport. I don't think they stayed the night that time, but they've stayed many times since. We just decided we were going to play with the character; to find Mason. I remember putting a whole bunch of dressing-up clothes in our drawing room. Catherine had brought all sorts of things as well. One of the first things I did was get the sellotape and put my nose up. And we just played like a bunch of six-year-olds, really—dressing me up. There was one photograph that Director Bong had produced, which was a photograph that he'd found of a woman who we called the "Parrot Lady." I've no idea who she was. She just looked like a parrot. She was a more naturalistic version of Mason. Mason was an extreme, [Hayao] Miyazaki version of this woman. She was sort of the first indication. She was slightly hunched, wearing a uniform of some kind. I can't really remember—she was a librarian or something. And there was something about her hair, which was cut like that. But then we just took it to the psychedelic level, and we realized we needed to have a fake wig. We didn't want her to look naturalistic at all. And we started putting uniforms on me and ribbons, and the idea of all the fake medals. This whole thing took about an hour, and I know that because I had a pie in the oven. I said, "Okay, I'm putting the pie in the oven and when it's ready then we'll eat lunch." And by the time the pie was ready we'd kind of got it.

That's incredible. Did you develop her voice during that session, or did it come later down the line?

I think it came then. This is how it works with Director Bong. He's so encouraging and welcoming of these flights of fancy. Certainly with me and Catherine, he really encourages us to just go there, and to not second-guess even the most surreal ideas, certainly in the work that I've made with him to this point. We'll have various conversations about other things that will have a slightly different caliber, which won't be so extreme or so grotesque. Because the three portraits that I've made with him so far, which are Mason and the two Mirando sisters, have been pretty out–there, pretty grotesque—and burlesque, even. So we have plans to make something more naturalistic, and maybe a little less fanning the flames. He definitely has fanned the flames so far with me.

That pretty naturally brings us to the characters of Lucy and Nancy. I understand that you were brought onto *Okja* a lot earlier than you were with *Snowpiercer*—at the point where they were still working out the script and the story. When did Bong first show you the sketch that he'd done of *Okja* or tell you what the story was going to be?
We were in Seoul for the premiere of *Snowpiercer*, and the next morning he was taking us to the airport. Someone else was driving and he was in the front seat, and he leaned over the back and showed me this little drawing. He'd made this little doodle of this little girl standing beside this big pig, and he said, "This is the next film," and I said, "What the . . . " I've mentioned Miyazaki before—one of the many strands of the bond we share is a great love of Miyazaki, in particular *My Neighbor Totoro* [*Image bottom left*], which is a sort of totemic film for both of us. Also *Spirited Away*—we love those twins, those women who start as monsters and end up as these very sympathetic characters, or godmothers rather. So this very first drawing to me indicated—not in a sort of plagiaristic way, but in a sort of reverential way—that it felt like an homage to something in Miyazaki Hayao that we loved.

On that note, the characters you're talking about, the characters of Yubaba and Zeniba, the funny thing is that they are identical, whereas with the characters of Lucy and Nancy, even though their faces are the same, their aesthetic choices are so different. Was there ever a point where you thought they'd look exactly the same, or how did you come up with their respective looks?
Our idea was that they were actually identical. They are identical, it's just that one of them has sort of let herself go, whereas the other has spent a lot of money on cosmetics and her hair and all the rest of it. But we didn't really employ much prosthetic [stuff] with Nancy, the structure of her face hasn't changed—she's just got a really difficult haircut and clothes, and maybe hasn't moisturized as much as Lucy has. The idea was they were actually almost a bit Dorian Gray [*Image next page*] that Nancy kind of came down from the attic, and Lucy was, you know, the portrait, the public face of Mirando. So in the beginning in the first section, she's wearing those training things on her teeth, and then in the next section her teeth have been all straightened and whitened.

I read that there was a specific detail that you came up with for Nancy, which was the idea of her carrying around a neck pillow all the time. Where did that come from?
I don't know, it was just one of those things. Now, of course, I see them everywhere, not just airports but everywhere you walk you see people with neck pillows. But for some reason I just thought it was very funny, and we'd never seen it in a film—just somebody walking around with a neck pillow. But I don't know. I just thought she needed to have one. There's just something slightly shameless about someone who walks around with a neck pillow, very admirable about someone who goes, "I don't care who knows I need my neck pillow when I'm on the plane or the bus or whatever." It's someone who doesn't care how it looks, so we felt that was good for her. And her clothes: The whole idea was that she was a big golfer, so she wears golf clothes, whatever those are.

You mentioned that part of Nancy's backstory is that she's a golfer. How deep do you go into creating stories for these characters? Because from what I've heard and read, Bong doesn't really give a lot of detail in terms of back story, or rather he allows the actors to run with it as opposed to spelling it out for you.
I don't know that I've ever done this, really, with anyone else. Everyone I work with I feel like we have a different set of practices and rituals. I'm not sure it's necessary or even part of the work, but we just have fun thinking about these . . . not even back stories, but these side stories, rather. We had this whole fantasy about Mason: I kept thinking what Mason's cabin might be like on the train and what she's got in there. You know, my fantasy was—because that wig

is so clearly like a hat, we didn't even glue it down, we just plonked it on my head—and so the idea was that, maybe in her cabin she's got a wig block and the hat goes on. And so, is she bald underneath? And I was trying to persuade Director Bong to let me lose the wig, for the wig to fall off at one point and you see me bald underneath, but finally we didn't do that. She does take her teeth out at one point. I also like the fantasy that, who knows whether Mason is a woman or not? I mean, I'm not really sure what Mason is. Mason could be anything. Mason could take off her breasts and hang them up on a body. We just had so much fun thinking about these strange things, and we had all these side stories for the Mirandos as well. But it's just fun. It would be perfectly easy to get the scenes without them, but it's just something that we amuse ourselves with.

That actually leads me to a quote of yours that I really love, wherein you say that you do the work before you come to set, and then you can play in that world. What else is involved in the kind of work that you do prior to filming as these characters?

As I say, the work that I've done with Bong so far have been these quite broad constructions—they're not really characters, they're not really people, they're sort of . . . put together? And so there's an element of a game about it all. I think it's possible that if we worked, as we plan to, with a different kind of caliber, it may not be like that, it may be much more interior, one may not have these kinds of silly jokes, or not to the same extent. But it's just like a sort of fancy dress costume really, just enjoying this inner pantomime of these characters, and imagining their other lives. It goes on when we're shooting as well—it's just constant silliness. But, as I say, I don't know if I've worked in that way with anyone else. It's really specific to him. And I don't know whether he works in that way with anyone else either, it just so happens that those particular characters . . . I can't think of a better way of describing working with Bong when we're shooting: He wants you to be really free. He works in this disciplined, constructed way, working with his editor beside him. He shows his cut constantly to the people that he's working with—that may sound like it would be quite constraining, but I find it very freeing because he'll say, "So this is exactly the way you left the frame in the last bit, and that next bit is the way you enter the frame." So you're free within the bit that you're just about to do, to fill it however you want. And that precision is, I find, really liberating. So that sense of play, and that sense of riffing, seems to me to be very much a part of what he's interested in. He's interested in all his comrades being very free and into it and enjoying themselves.

One other aspect of the Mirando sisters that I wanted to ask about is the voices, because that's such a clear delineation between the two of them. What were the steps leading up to saying, "This one sounds like this, and the other one sounds like this"?

Of course, we were having to differentiate them, and having made the decision that they were going to be as different as we wanted them to be, that meant their voices too. And we wanted Nancy to be very much identified with their terrible father, who we never see but we kind of feel we've seen because of Nancy, because she's so much her father's daughter, or maybe her father's son in a way. And the idea about Lucy is that she's sort of infantilized—maybe she's the younger twin. It's funny because I've got twins myself, and they're only four minutes apart, but my daughter likes to describe herself as the younger twin, and my son likes describing himself as the older twin. For some reason it's very important. My sense is that Lucy very much attaches her sense of identity to being the younger, and Nancy is the older. So there's this very disparate sense of authority. I mean, maybe there's only a few minutes between them, but Nancy took her role as CEO very seriously, and adopted this sense of being her father's daughter. And then Lucy was this younger, very modern woman, who desperately tries to be as different to Nancy as she possibly could be.

The idea of Lucy wanting to appear hip or young comes across in her color palette—she's wearing this "millennial pink" that is almost ahead of the curve.

Yeah, millennial pink and white. I love her white. We always said the dress that she does the big presentation in, she almost looks like a sort of therapist from a spa. The idea of her wearing spa gear was very important.

Is it true that your son's Springer Spaniel served as inspiration for Okja?
Yes. Director Bong met Rosie, who is the matriarch—we have a dynasty of five now but she was the first, she's the grandmother. And he first met her when he came to work with me on Mason, and loves her. I mean, she's a pretty loveable animal. So when we started talking about Okja we talked a lot about, "Who is this creature?" In the very early days she was just a big pig, there wasn't much of a sense of her character. And Rosie was a very early model. There's something about Rosie, she has a sort of gravitas. You could rest in her. As I say, she's a matriarch, she's now a grandmother. We call her the OG Doggie—she's the Original Gangsta doggie. There's this sense that Okja is [like that], because Mija rests in her. We talked about that scene in *Totoro*, when they land on Totoro's stomach and sort of bounce. We took lots of footage of Rosie as reference: took lots of photographs of her expressions; her eyes. When she looks worried, she does this thing with her triangle eyebrows. That was something we talked about a lot with Okja, whether she would have eyebrows. Yeah, so she was the source, she was the OG Okja.

I'm curious if you could describe your working relationship with Bong, because it seems as if it goes beyond a typical actor–director relationship where you talk about the ideas he has for a movie even beyond "what's my part in it, and what am I going to do?" How much do you talk with him about the projects that you aren't involved in, with *Parasite* and with some of his upcoming works?
Quite a lot. I mean, I've also worked with him as a producer. I'm a producer on *Okja*. And I love that. I love that part of our conversation. The planning, the plotting, the developing—it's very dear to me. And we have an ongoing conversation with all sorts of different branches into different projects. We're constantly talking about projects that I don't think I'll be in, and I'm very happy with that.

Awful though they are, *Snowpiercer*'s Minister Mason (Tilda Swinton), with their molasses-like hair and a nose reminiscent of a Dr. Seuss character, is also an undeniably attention-grabbing and fascinating presence, not least because of Swinton's chameleonic performance.

Okja's Mirando sisters (both played by Swinton) are similarly memorable, though both push different aesthetic and moral extremes. Lucy, the more outwardly inviting of the two, represents an attempt at forward thinking that is ultimately empty, while the remorseless Nancy is exactly as she appears.

JUNG JAEIL

Composer

Collaborations

Okja

Parasite

Composer Jung Jaeil is now responsible for some of the most recognizable music coming out of the South Korean film and TV industry, from *Parasite*'s score (which filled the Dolby Theatre during the 2020 Academy Awards) to the eerie sounds of *Squid Game* (2021). A graduate of Seoul Jazz Academy—and passionate about music from a young age—Jung's oeuvre includes work as a solo artist as well as in various bands. His first credit as a film composer appears in the 1997 Jang Sun-woo film *Bad Movie*, where he is cocredited with Dalpalan. Having worked regularly across a range of movies in the '00s and '10s, a meeting with Bong Joon Ho led to a pair of key collaborations: 2017's *Okja* and 2019's *Parasite*. Jung's work yielded two of the most memorable and musically diverse scores in the Bong corpus.

You first worked with Director Bong on the 2014 film *Sea Fog*. Do you remember the first time that you actually met?

There was a very tragic event in Korea [around that time], the Sewol ferry incident. And *Sea Fog* was a movie about a sinking ship . . . so that was somewhat difficult. The first time I met Director Bong, he came with his head shaved, so I remember thinking he was probably having a hard time over the ferry incident as well.

How did you come to be hired to work on *Okja*?

Before Director Bong left for New York, he came to me and gave me the script and asked me to work on it. That was all he said. He didn't have any thoughts on it. I thought to myself, "This is very unusual." With *Parasite*, Director Bong had very concrete ideas. But with *Okja*, he didn't really have anything. So I did whatever I wanted.

One of the ideas your music gets across in *Okja* is the divide between the countryside and the city. How did you achieve that?

For *Okja*, from beginning to end, the locations of the movie are clearly divided. The countryside, the capital, and then the sort of super capital at the end. From the start, there was the idea that the sound should be different for each location. And it's really kind of a road movie, so we kept that in mind when we were working on it.

In the sequence when Mija is first trying to retrieve Okja, they run through an underground mall in Seoul. The music is so fun in terms of the use of brass—it's also weirdly reminiscent of Balkan music. Could you tell me a little bit about composing for that sequence?

Thank you for noticing that. That was Balkan music. Bong Joon Ho doesn't like proper music. I think he's someone who likes music that's a bit distorted. I remember, I tried to give him something that followed more of a Hollywood-style approach. And then Emir Kusturica popped into my head. Kusturica is a director that both myself and Bong adore, and he uses Balkan music in his films. We decided to try using Balkan music, and most people might not know what you're talking about if you mention films like *Time of the Gypsies* (1988) [*Image next page*]

or *Black Cat, White Cat* (1998), but Director Bong got it right away. Compared to *Parasite*, the locations for *Okja* were very diverse, which is why I could go all the way to the Balkans. And when we were doing *Okja*, Director Bong told me to do whatever I wanted, which is not normal for someone making such a big movie. I remember that. But with *Parasite*, it was different. For *Parasite*, he gave me this completely predetermined format that came from the things he was thinking. But with *Okja*, he said the creative director has free rein. I loved *Okja*, because I am currently in love with a cat, and Okja was like a cat.

Later, when Okja arrives in New York and the Animal Liberation Front are tailing her, she goes to a warehouse and there's a little bit of something that sounds like a concertina. What made you choose that sound?

It's actually a bandoneon [*Image below left*], not a concertina. An Argentine bandoneon. Director Bong selected that instrument. Can I add that I'm a total cinephile, and if you look at movie history, there are some truly outstanding music selections. Like, for example, "St. Matthew Passion" in Andrei Tarkovsky's *The Sacrifice* (1986). But Bong's decision to use "Annie's Song" too, I really marvel at his judgment. That's what I wanted to say.

On the other side of that coin, there are moments in both movies where there pointedly isn't any music at all. How do you decide when a scene should be silent?

That's always the same when I'm working on movies. Once the edited version is out, we meet to discuss. "Let's put in music here, let's not put in music there, etc."

It sounds like your work process was pretty different for both films, and I'm curious if you prefer one method over the other, or if you actually feel more pressure when you have free rein?

It's all different. But with *Okja*, there really was nothing, so I was able to work with a lot more freedom, and I really was ecstatic when my idea for using Emir Kusturica was accepted. With *Parasite*, things were definitely different. There were only two locations, and Director Bong asked for a concentrated sound. I was constantly searching for what that concentrated sound could be. As I mentioned before, *Okja* was a road movie, and at least one of those sounds must've been good. It was that kind of a time. But really, both methods are hard. I still have to get approval, and I remember, when I went to Skopje in Macedonia to search for underground music, there was a moment when I thought, "Oh, I'm screwed. What should I do? How am I going to apologize to Director Bong? I might have to live as his servant forever." A lot of that kind of stuff. Even today.

What was it that you felt hesitant or nervous about during the research process for *Okja*?

With *Okja*, the important thing was always not to have music that fit the scene perfectly—as that would make it like the Hollywood movies we know so well—but rather, to have music that seems to fit, but is, in a way, a bit wonky. Like running smoothly, and then suddenly tripping and falling over, or to be working hard on something and having it fail. I think that kind of attitude was very important, and it influenced the making of the entire movie. Even at the end, the peace that we find is not really peace. We've gone through all of this, but now what do we do? Music that provokes those kinds of thoughts, that the audience feels that way through the movie's music. That's what I was thinking about.

I love what you said previously about "concentrated sound." Do you think you can define it or characterize it now?

I don't really know. With music, because music isn't a language, it's a bit more difficult. With *Parasite*, I'm still not sure if Director Bong got the kind of sound he wanted. So now I just live life hoping that he got it.

You've spoken about how difficult the process of coming up with the music for *Parasite*'s "Belt of Faith" sequence was. What were your initial ideas for the sequence, and how did they compare to the score that made it to the final film?

With music, Director Bong doesn't like music that's sane, or normal music. So he

doesn't really like it when I bring him music that I worked hard on. It has to be a little nutty. Something has to be weird. It has to have a subject. I've had to adjust to that, which actually started with *Okja*. In *Okja*, there's music in the scene where the ALF is convincing Mija that they need to send Okja to America, and we redid that music about ten times. Director Bong was saying that this isn't it, that there needs to be a moment when a can gets kicked. That is, it needs to have this steady pace of walking along, and then suddenly something collapses. That's what he said. And it was the same for the "Belt of Faith" sequence. So this is a really big, really long sequence, and he had the idea that the music needed to seem distorted.

With *Okja*, you joined the project after the film had begun shooting. With *Parasite*, you joined right at the beginning and your proposals for the music came at an earlier stage in the process. How did Director Bong explain *Parasite* to you?
With *Parasite*, I got the script first. As he was giving me the script, he also showed me the model for the fancy Park house. So I thought, "Wow, this guy really does have a plan." Which actually led to my being more nervous about it, because with *Okja*, it was more of an exploration. What with going to Skopje and, even with the opening credits, I got super excited and kind of did a rock music–type thing. But with *Parasite*, it was a very tailored feeling. Like a Persian carpet—I felt like my work process was like tailoring something.

Having worked on two films with Director Bong, do you have a sort of agreed-upon work process, or a method of collaboration?
It's always the same with a film musician and a film director. It's either, they like it or they don't. So even if I send him a bunch of stuff, if he doesn't like it, that's that. With the "Belt of Faith" sequence, in the beginning, I tried to use [computer-generated] string instruments, but in the end the sound wasn't good enough, so I just played the piano and gave it to him. And he liked it, which made me realize that I should try different things. Even if it's not a completed piece of music, I should try to get him something that fits the sequence—in theory, at least. In the end though, I give him something, and if he doesn't like it, he doesn't like it. If he likes it, he likes it.

How much do you discuss end credits music with Bong, because in *Okja*'s case, the music that plays over the credits is very much from the score, whereas with *Parasite*, there's an original song that accompanies the credits.
In *Okja*, after everything, Okja and Mija do come back home. But that's not really happiness. All of these things have happened and these scars remain in our heart. We said that we wanted to convey that it wasn't a simple and happy kind of peace at the end of the film, and that's the direction I went with the music.
With *Parasite*, Bong said that he wanted people to feel like they wanted to go get a bottle of soju [*Image below left*] after seeing the movie at the theater. In Korea, soju is a kind of symbol of something people drink when they feel a certain bitterness, or when life feels lonely and blue. So he asked me to create an ending song that would lead the audience to feel that they want to go get a bottle of soju, and feel that, yeah, this is how the world is.

What were you feeling when you wrote the theme for *Okja*?
Like I was saying, I started with music that conveys that the peace we found is a peace that comes only with all of these scars that we still carry. But personally, there was a person with whom I was very much in love with at the time, and I had the thought that I wanted to be with that person for a long time. It was just a variety of emotions coming together, and so, for example, I made this simple melody, like, mi-sol-mi, la-sol-sol. And before I realized it, I had sent it to Director Bong. It wasn't really even a finished melody. But Director Bong said, "Let's try it." So here we are.

It seems like there are generally two modes to film scoring, and to the music you make. The first kind is when the music follows the action on the screen, and the second is when music enhances the tone of specific moments. How do you select which mode of music to use in which situation?
I think that depends on the style of the director. For example, if there's a chase scene, I would compose something with

a really tense feeling. But sometimes the director doesn't want that. I keep talking about the Balkan music, but then it was also like, "Let's try Balkan music, something that's tense but also a little quirky." Similar to this kind of approach, I think it's always a case–by–case joint effort to find the best option, based on the director's style and also what the script demands. Really, what the director wants is vague: "This would be good, or that would be good." So we make something, and realize it's not what we want. Then we try again. It's that kind of a repeated process.

I want to return to the musical characters in *Parasite*; can you tell me about casting the score, so to speak?
It's really not a very logical process. If there were any larger concepts, it was that it's a concentrated kind of sound, and that it's probably a string instrument sound. And also that it might be a Baroque sound. But the most important thing was to find the logic of why this person killed someone, how they got to the place where they committed this act that was probably the most serious act of their life. That was it. So I think he continuously emphasized that I needed to think about how the music goes from those incidental moments, like with the "Belt of Faith" scene, all the way to this act of murder. One scene that I still remember, when the father is holding the daughter, and the daughter is dying with the stab wound, and she says, "Don't press it. It hurts more when you press it." That's one of my favorite scenes in the movie. I tried not to lose that element of humor, even at the very end.

You mentioned that the "Belt of Faith" sequence was somewhat difficult. Was there any music in *Parasite* that you felt was easier to compose?
None. And this is sort of an unknown fact, but as far as I know, Director Bong was thinking that I really wasn't working out, and he went as far to think that he was going to have to fire me, or take some kind of action. But he didn't.

CHOI WOO SHIK

Actor

Collaborations

Okja

Parasite

One of the more recent additions to Bong Joon Ho's stable of actors is Choi Woo Shik, who appears in both *Okja* (2017), as a Mirando Corporation employee, and in *Parasite* (2019), as the hapless Ki-woo. Best known to Western audiences for the latter role and his turn as a high school baseball player in *Train to Busan* (2016), Choi has been active in the Korean film and TV industry since 2011, with roles ranging from a young man who pretends to be a priest in order to prolong his stay at a group home (2014's *Set Me Free*, for which he won Actor of the Year at the Busan International Film Festival), to a sadistic supernatural assassin (2018's *The Witch: Part 1. The Subversion*). That said, his performance as Ki-woo remains a stand-out, as he shoulders the burden of introducing the audience to the world of the film as well as escorting them out of it.

I wanted to start off with your role in *Okja*. I read that you were recommended to Director Bong by one of his assistants who'd seen you in Kim Tae-yong's *Set Me Free*. Is that right?

Yeah. I think his assistant watched *Set Me Free* [*Image right*] first, and then told Director Bong to contact me after. I don't recall if that's really what happened, but that's what I heard. We first met after he called me, he wanted to see me for this movie called *Okja*, but I didn't know what he was referring to because in Korea we had no idea what he was doing at that time. We had no information about the character or the movie. He told the crew not to tell me about the role or about the movie, and I had to sign this contract with Netflix. When we met, he told me how good my performance was in *Set Me Free*, and that he had wanted to see me in person. When we met for the first time, he mentioned that I looked really young, like a junior high schooler, but he wanted someone around their early twenties, so he wanted to change my appearance to make me look older. He gave me no further information, so I was just waiting for his next call after that meeting.

You said that Bong wanted you to look a little bit older for *Okja*. What kind of stuff were you figuring out in order to try to match his mental image of that character?

Regarding the appearance that Director Bong wanted for my character, we didn't necessarily need to talk to the visual coordinator, he just said "shaggy hair and no real attention to appearance." I guess his first impression of me was very clean-looking, like, young and pretty, but he wanted something more rough, so I intentionally didn't shave. But I actually don't have a lot of facial hair to begin with. I remember I grew a messy beard for that role.

Once you did get the part, how did he describe the character to you?

Director Bong's scripts are really, really well-written. Every character has their specific nuances—like cadences of speech. Even in *Parasite*, or any movies that he did, all the characters had, even in writing, a specific manner of speaking and gesturing. So when I was acting as Kim, he wanted something new, like a new

generation, someone very young, but also bold—something not seen before, at least in Korea. I think there was an element of showing a kind of generation that didn't exist before in Korea. In Bong's scripts, the characters are always explained so well that the actors don't really need to create new personas.

With regard to both Kim in *Okja* and then Ki-woo in *Parasite*, were there specific things in the script that were really helpful for you?

When I was playing Ki-woo, it almost felt like I was supposed to act like . . . I don't know how to put it in English, but like, a failure? He's trying hard, but he also fails to go to university. He does poorly on tests and exams, but he's not actually dumb. But I really didn't know how to act that out. Am I supposed to act not stupid or not intelligent? So I asked Bong, "Am I dumber than Ki-jung? Is Ki-jung smarter than me? Or am I the dumb one of the family?" But he told me, "No, no, he's not dumb—he's really smart. And he's really caring—he has a really big heart, but his shortcoming is that, when he plans things out and the plan goes wrong, he just panics and he fails at everything. He's not able to do anything from the point of failure." This idea that whenever he feels pressure, he just switches off—that was really helpful. When it comes to *Parasite*, everything is his plan, right? He invites Ki-jung as a tutor. And when that plan fails, he kind of goes a bit numb. I think Bong and I found a good solution to portraying that. If we had messed that up, Ki-woo would have come off as an idiot who acts like a child to his parents. It would have been an overly simplistic portrayal, with Ki-jung being the smart one and Ki-woo being the dumb one.

I read that Bong first started talking to you about *Parasite*, at least in a very abstract way, while you were still working on *Okja*, basically asking you what you were doing next and then telling you to stay skinny.

Yeah, he did. I believe it was after the parade sequence at the end of *Okja* that I told him that I was planning to bulk up. At that time, I had had a few similar roles, all skinny types, and I wanted to change. I told Bong that I was gonna bulk up and be different, and then he told me to stay skinny for no reason. I was like, "Well, why?" He told me, "Oh, just stay skinny because I wanna . . . I don't know, I don't know." I had no next film planned, so I was like, "Well, okay." That was it. We had no conversations about anything after that. Steven Yeun and I were having a beer together, and he was like, "Oh, congrats, man. I heard you're gonna do something with Bong next." I was like, "What?" I had no idea. After that night, Bong asked me what I was doing for the next couple of months, and I was like, "Nothing. I was going to bulk up." He said, "No. Stay skinny. Come to my office, and then we'll talk about some roles." Then he told me that he couldn't tell me about anything else, so I was like, okay.

What was the interval between that and you actually being told about what *Parasite* was going to be?

I think it was five or six months after that. For all that time, I was just wondering when he would call. I couldn't tell anyone about it. My parents kept asking me why I wasn't working, and I didn't have anything I could tell them. I just waited. He would send me texts in the meantime asking what I was doing. "What are you doing these days? Staying skinny?"

Do you remember the chemistry tests that you did with Park So-dam?

Bong knew that I liked drinking. He also likes drinks, casually speaking. And So-dam is also a very fun drinker. So he told me to come out for a drink. He invited us to an izakaya [*Image bottom left*], and told us to wear very grungy clothing. He told us not to shower and not to put on makeup, and just wear really comfortable and shabby clothing. I didn't shower or shave starting the day before, and just went as I was. So-dam also looked extremely shabby. I had this spotty stubble. So-dam and I had really similar vibes. I had seen her and knew who she was, but I never thought that we looked alike. It was my first time meeting her, and both of us were really out of shape. It was kind of awkward at first, but also very fun. We didn't do any readings after that. But when I was preparing for this interview, I was backtracking about the work we did on *Parasite*, and when I think about it, we never did any readings. I don't know about anyone else, but I think he never had

any readings with anyone. I don't think we had an audition either. I don't think anyone had one—maybe the girl and boy from the Park family—so I was curious about this process. What if one of us was not performing well? That was kind of weird.

Do you remember what that first meeting with So-dam was like? Was it just a normal conversation, testing your rapport?

The meeting was casual. Bong took a photo of us, and asked us what we were up to. He told us that he had some characters in mind, and that we would play siblings in a house, with the father being played by Song Kang-ho. I think that was the second or third time that I heard that Song Kang-ho was going to play my father, but at that point we didn't even know the purpose of these characters and the storyline or anything.

Was there anything similar in terms of chemistry tests between you and Song Kang-ho or Jang Hye-jin to figure out the overall family dynamic?

During preproduction we—the Kim family—got together in one space. We rented a semi-basement space, and we wore really worn-out PJs, and just did some shooting like that. It wasn't really even a chemistry reading, it was just to see visually what we were like.

You've spoken a little bit about developing your relationship with Song Kang-ho and calling him "papa" during shooting. Can you tell me about getting to know him and working with him on the film?

In Korea, the idea of the senior-junior relationship is really strong. It's less like a working partner relationship and, honestly, if you're of different ages, it's difficult to be close. You have to be sure you're minding your manners on set. There's just something culturally, and this concept of seniors and juniors is very hardwired. But in *Parasite*, all the senior actors in that generation were so great. I can be pretty shy, and I thought if I approached Song Kang-ho calling him my senior, we would both have a hard time getting close, so I started calling him papa. Frankly, you can't be all that easygoing on set with older actors or seniors that you meet through work. The slightest misstep could come across as impolite, which could lead to rocky relations. Shooting *Parasite*, though, we all stayed together at the same hotel for about three or four months, so we had gotten pretty close even before that since we were spending all our time off-set together. It felt like we were really a family, and really little sister and older brother and mother and father. I think I tried to maintain that kind of relationship with all the actors, not just Song Kang-ho. And we would call each other by our role names, like Yeon-gyo or Ki-jung.

Was there ever a time when Bong laid out his vision of what the family dynamic should be?

Unlike other directors, Director Bong isn't very direct about giving instructions on set. I think he gives very broad directions, and we have to think about what he actually wants, so we try different versions, which is what I think Bong wants. We try this, and then that, and then something else. Through that, we find a kind of harmony. The acting comes from a mix of three elements—what we read in the script; the gestures or lines of movement that were in the storyboard; and then the ideas that Director Bong would give us on set.

Was there ever a moment where you were nervous about finding that right version or harmony?

There was a scene. I truly didn't sleep for, like, four days over it. I was very whiny about it with Director Bong. I felt this immense pressure about having the movie end with a shot of my face. I didn't even know what I was supposed to look like when I'm acting in that scene. The guy has lost his family. His little sister's dead. His father is missing. He doesn't even know for sure where he's at. And I needed to show that in an expression at the end of the film, just looking at the camera. There's a scene like that in *Memories of Murder* as well. I was whining, asking Director Bong, "What do I do here, should I cry, what do I do?" He was just like, "We'll get it. We'll get the face we need." He just trusted me one hundred percent, but that was actually bothering me for four days. With *Memories of Murder*, Song shot that scene really early on in the process, and it was the same for me, because we had to build the set and then take it down. The flood scene and the very last scene of the movie, we shot in the early-to-mid stages of filming. I'm not completely sure, but I heard that Song filmed that scene on the first or second day of shooting. I was agonizing over what to do. We did quite a few takes because Bong was also like, "Maybe we can try this," or "Let's try doing that. Let's up the emotion a little, or pull back." We tried smoking, not smoking. We got to the set and Director Bong, plus all the staff, were really quiet for me. Bong played a song for me on the set, just so I could be calm. The way I felt, it was like he was telling me one hundred percent that it was okay if I didn't act it perfectly. Like, "I'll cover it up!" His vibe was like, "Don't worry about it. If you don't like it. It's okay. I'll make it better afterward." That scene was really difficult.

Was there a take where you felt that you'd nailed it? How did that situation ultimately end?

We kept a few takes that Bong liked. We kept a take with me crying, and we kept one without the crying. We did several versions, and we got an okay for one of each version. I think, for Director Bong too, he wanted to have the best shots of all these different faces because he would have to see which of them went with the entire movie after all the editing was over. So we would get the okay for one, and then move on to the next.

Which take is the one that ended up in the final film? Do you have any feelings about that particular take?

After I did a take crying my eyes out, we did a take without the crying, without me moving at all. I think that was the one that finally got confirmed. But honestly, I liked all of them. Whichever take got picked in the end, I was just so happy to see that that scene didn't get edited out.

Do you remember what kind of music Bong played you on set?

He sent me this playlist. I liked it so much, I asked him what the playlist was and he sent it to me. It's kind of all classical music. *The Four Seasons*. I don't know anything about classical music, so I don't know if it's popular or famous.

With regard to that final scene and its parallels to the one in *Memories of Murder*, did you talk to Song Kang–ho about how he did it?

Yeah. I asked him what he was thinking during that scene. But Song Kang–ho, he's not really the type to talk to other people about acting. He was kind of like, "Just do it. Figure it out." He doesn't ever comment on other people's acting.

You mentioned that you all stayed at the same hotel for three or four months. What was that experience like? Were there any particular scenes that you all talked about more than others?

That was kind of a space where we could all relax. On set, we were really under pressure. We all wanted to perform our best, and we were wondering how to act better. But Bong doesn't really give out compliments or even feedback on set. He's generally just like, "Okay, good, okay, let's go to the next scene." So it was hard to gauge if we were doing well or not. I think everybody felt like that. When we ate, or when we drank, we would ask each other, "I'm doing alright, right?" And the person next to us would say, "Yeah you're doing great." Everyone was giving everyone else good vibes. There's a scene where we're all rolling around in the Parks' living room with the peaches. That scene was a lot of fun to shoot, and we would talk about preparing for that scene. "Let's do this, you're going to do that, and I'll do this, etc." And we came back and talked about it after shooting the scene. We all had ambitions for this movie, and also for acting in general—we all wanted to be better, which is why we constantly wondered whether or not we were doing well. That was true even for Song Kang–ho. He would ask himself whether he was doing well. And then we were just drinking. Bong would come by, and when he came, he would say things that he couldn't always say on set, like that he liked a certain scene. If he said that he liked a scene, that would encourage us to work harder.

I read that the scene where the Kims are all hiding under the Parks' living room table felt like it was very comedic while you were shooting it, and it felt like you guys were playing it that way, but then when you actually saw the film it was much more serious and tense.

When we were hiding under the table, we thought it was really funny. We had to stop two times, because we couldn't hold back our laughs. But the outcome was very deep

and kind of weird, almost eerie. There is a scene where Moon–gwang falls down the stairs [*Image left*]. We thought it was really pitiful and cruel, but at the premiere at the Cannes, everyone was laughing. They were cheering. And then when I went to New York and when I was watching with an audience, they were clapping and laughing at that time, too. It was weird. Sometimes the audience sees a scene differently from the way we thought about it while shooting. A similar scene was rubbing the peach in Moon–gwang's face. During shooting, we were like, "Is this okay?" But then on screen we could see Ki–jung's desperation and our family's desperation, that we had no choice but to take that action. So that was interesting.

I understand that Director Bong refused to answer questions about the metaphors in the film. One of the main discussion points after the film came out was what is the meaning of the scholar's rock. I'm curious how much you discussed those kinds of hidden meanings when you were making the film.

I think that's Bong's personality. He doesn't really explain things to you, but allows you to figure it out on your own. He doesn't give you the right answers. When we all had dinner together at the hotel, I talked a lot with Cho Yeo–jeong, Park So–dam, and Lee Sun–kyun. We just kept talking over drinks. Nothing serious, just light guessing. "This must be this? Doesn't it mean this? Isn't it a metaphor for this? Or that? The rock, couldn't it mean this?" We all had completely different ideas. I thought the rock was the responsibility that Ki–woo was feeling, and Cho Yeo–jeong thought it symbolized a shortcut to success. I think it was more interesting that we had different ideas about what it symbolized.

This may be more of a production question, but do you have any sense of where the scholar's rock that ended up in the movie came from?

I think they wanted to rent this really expensive rock, but they figured that if they actually used an expensive rock, it's not funny. So the rock that Ki–woo's friend brings, the scholar's rock, isn't expensive, but Ki–woo thinks it is and we think it is. I think that makes it funnier. But that's why they didn't use a really rare or precious rock. It's a rock from somewhere. So we rented a rock and then returned it, and we had prop rocks that we used while we were acting. There were three of them, and one is in my house.

Did you ask for it or did they give it to you?

There were a bunch of people wanting that rock. Because it was just a prop, people just could take it. But there were just three of them. One was the prop that was used to hit my head, so it was kind of light. Not too light, but heavy enough so it doesn't bounce off the ground and is obviously a fake prop. And then there was a really light prop rock, and also a really heavy one. I got the heavy one. That's the one that everyone wanted. I think they were all trying to bid on the rocks, and then someone actually took it, so it was nowhere to be found, but Director Bong told the producer and then he was like, "Oh, I think we have to give Ki–woo one."

When did Bong tell you that he wanted you to sing the song that plays over the end credits?

I thought he was joking at first. It was after the shoot, I think midway through the editing. I would go to a booth in a studio to record my lines—ADR—and he said to me, "Ahh, I was talking to our music director and, you know, I think it would be nice if you sing a song for us." I thought he was joking, so I was like, "Yeah, I'll sing." I told him I'm not a good singer, but I was joking, and I thought he was joking, too. He'd heard me singing karaoke, so he knew how good I was. Then he's like, "Oh yeah, I wrote the lyrics too, so, you know, it would be fun." I went home and then when I went in for the next recording, he told me the music was done and that I'd have to come back in a week to record the song. I asked him, "Are you serious?" The music director gave me this really roughly recorded music. The pitch was really high, so high that I couldn't sing it. I was like, "Director Bong, I don't think I can sing," and he's like, "Nah, it's okay, it's okay. We'll do some post–production on it, then it will be okay." They pitched it down two keys or something, but it was still really high. But I did it. Song Kang–ho loves it. He always teases me whenever we have dinner together. He always makes me sing the song.

As *Parasite*'s Kim Ki-woo, Choi Woo Shik delivers a masterful performance. It's Ki-woo who sets the plot in motion, and the character serves as something of an anchor, bookending the film.

Octobre 2018
Claire DENIS
Octobre 2018
Douglas TRUMBULL
Octobre 2018
Alice ROHRWACHER
Novembre 2018
Brian DE PALMA
Mars 2019

INSTIT

OUTRO

When Bong Joon Ho's films come to a close, the sense is not that the story has ended, nor that these characters will disappear once the credits roll. The prevailing feeling is, instead, of bidding adieu to a friend. Bong's characters are so thoroughly and intricately realized that it takes very little stretch of the imagination to think that these lives—fictional though they are—will continue after the credits have rolled. What the characters have just experienced isn't the be-all and end-all of their lives, and the idea that they will continue on is less about setting up any kind of sequel than it is acknowledging that this is the way life is. In Bong's films, moments of comedy and tragedy are often intertwined rather than discrete. In a similar vein, the events and experiences depicted often feel cataclysmic in the moment, yet Bong makes it clear that it's imperative to move on and look to the promise of the future. We, as audience members, are lucky just to have been along for the ride.

This idea that Bong's works reflect and reveal aspects of our world is a vital part of what makes his films so thrilling. The overlapping themes, such as the inherent pitfalls of a society based on the ceaseless flow of capital, and the empathy necessary to survive within it, avoid prescriptiveness because Bong's aim is never to create a morality play. His films always have something to say, but those messages are woven into the stories he tells rather than the story's entire purpose. Again, art imitates life; the things we experience are almost never (if ever) specifically meant as teaching moments—that we do learn from them is a natural part of growing up. And in the critical and commercial success he has achieved while eschewing Hollywood conventions (dashing heroes, neat finales, not to mention a refusal to relinquish the privilege of final cut of his films), he has remained unpredictable, telling stories that defy any sense of a safety net, both in terms of whether or not characters will make it to the end of a given movie and in terms of how that ending will take shape. *Parasite*'s stupendous mid-film reveal; the betrayal at the center of *Okja*; the true nature of *Snowpiercer*'s lead character . . . it's practically impossible to see any of these twists coming.

The question, now, is what comes next for Bong himself. It would be churlish to say that Bong is in the prime of his career—that he has evolved as a filmmaker does not preclude the fact that his earlier films are masterworks in their own right. But in the wake of *Parasite*'s blindingly bright success, there's no question that, at the very least, this is the greatest number of eyes the filmmaker has ever had focused on him. During a 2021 conversation with Rian Johnson for the DGA's *Director's Cut* podcast, Bong mentioned that he was working on two screenplays: one in Korean, based in Seoul and mixing horror and action; and one in English, based on true events from 2016. Since then, it has been announced that he will be helming the film adaptation of Edward Ashton's 2022 science fiction novel *Mickey7*, and it has been reported that he has also been at work on a Korean animated film involving deep-sea creatures. That is to say, there are myriad Bong projects on the way, each one radically different from the others—just as his previous films are.

It's a particular skill that Bong, even though his films vary wildly in tone and subject matter, is able to cast an eye back into the past as well as charge ahead into hypothetical futures. Films such as *Memories of Murder* and *Snowpiercer*, disparate as they appear at first glance, still feel resolutely like the work of one brain. He is unquestionably an auteur (though his shyness and tangible love for his coconspirators suggest he might reject the label)—his films boast a stylistic expressiveness and continuity that is near-instantly recognizable, on top of a steadfast refusal to submit to moral absolutes. Upon being asked how he achieves such fluidity with genre and tone, he has said on more than one occasion that it's not actually something he's conscious of. He compares his filmmaking habits to bartending or cooking—an apt comparison, as both arts, though certainly dependent upon an amount of calculation, are often described more as endeavors of love and intuition—and to continue that tangible sort of description, his fingerprints are always visible on the films he makes, shaping his coterie of lovable losers and grotesques.

And even if Bong may feel cynical about the future—his characters never quite achieve what they set out to do—his works rarely let go of a sense of hope. That the two modes seem incompatible is a part of his films' appeal—he is unflinching and practical, but not without offering an alternative way forward. This is the key to his dissident nature: an iconoclast with politically forthright views and no small amount of anger, but also someone who sees a transcendent duality in human nature. As awful as the system—and the people created by it—can be, everyone and everything is worth saving. Whether it's doing away with flawed power structures entirely, as in *Snowpiercer*, or learning how best to live within them, as in *Okja*, he provides a torch, even if the light at the end of the metaphorical tunnel may be too faint to initially make out. To proselytize further would be to welcome triteness, so I'll leave it at this: Bong, a lifelong cinephile, is now himself a part of cinema's grand tapestry. His love for the work of Alfred Hitchock, Martin Scorsese, and Kim Ki-young, to name a few of the directors for whom he's professed admiration, means that his films are often in conversation with theirs. And yet he has also created a filmic language of his own, one that spans an enviably original and extraordinary body of work. That it's impossible to guess what kind of story Bong will tell next is part of his appeal as a storyteller—it's a pleasure to be swept away.

ACKNOWLEDGEMENTS

THE AUTHOR WOULD LIKE TO THANK . . .

There are many acknowledgments that need to be made with regard to the shepherding of this book from start to finish—I certainly could never have done this on my own, and count myself incredibly lucky to have worked with such a brilliant cohort in bringing this book to life. Particularly crucial among them is Dooho Choi, whose generosity opened a lot of doors, and who remained superhumanly patient and kind over the course of countless email chains. And, of course, Bong Joon Ho, without whom this book—in the most literal sense possible—would not exist.

Thank you, too, to Choi Tae-young, Choi Woo Shik, Hong Kyung Pyo, Jung Jaeil, Tilda Swinton, and Yang Jinmo for taking the time to share their experiences with me—it was an honor and a pleasure to pick the minds of such luminary talents. And, on the subject of luminary talents, many thanks to [David Lowery] for providing this book's foreword, and whose involvement is nothing less than a blessing.

This book also owes a considerable debt to David Jenkins, who brought me into the Abrams/Little White Lies family and took a gamble on me as an author, and whose endless graciousness and support have been invaluable to this monograph seeing the light of day. I could not have asked for a more perspicacious and thoughtful editor—I hope our chats about movies, video games, and the world at large will continue even after this book is out of our hands. I am also endlessly grateful to Clive Wilson and Meredith A. Clark for their oversight of this project, and to the brilliant Han Nightingale, Tertia Nash, and Fabrizio Festa for making this book look so beautiful.

To note a few other key collaborators: I would never have been able to put this book together without the assistance of Sharon Choi and Jungmin Kang, who went above and beyond as interpreters/translators for the interviews conducted for this book, nor without Anna Swanson and her hard work as research assistant.

To all of my dear friends in their various roles as confidantes, readers, and supports—thank you, thank you, thank you. I hope to thank you in person. Of those loved ones, thanks in particular to Brian, for sticking with me through it all.

Finally, this book is dedicated to my wonderful 엄마, Myung-Ja Han, and to the memory of my 아빠, Shin-Kap Han, who had everything to do with igniting my love of film. Love you, miss you, wish you were here.

LITTLE WHITE LIES WOULD LIKE TO THANK . . .

Due to the birth of my one and (at time of writing) only daughter, I did not attend the Cannes Film Festival in 2018—the first time I'd skipped it since 2011. I won't lie: It was a bummer to miss the world premiere of a new work by Bong Joon Ho, whose films had captivated me since I succumbed to the hype of *The Host* back in 2006. Removed from the action, I experienced the festival vicariously through Twitter, and one thing that became noticeable quite quickly is that the US writer and journalist Karen Han had become the nucleus for passion and anticipation when it came to the world premiere of Bong's new one, *Parasite*. I was scrolling at the very moment she founded the #BongHive, a nomenclature that persisted and expanded through Bong's slow but steady conquering of the entire globe. For me, the best thing about Bong winning the Best Picture Oscar in 2019 was the reaction video featuring Karen at home, screaming/yelling/weeping/wooping at the exact moment those fateful words inside the envelope were read aloud. It was not long after that glorious moment that the wheels were in motion for this book, and her affirmative response to my initial, sheepish DM was a great day indeed. It has been a joy and a pleasure to edit Karen in the process of writing this book. Karen's forensic, deep-dive insights into the formal and emotional minutiae of Bong's cinema are more than fitting for a man who made *Memories of Murder*, and her intimate affection for the material is implicit in every word. The last big piece of the puzzle that came in for this book was the interview with Tilda Swinton, so things ended as fun and exciting as they began.

Elsewhere, I'd like to thank the whole TCO design team (Teria, Han, Fabs, et al) the head of TCO Printworks, Clive Wilson, plus Wendy Klerck and Vince Mederios for allowing us to plunge so much time and energy into books like this. Also my colleagues on Little White Lies magazine, Adam Woodward, Hannah Strong, and Marina Ashioti for all their advice along the way. Thanks to Eric Klopfer and Meredith A. Clark, our guardian angels at Abrams who have, once again, allowed us to push and prod the traditional form of the film monograph. I'd like to thank Joonho Brian Ko and Youn Soo Kwack for the amazing illustrations they provided for this book, and also to Chris Gonzalez at Netflix for supplying us with amazing behind-the-scenes materials. Sharon Choi and Jungmin Kang were essential for translating this set of wonderful interviews with Bong's collaborators, and to Saskia Lloyd-Gaiger for help with transcription. And also thanks to Dooho Choi who helped with some incredible dot connecting while in the works with a new Bong opus. And lastly to Adam Nayman, who instigated this series for us with his books on the Coen brothers, Paul Thomas Anderson, and David Fincher.

INDEX

J

K

L

M

N

O

P

BIBLIOGRAPHY

Anime Anime. "*Snowpiercer* Interview with Bong Joon-Ho," February 6, 2014.

Bitel, Anton. "Discover the Hypnotic Mystery of This Nihilistic Thriller." *Little White Lies*, April 23, 2018.

Bloom Ingam, Livia. "Bong Joon-Ho, *Mother*." *Filmmaker Magazine*, March 10, 2020.

Bong, Joon-Ho. "Bong Joon-Ho." *British Film Institute*, 2012.

Bong Joon-Ho on His Creative Process, *Barking Dogs Never Bite*, *The Host* & More | *On Writing*, 2020.

Bong Joon-Ho Talks about *The Host*, 2007.

Brzeski, Patrick. "Making of *Parasite*: How Bong Joon Ho's Real Life Inspired a Plot-Twisty Tale of Rich vs. Poor." *Hollywood Reporter*, November 8, 2019.

Chan, Yuan-kwan. "Quentin Tarantino, Bong Joon-Ho Make Surprise Appearance in Busan." *Meniscus Magazine*, October 29, 2013.

Chang, Kee. "The Lost Interview: Bong Joon-Ho." *Anthem Magazine*, April 13, 2017.

Chen, Nick. "Bong Joon-Ho on *Babe*, Bin Laden and Why *Okja*'s on Netflix." *Dazed*, June 21, 2017.

Choe, Sang-hun. "Bong Joon Ho's Path From Seoul to Oscar Dominance." *New York Times*, February 13, 2020.

Cinematographer Hong Kyung-Pyo on *Parasite* (Bong Joon-Ho, 2019), 2021.

Condit, Joe. "Joon-Ho, Bong (*The Host*)." *Dread Central*, January 4, 2007.

Cunningham, Jake. "*Parasite* | The Curzon Film Podcast Feat. Bong Joon Ho + Tilda Swinton." *The Curzon Film Podcast*, February 7, 2020.

Dargis, Manohla. "Unprepared and Ill-Equipped for a Serial Killer at Large." *New York Times*, July 15, 2005.

Desowitz, Bill. "*Parasite*: Shooting Bong Joon Ho's Social Thriller Through the Lens of Class Divide." IndieWire, November 15, 2019.

Desta, Yohana. "Bong Joon-Ho Looked to Hitchcock When Making *Parasite*: 'He Always Gives Me Very Strange Inspiration.'" *Vanity Fair*, October 11, 2019.

Ebert, Roger. "The Wages Of Fear." RogerEbert.com, March 6, 1992.

[ENG SUB] MMTG Choi Woo Shik & Kim Dami Interview about Our Beloved Summer #그해우리는. *MMTG*, 2022.

Grobar, Matt. "How Editor Jinmo Yang Refined The Pacing Of *Parasite*, Bong Joon Ho's Darkly Comedic Thriller." Deadline, November 5, 2019.

Hammond, Pete. "Oscars: 'Snowpiercer's Tilda Swinton On Her Transformation Into A Creepy Dictator." *Deadline*, December 30, 2014.

Han, Karen. "Bong Joon-Ho and His Parasite Composer Struggled to Perfect the Film's Key Song." *Polygon*, April 8, 2020.

Harris, Hunter. "*Parasite*'s Choi Woo-Shik Is Optimistic About the Movie's Overwhelming Ending." Vulture, October 16, 2019.

Hu, Elise. "Bong Joon Ho's Tips on How He Stays so Chill: 'I'm Actually Very Anxious.'" *Los Angeles Times*, February 13, 2020.

Hunt, Aaron. "Sibling Subterfuge: Choi Woo-Shik and Park So-Dam on *Parasite*." *Filmmaker Magazine*, October 15, 2019.

IndieWire. "IndieWIRE INTERVIEW: *The Host* Director Bong Joon-Ho," March 13, 2007.

Jang, Seong-ran, and Hyo-eun Kim. "Useful Things to Know about Bong Joon Ho." *The JoongAng*, July 31, 2017.

Jun, R. "*Parasite* Director Bong Joon Ho Talks About His Beginnings As A Director." *Soompi*, February 10, 2020.

Jung, E. Alex. "Bong Joon-Ho's Dystopia Is Already Here." Vulture, October 7, 2019.

Jung, E. Alex. "The Face of Korean Cinema Is Anxious, Afraid, and Full of Metaphors." Vulture, October 23, 2019.

Kampakis, Demitra. "*Parasite* Stars Park So-Dam and Choi Woo-Shik on Breaking Barriers and Cultural Differences." *The Film Stage*, November 13, 2019.

Kim, Jye-hee. "The Title Is *Parasite*, But the Film Is about Symbiosis." *The Kyunghyang Shinmyn*, May 30, 2019.

Laverty, Christopher. "*Snowpiercer*: Q&A with Costume Designer Catherine George." *Clothes on Film*, n.d.

Lee, Claire. "Tilda Swinton: Making *Snowpiercer* Was like 'Being in Kindergarten.'" *Asia One*, July 20, 2013.

Lee, Hyo-won. "Quentin Tarantino: 'Korea's Bong Joon Ho Is Like Spielberg in His Prime.'" *Hollywood Reporter*, October 11, 2013.

Lee, Kevin B. "The Han River Horror Show: Interview with Bong Joon-Ho." *Cineaste*, 2007.

Lee, Nikki J. Y., and Julian Stringer. "From 'Screenwriting for Sound' to Film Sound Maps: The Evolution of Live Tone's Creative Alliance with Bong Joon-Ho." *The New Soundtrack 8, no. 2* (September 4, 2018): 145–59.

Lee, Suh-yoon. "Police Narrowly Missed Serial-Killer Suspect 25 Years Ago." *Korea Times*, September 20, 2019.

Mazur, Matt. "Mama Said Knock You Out: An Interview with *Mother* Director Bong Joon-Ho." *Pop Matters*, March 11, 2010.

McNamara, Lisa. "*Parasite* Editor Jinmo Yang on the Road From South Korea to the Oscars." *Frame.io*, February 6, 2020.

Memories of Murder Q&A with Director Bong Joon-Ho, 2020.

[MOVIE & I] FILM EDITOR, YANG JINMO (기생충, 옥자, 부산행… 편집한 사람 나야 나). *Movie & I*, 2021.

Murphy, Mekado. "Bong Joon Ho Narrates a Scene From '*Okja*.'" *New York Times*, July 3, 2017.

Nash, Kate. "This Is Something I Wrote about Why I Personally Chose to Go Vegan . . ." *Instagram*, May 4, 2020.

Paquet, Darcy. "The Bong Joon-Ho Page." *Korean Film*, February 14, 2008.

Paquet, Darcy. "*The Housemaid* (1960)." *Korean Film*, August 6, 2018.

Park, Ed. "Memories of Murder: In the Killing Jar." Criterion Collection, April 20, 2021.

Parker-Dalton, Jacob. "Bong Joon-Ho Reveals Respect for Naoki Urasawa in Asadora! Comment." *Otaquest*, April 30, 2021.

Park, S. Nathan. "Opinion: How *Parasite* Almost Never Saw the Light of Day." *Washington Post*, February 10, 2020.

Poenisch, Emily. "*Okja* Director Bong Joon Ho Says Working With Tilda Swinton Gives Him '*Nuclear Power*.'" *Esquire*, June 29, 2017.

Polygon. "Bong Joon-Ho on Weaving His Personal Memories into *Parasite*," October 14, 2019.

Radish, Christina. "Bong Joon Ho Looks Back on *The Host*, *Snowpiercer*, *Parasite* and More at SBIFF." *Collider*, January 28, 2020.

Radish, Christina. "Tilda Swinton Talks Snowpiercer, Creating Her Outrageous Character, Playing a Character Originally Written as a Man & the Film's International Production." *Collider*, June 23, 2013.

Raup, Jordan. "Bong Joon Ho on Family and Class in *Parasite*, Collecting Films, and Memories of Murder." Film at Lincoln Center, November 19, 2019.

Rayns, Tony. "'Alan Moore Pushed Me to Think Less about the Killer and More about the Spirit of the Times': Bong Joon Ho on *Memories of Murder*." *British Film Institute*, September 11, 2020.

Rayns, Tony. "The Makings of Bong Joon Ho." *British Film Institute*, February 12, 2020.

Russell, Mark. "Unlike His Peers, the Director Bong Joon-Ho Likes Ideas and Metaphors." *New York Times*, May 28, 2008.

SBIFF 2020 - Bong Joon Ho Discusses "*Memories Of Murder*," 2020.

Schou, Solvej. "Top South Korean Directors on Hitting Hollywood - EXCLUSIVE." *EW*, October 29, 2012.

SciFi Japan. "*The Host* Press Notes and Director's Interview," 2006.

Sedia, Giuseppe. "An Interview with Bong Joon-Ho." *Korean Film*, October 2007.

Selavy, Virginie. "Mother: Interview with Bong Joon-Ho." Electric Sheep Magazine, August 1, 2010.

Shaffer, Marshall. "*Parasite* Editor Jinmo Yang On Subtlety And The Time Director Bong Joon-Ho Apologized To Him [Interview]." *Slashfilm*, January 28, 2020.

Shark, Zack, and Christian Zilko. "Bong Joon Ho's Favorite Movies: 44 Films the Director Wants You to See." IndieWire, February 25, 2022.

Swinton, Tilda. "Bong Joon Ho." *Time*, September 22, 2020.

Tan, Sandi. "Parasite Power: Director Bong Joon Ho on His Edgy Oscar Contender." *Vanity Fair*, January 27, 2020.

Tauer, Kristen. "Tilda Swinton Reunites With Bong Joon-Ho for *Okja*." *WWD*, June 28, 2017.

"The Craft of the Director with Bong Joon Ho." *The Director's Cut*, n.d.

The Host Q&A with Director Bong Joon-Ho, 2020.

Todoroki, Yukio. "Naoki Urasawa x Bong Joon Ho." *Pia*, July 31, 2006.

Tsui, Curtis. "10 Things I Learned: *Memories of Murder*." Criterion Collection, April 22, 2021.

Vélez, Diva. "Interview: Bong Joon-Ho on *Okja*'s Inspirations and Controversies." *ScreenAnarchy*, July 2, 2017.

Vineyard, Jennifer. "Director Bong Joon-Ho Explains Harvey Weinstein's Problem With *Snowpiercer*." Vulture, November 6, 2013.

Walden, Jennifer. "Perfecting *Parasite*'s Award-Winning Sound – with Ralph Tae-Young Choi." *A Sound Effect*, February 19, 2020.

Williams, Mary Elizabeth. "*Parasite*'s Bong Joon-Ho: 'Voyeurism Is an Essential Part of Cinema.'" *Salon*, October 15, 2019.

Wojnar, Zak. "*Parasite* Interview: Editor Jinmo Yang Interview." *Screenrant*, January 9, 2020.

Zuckerman, Esther. "*Okja*'s Tilda Swinton and Bong Joon-Ho Crafted Their Greedy Capitalist Tale Long before Trump's Presidency." AV Club, June 28, 2017.

IMAGE CREDITS

4	PA Images/Alamy Stock Photo
8	REUTERS/Alamy Stock Photo
13	Everett Collection Inc/Alamy Stock Photo
15	Peter Phillips/Alamy Stock Photo
16	Everett Collection Inc/Alamy Stock Photo
18	dpa picture alliance/Alamy Stock Photo
20	CTK/Alamy Stock Photo
23	Paul Smith/Alamy Stock Photo
28	The History Collection/Alamy Stock Photo
46	Photo 12/Alamy Stock Photo
49	BFA/Alamy Stock Photo (*tl*)
	Pictorial Press Ltd/Alamy Stock Photo (*tm*)
	Collection Christophel/Alamy Stock Photo (*tr*)
	colaimages/Alamy Stock Photo (*bl*)
	Moviestore Collection Ltd/Alamy Stock Photo (*br*)
56	TCD/Prod.DB/Alamy Stock Photo
69	Collection Christophel/Alamy Stock Photo
72	Album/Alamy Stock Photo
75	TCD/Prod.DB/Alamy Stock Photo (*tl*)
	Photo 12/Alamy Stock Photo (*tm*)
	Photo 12/Alamy Stock Photo (*tr*)
	Collection Christophel/Alamy Stock Photo (*bl*)
	TCD/Prod.DB/Alamy Stock Photo (*br*)
84	Moviestore Collection Ltd/Alamy Stock Photo
93	United Archives GmbH/Alamy Stock Photo
98	Photo 12/Alamy Stock Photo
100	Chungeorahm Film
	Chungeorahm Film
	Chungeorahm Film
101	Chungeorahm Film
	Chungeorahm Film
	Chungeorahm Film
103	Everett Collection Inc/Alamy Stock Photo (*tl*)
	Photo 12/Alamy Stock Photo (*tm*)
	TCD/Prod.DB/Alamy Stock Photo (*tr*)
	Everett Collection Inc/Alamy Stock Photo (*bl*)
	Collection Christophel/Alamy Stock Photo (*br*)
111	ScreenProd/Photononstop/Alamy Stock Photo
126	Photo 12/Alamy Stock Photo
129	Allstar Picture Library Limited./Alamy Stock Photo (*tl*)
	Allstar Picture Library Limited./Alamy Stock Photo (*tm*)
	SilverScreen/Alamy Stock Photo (*tr*)
	TCD/Prod.DB/Alamy Stock Photo (*bl*)
	cineclassico/Alamy Stock Photo (*br*)
150	TCD/Prod.DB/Alamy Stock Photo
153	Newscom/Alamy Stock Photo (*tl*)
	CLEMENT CAZOTTES/Alamy Stock Photo (*tm*)
	Cronos/Alamy Stock Photo (*tr*)
	Newscom/Alamy Stock Photo (*bl*)
	Cronos/Alamy Stock Photo (*br*)
170	TCD/Prod.DB/Alamy Stock Photo
173	Everett Collection Inc/Alamy Stock Photo
175	Pictorial Press Ltd/Alamy Stock Photo
178	Photo 12/Alamy Stock Photo
180	All images: © 2022 Netflix, Inc.
181	All images: © 2022 Netflix, Inc.
183	Everett Collection Inc/Alamy Stock Photo (*tl*)
	Everett Collection Inc/Alamy Stock Photo (*tm*)
	Pictorial Press Ltd/Alamy Stock Photo (*tr*)
	AA Film Archive/Alamy Stock Photo (*bl*)
	GRANGER -Alamy Stock Photo (*br*)
206	TCD/Prod.DB/Alamy Stock Photo
209	TCD/Prod.DB/Alamy Stock Photo (*tl*)
	TCD/Prod.DB/Alamy Stock Photo (*tm*)
	TCD/Prod.DB/Alamy Stock Photo (*tr*)
	TCD/Prod.DB/Alamy Stock Photo (*bl*)
	TCD/Prod.DB/Alamy Stock Photo (*br*)
219	TCD/Prod.DB/Alamy Stock Photo
222	Collection Christophel/Alamy Stock Photo
225	Prisma by Dukas Presseagentur GmbH/ Alamy Stock Photo (*bl*)
227	Photo 12/Alamy Stock Photo
228	Photo 12/Alamy Stock Photo
230	TCD/Prod.DB/Alamy Stock Photo
231	Pictorial Press Ltd/Alamy Stock Photo (*tl*) Moviestore Collection Ltd/Alamy Stock Photo (*bl*)
238	TCD/Prod.DB/Alamy Stock Photo
239	Lifestyle pictures/Alamy Stock Photo
240	Moviestore Collection Ltd/Alamy Stock Photo
242	Sipa US/Alamy Stock Photo
243	Album/Alamy Stock Photo
244	Art Collection 3/Alamy Stock Photo
246	(*From top to bottom*) Entertainment Pictures/Alamy Stock Photo Entertainment Pictures/Alamy Stock Photo Everett Collection Inc/Alamy Stock Photo Album/Alamy Stock Photo
247	(*From top to bottom*) Everett Collection Inc/Alamy Stock Photo Moviestore Collection Ltd/Alamy Stock Photo Everett Collection Inc/Alamy Stock Photo Album/Alamy Stock Photo
249	Everett Collection Inc/Alamy Stock Photo (*tl*) tilialucida/Alamy Stock Photo (*bl*)
250	Seoul, South Korea/Alamy Stock Photo
253	Sergio Torres Baus/Alamy Stock Photo (*bl*)
257	(*From top to bottom*) BFA/Alamy Stock Photo Album/Alamy Stock Photo
258	Abaca Press/Alamy Stock Photo
261	REUTERS/Alamy Stock Photo

Key

(*tl*)	top left
(*tm*)	top middle
(*tr*)	top right
(*bl*)	bottom left
(*bm*)	bottom middle
(*br*)	bottom right

Author Image Carly Hildebrant
Cover Image Album/Alamy Stock Photo
Endpapers Han Nightingale
Typefaces Fortescue, Atlas Grotesk
Chapter Opener Illustrator Younsoo Kwack
Chapter Close Illustrator Joonho Brian Ko

FOR LITTLE WHITE LIES
Editor *David Jenkins*
Art Director *Fabrizio Festa, Tertia Nash*
Designer *Han Nightingale*
Head of Books *Clive Wilson*
Publisher *Vince Medeiros*
Translation *Sharon Choi and Jungmin Kang*
Transcription *Jungmin Kang and Saskia Lloyd-Gaiger*
Research *Anna Swanson*

FOR ABRAMS
Editor *Meredith A. Clark*
Managing Editor *Mike Richards*
Design Manager *Jenice Kim*
Production Manager *Larry Pekarek*

—

Library of Congress Control Number: 2021932419

ISBN: 978-1-4197-5812-6
eISBN: 978-1-64700-535-1

Printed and bound in the United States
10 9 8 7 6 5 4 3 2 1

ABRAMS The Art of Books
195 Broadway, New York, NY 10007
abramsbooks.com

ABOUT THE AUTHOR

Karen Han is a culture writer and screenwriter whose work has appeared in the *New York Times*, *The Atlantic*, *Vanity Fair*, *Village Voice*, *New York Magazine*, and *Slate*. This is her first book. She lives in Los Angeles with her partner Brian and a stuffed Okja.